First World War
and Army of Occupation
War Diary
France, Belgium and Germany

38 DIVISION
Divisional Troops
Royal Army Service Corps
Divisional Train (330, 331, 332, 333 Companies A.S.C.)
5 November 1915 - 16 June 1919

WO95/2550/5

The Naval & Military Press Ltd
www.nmarchive.com
Published in association with The National Archives

Published by

The Naval & Military Press Ltd

Unit 10 Ridgewood Industrial Park,

Uckfield, East Sussex,

TN22 5QE England

Tel: +44 (0) 1825 749494

www.naval-military-press.com

www.nmarchive.com

This diary has been reprinted in facsimile from the original. Any imperfections are inevitably reproduced and the quality may fall short of modern type and cartographic standards.

© **Crown Copyright**
Images reproduced by permission of The National Archives, London, England, 2015.

Contents

Document type	Place/Title	Date From	Date To
Heading	WO95/2550/5 Divisional Train		
Heading	38th Division 38th Divl Train ASC. Nov 1915-Jun 1919 (330 To 333 Coys ASC)		
Heading	38th Divl Welch Vol V Dec 15 June 19		
War Diary	Winchester	05/11/1915	04/12/1915
War Diary	At Sea	04/12/1915	04/12/1915
War Diary	At Sea and Le Havre	05/12/1915	05/12/1915
War Diary	Le Havre	06/12/1915	06/12/1915
War Diary	Aire	07/12/1915	07/12/1915
War Diary	Ligne.	07/12/1915	19/12/1915
War Diary	St Floris	20/12/1915	20/12/1915
War Diary	St Venant	21/12/1915	31/12/1915
Heading	38th Divl. Train Vol: 2 Jan 16		
War Diary	St Venant	01/01/1916	23/01/1916
War Diary	Lestrem	24/01/1916	18/02/1916
War Diary	Locon	19/02/1916	29/02/1916
Heading	38th Divl: Train Vol: 3		
Heading	38 Div Train Vol 4		
War Diary	Locon	01/03/1916	21/04/1916
War Diary	La. Gorgue	22/04/1916	12/06/1916
War Diary	St Venant	13/06/1916	15/06/1916
War Diary	Tinques	16/06/1916	26/06/1916
War Diary	Bonnieres.	27/06/1916	27/06/1916
War Diary	Vacquerie	28/06/1916	29/06/1916
War Diary	Rubempre	30/06/1916	30/06/1916
Heading	War Diary Of Lieut Colonel T.E. Bennett A.S.C. Commanding 38 (Welsh) Divisional Train From 1/7/16 To 31/7/16 Vol 8		
War Diary	Rubempre	01/07/1916	01/07/1916
War Diary	Acheux	02/07/1916	02/07/1916
War Diary	Treux	03/07/1916	04/07/1916
War Diary	Morlancourt	05/07/1916	12/07/1916
War Diary	Poulainville	13/07/1916	13/07/1916
War Diary	Pont Remy	14/07/1916	14/07/1916
War Diary	Pont. Remy Area	15/07/1916	15/07/1916
War Diary	Famechon	16/07/1916	31/07/1916
War Diary	Esquelbecq	31/07/1916	31/07/1916
War Diary	War Diary Of Lieut T.E. Bennett. A.J.C. Commanding 38/Welsh/Divisional Train From 1/8/16 To 31/8/16 Vol 9		
War Diary	Esquelbecq	01/08/1916	24/08/1916
War Diary	St Jean Ter. Biezen	25/08/1916	31/08/1916
Heading	War Diary Of Lieut Colonel T.E. Bennett A.S.C. Commanding 38/Welsh/Divisional Train From 1/9/16 To 30/9/16 Vol 10		
War Diary	St Jean Ter. Biezen.	01/09/1916	30/09/1916
Heading	War Diary Of Lieut Colonel T.E. Bennett A.S.C Commanding 38/Welsh/Divisional Train From 1/10/16 To 31/10/16 Vol 11		
War Diary	St Jean Ter. Biezen	01/10/1916	31/10/1916

Miscellaneous	War Diary Of Lieut Colonel T.E. Bennett A.S.C. Commanding The 38th (Welsh) Divisional Train From 1.11.16 To 30.11.16 Vol 12		
War Diary	St Jan Ter. Biezen	01/11/1916	30/11/1916
War Diary	War Diary Of Lieut Colonel T.E. Bennett. A.S.C. Commanding The 38th (Welsh) Divisional Train From 1.12.16 To 31.12.16 Vol 13		
War Diary	St Jan Ter. Biezen	01/12/1916	14/12/1916
War Diary	Esquelbecq	15/12/1916	31/12/1916
Heading	War Diary Of. Lieut Colonel T.E. Bennett A.S.C. Commanding 38/Welsh/Divisional Train From 1/1/17. To 31/1/17 Vol 14		
War Diary	Esquelbecq	01/01/1917	16/01/1917
War Diary	St Jan Ter Biezen	17/01/1917	31/01/1917
Heading	War Diary Of Lt Col. T.E. Bennett A.S.C. Commanding. 38th (Welsh) Divisional Train From Feb 1st 1917 To Feb 28th 1917. Vol 15		
War Diary	St Jan Ter Biezen	01/02/1917	28/02/1917
Heading	War Diary Of Lieut Colonel T.E. Bennett Commanding. 38/Welsh/Divisional Train From 1/3/17 To 31/3/17 Vol 16		
War Diary	St Jean Ter Biezen	01/03/1917	31/03/1917
Heading	War Diary Of. Lieut Colonel T.E. Bennett A.S.C. Commanding 38/Welch/Divisional Train. From 1/4/17 To 30/4/17 Vol 17		
War Diary	St. Jan Ter. Biezen	01/04/1917	30/04/1917
Heading	War Diary Of. Lieut Colonel T.E. Bennett A.S.C. Commanding 38/Welsh/Divisional Train. From 1.5.17. To 31.5.17. Vol 18		
War Diary	St Jan Ter. Biezen.	01/05/1917	31/05/1917
Heading	War Diary Of Lieut Colonel T.E. Bennett A.S.C. Commanding 38/Welsh/Divisional Train From 1/6/17 To 30/6/17. Vol 19		
War Diary	St Jan Ter Biezen	01/06/1917	24/06/1917
War Diary	International Corner.	24/06/1917	30/06/1917
Heading	War Diary Of Lieut Colonel T.E. Bennett A.S.C. Commanding. 38th (Welsh) Divisional Train 1/7/17 To 31/7/17 Vol 20		
War Diary	Norrent Fontes	01/07/1917	19/07/1917
War Diary	Proven	20/07/1917	21/07/1917
War Diary	International Corner.	22/07/1917	31/07/1917
Heading	War Diary Of Lieut Colonel T.E. Bennett D.S.O. A.S.C. Commanding 38th (Welsh) Divisional Train. 1/8/17 To 31/8/17 Vol 21		
War Diary	International Corner	01/08/1917	05/08/1917
War Diary	Proven	06/08/1917	18/08/1917
War Diary	Dragon Camp.	19/08/1917	31/08/1917
Heading	War Diary Of Lieut Colonel T.E. Bennett D.S.O. A.S.C. Commanding 38th (Welsh) Divisional Train From 1/9/17 To 30/9/17 Vol 22		
War Diary	Dragon Camp.	01/09/1917	10/09/1917
War Diary	Proven Road.	11/09/1917	13/09/1917
War Diary	Estaires	14/09/1917	16/09/1917
War Diary	Sailly-Sur-La-Lys.	17/09/1917	30/09/1917

Heading	War Diary Of Lieut Colonel T.E. Bennett D.S.O. A.S.C Commanding 38th (Welsh) Divisional Train 1/10/17 To 31/10/17 Vol 23		
War Diary	Sailly-Sur-La-Lys.	01/10/1917	31/10/1917
Heading	War Diary Of. Lieut Colonel T.E. Bennett. D.S.O. A.S.C. Commanding 38th (Welsh) Divisional Train 1/11/17 To 30/11/17 Vol 24		
War Diary	Sailly-Sur-La-Lys	01/11/1917	30/11/1917
Heading	War Diary Of Lieut Colonel T.E. Bennett D.S.O. Army Service Corps Commanding 38/Welsh/Divisional Train From 1.12.17 To 31.12.17 Vol 25		
War Diary	Sailly	01/12/1917	31/12/1917
Heading	War Diary Of. Lieut Colonel T.E. Bennett D.S.O. Army Service Corps Commanding 38th (Welsh) Divisional Train 1/1/18. To 31/1/18 Vol 26		
War Diary	Sailly Sur-La-Lys.	01/01/1918	06/01/1918
War Diary	Sailly	07/01/1918	14/01/1918
War Diary	Merville	15/01/1918	31/01/1918
Heading	War Diary Of Lt Colonel T.E. Bennett. Commanding 38/Welsh/Divisional Train. From 1.2.18. To 28.2.18. Vol 27		
War Diary	Merville	01/02/1918	15/02/1918
War Diary	Steenwerk	16/02/1918	28/02/1918
Heading	War Diary Of Lieut Colonel T.E. Bennett D.S.O. Army Service Coys Commanding 38th (Welsh) Divisional Train. From 1.3.18 To 31.3.18 Vol 28		
War Diary	Steenwerck	01/03/1918	31/03/1918
Heading	War Diary Of Lieut Col. T.E. Bennett D.S.O. Army Service Corps Commanding 38th (Welsh) Divisional Train. From 1.4.18 To 30.4.18 Vol 29		
War Diary	Toutencourt	01/04/1918	12/04/1918
War Diary	Contay	12/04/1918	30/04/1918
Heading	War Diary Of Lt Col. T.E. Bennett D.S.O. Army Service Coys Commanding 38th (Welsh) Divisional Train From 1.5.18 To 31.5.18 Vol 30		
War Diary	Contay	01/05/1918	06/05/1918
War Diary	Toutencourt	07/05/1918	20/05/1918
War Diary	Herissart	21/05/1918	31/05/1918
Heading	War Diary Of Lt Col. T.E. Bennett D.S.O. Army Service Corps Commanding 38th (Welsh) Divisional Train From 1.6.18 To 30.6.18 Vol 31		
War Diary	Herissart	01/06/1918	05/06/1918
War Diary	Lealvillers	06/06/1918	30/06/1918
Heading	War Diary Of Lt Col. T.E. Bennett D.S.O. Army Service Corps Commanding 38th (Welsh) Divisional Train From 1.7.18 To 31.7.18 Vol 32		
War Diary	Lealvillers	01/07/1918	31/07/1918
Heading	War Diary Of Lt Col. T.E. Bennett D.S.O. Army Service Corps Commanding 38th (Welsh) Divisional Train From 1.8.18 To 31.8.18 Vol 33		
War Diary	Lealvillers	01/08/1918	24/08/1918
War Diary	Hedauville	25/08/1918	25/08/1918
War Diary	Usna Hill	26/08/1918	31/08/1918
Heading	War Diary Of Lt Col. T.E. Bennett D.S.O. Army Service Corps Commanding 38th (Welsh) Divisional Train From 1.9.18 To 30.9.18 Vol 34		

War Diary	Contalmaison	01/09/1918	02/09/1918
War Diary	High Wood	03/09/1918	04/09/1918
War Diary	Les Boeufs	05/09/1918	10/09/1918
War Diary	Etricourt	11/09/1918	16/09/1918
War Diary	Rocquigny	17/09/1918	30/09/1918
Heading	War Diary Of Lt Col. T.E. Bennett D.S.O. Army Service Corps Commanding 38th (Welsh) Divisional Train From 1.10.18 To 31.10.18 Vol 35		
War Diary	Sorel Le Grand	01/10/1918	06/10/1918
War Diary	Epehy	07/10/1918	07/10/1918
War Diary	De La L'eau	08/10/1918	09/10/1918
War Diary	Villers Outreaux	10/10/1918	10/10/1918
War Diary	Clary	11/10/1918	11/10/1918
War Diary	Bertry	12/10/1918	23/10/1918
War Diary	Troisvilles	24/10/1918	24/10/1918
War Diary	Forest	25/10/1918	29/10/1918
War Diary	Richemont	30/10/1918	31/10/1918
Heading	War Diary Of Lt Col. T.E. Bennett D.S.O. Army Service Corps Commanding 38th (Welsh) Divisional Train From 1.11.18 To 30.11.18 Vol 36		
War Diary	Richemont	01/11/1918	04/11/1918
War Diary	Englefontaine	05/11/1918	05/11/1918
War Diary	Locquignol	06/11/1918	08/11/1918
War Diary	Aulnoye	09/11/1918	30/11/1918
Heading	War Diary Of Lt Col. T.E. Bennett D.S.O. Royal Army Service Corps Commanding 38th (Welsh) Divisional Train. From 1.12.18 To 31.12.18 Vol 37		
War Diary	Aulnoye	01/12/1918	29/12/1918
War Diary	Inchy	30/12/1918	30/12/1918
War Diary	Glisy	31/12/1918	31/12/1918
Heading	War Diary Of Lt Col. T.E. Bennett D.S.O. Royal Army Service Corps Commanding 38th (Welsh) Divisional Train. From 1.1.19 To 31.1.19 Vol 38		
War Diary	Glisy	01/01/1919	14/01/1919
War Diary	Pont Noyelle	15/01/1919	31/01/1919
Heading	War Diary Of Lt Col. T.E. Bennett D.S.O. O.B.E. R.A.S.C. Commanding 38th (Welsh) Divisional Train From 1.2.19 To 28.2.19 Vol 39		
War Diary	Pont Noyelle	01/02/1919	28/02/1919
Heading	War Diary Of Lt Col: T.E. Bennett D.S.O. O.B.E. R.A.S.C. Commanding 38th (Welsh) Divisional Train From 1.3.19 To 31.3.19 Vol 40		
War Diary	Pont Noyelle	01/03/1919	31/03/1919
Heading	War Diary Of Major W.S. Cameron T/Commanding 38th (Welsh) Divisional Train From 1.4.19 To 30.4.19 Vol 41		
War Diary	Pont Noyelle	01/04/1919	07/04/1919
War Diary	Querrieu	08/04/1919	19/04/1919
War Diary	Blangy	20/04/1919	30/04/1919
Heading	War Diary Of Lt Col. T.E. Bennett D.S.O. O.B.E. R.A.S.C. Commanding 38th (Welsh) Divisional Train From 1.5.19 To 31.5.19		
War Diary	Blangy	01/05/1919	31/05/1919
Miscellaneous	D.A.G. British Troops in France & Flanders, (Records. Section),	18/06/1919	18/06/1919

Heading	War Diary Of Lt Col. T.E. Bennett D.S.O. O.B.E. R.A.S.C. Commanding 38th (Welsh) Divisional Train From 1.6.19 To 16.6.19 Vol 43		
War Diary	Blangy	01/06/1919	16/06/1919

WO95/2550/5
Dinsmore Train

38TH DIVISION

38TH DIVL TRAIN ASC.
Nov ~~DEC~~ 1915 - JUN 1919

(330 to 333 Coys ASC)

38th Sept. Mail
vol. V

9/6/78

Dec 15
June 19

Army Form C. 2118

WAR DIARY or INTELLIGENCE SUMMARY

(Erase heading not required.)

Welsh Divisional Train

Instructions regarding War Diaries and Intelligence Summaries are contained in F.S. Regs., Part II. and the Staff Manual respectively. Title Pages will be prepared in manuscript.

Nov- Dec 1915

Place	Date	Hour	Summary of Events and Information	Remarks and references to Appendices
Winchester	5/11/15	10 a.m.	Received orders from Divisional HdQrs (together with cpy of W.O. letter) to be prepared for embarkation for service in France with the Division on or about 22nd inst.	
		2.30 p.m.	175 Horses received for Train from Offr of Remounts.	W.t.t.
		5.30 p.m.	Lectured to Reg.tal Transport Officers in their duties generally.	W.t.t.
"	6/11/15		Routine.	
"	7/11	a.m.	Sunday. Went to Salisbury by car & interviewed A.D. of S.T.	
"	8/11		Inspection of horses by Inspg Genl of Remounts. Major Iredell applied officially to be relieved of appointment as S.S.O.	
"	9/11/15	p.m.	S.S. wagon of 332 Coy. arrived Supplies lorries and wire landed over to Divisional Remount Depot at 2 p.m. Orders received by Lt Col Yates to proceed overseas 15-15 Progress Report of Supply Train forwarded to Hd. Qrs.	C.H.M
"	10/11/15	a.m.	Instructions issued to Supply Officers fitted themselves in readiness a week before dep. embarkation of Division Lt Col Yates went to Records and London in a.m. S.O. 114th Inft Bde ordered to Salisbury Plain 3 Army Postal Service men to Sup. Train and 3 for Supply Column arrived. 13 G.S. wagons for 331 Coy. arrived in p.m. and wagons for 129th F Amb.	C.H.M

1875 Wt. W593/826 1,000,000 4/15 J.B.C. & A. A.D.S.S./Forms/C. 2118.

Army Form C. 2118

2

WAR DIARY
or
INTELLIGENCE SUMMARY   Welsh Divisional Train.
(Erase heading not required.)

Instructions regarding War Diaries and Intelligence Summaries are contained in F. S. Regs., Part II. and the Staff Manual respectively. Title Pages will be prepared in manuscript.

Place	Date	Hour	Summary of Events and Information	Remarks and references to Appendices
Winchester	11/11/15	a.m.	S.S.O. ordered hire S.O.C. at 10 a.m. Routine.	Ctw.
"	12/11/15	p.m.	331 Cdy horses less 15 trains mobilised. 40 lead horses obtained.	Ctw.
"	13/11/15		Routine. Lt.Col. Fisher ordered to join Staff train leaving for Marseilles via Gib – Havre on 16th and returning 20th.	
"	14/11		Sunday – Routine	
"	15/11		Routine	
"	16/11	P.M.	Lt.Col. Fisher left via Southampton for Marseilles on Staff train.	
"	17/11	P.M.	Squadron Wiltshire Yeomanry (Divisional Cavalry) arrived 8.40 p.m. Shed by wagon.	Ctw.
"	18/11	A.M.	Capt. H.W. Shove reported for duty as S.S.O.	Ctw.
"	19/11	A.M.	Capt. Shove met Major Iredell & went to Divl HQRS ordered to hand over. Change of supply officers full of instruction; S.O.s notified. £75 received from hotel Army Corps for conforts.	
"	20/11	A.M.	Capt. Shove assumed duties of S.S.O. Major Iredell granted sick leave till 10/12/15. Instructions about 2H.P.L. Junes reporting for duty received.	

1875 Wt. W593/826 1,000,000 4/15 J.B.C. & A. A.D.S.S./Forms/C. 2118.

Army Form C. 2118

Page 3

WAR DIARY
or
INTELLIGENCE SUMMARY
(Erase heading not required.)

Welsh Divisional Train.

Instructions regarding War Diaries and Intelligence Summaries are contained in F.S. Regs., Part II. and the Staff Manual respectively. Title Pages will be prepared in manuscript.

Place	Date	Hour	Summary of Events and Information	Remarks and references to Appendices
Lundala	21/11/15	a.m.	Return of unfit Officers for overseas rendered to Hd Qrs. Routine.	
"	22/11/15		Instructions received to 49th Rly Supply Ktchn to report to Aldershot. Exchanged Field Kitchen horses received at Hd Qrs. had kitchen running with rest to all units. Routine.	
"	23/11/15	a.m.	Orders received to Advanced Party of S.S.O. and 3 Rate S.O. Ordered overseas on 24th Nov. Requisitioning Officers' cars used to D.I.M.T. Reply received that cars would be detailed overseas.	
		p.m.		
"	24/11/15	a.m.	C.O. returned from overseas inspection. 10.30 am C.O. lectures on Supplies in the field at 5.30pm at Brush led Ors. began lectures men to units for Mobilization Parade.	
"	25/11/15	a.m.	Mobilization Parade 7.a.m. to WORTHY DOWN along ANDOVER ROAD. Bivouacked at Chew Calt apricks Camp broken up successfully used. Men worked together well. Eating and fed and tea had dinners. Packed up and moved off 3.40 pm under Capt Templeton and returned to camp at 6 p.m. Orders for practice parade issued. Wagon & Water cart for company.	
"	26/11/15	a.m.	Practice parade started 6.30 am. B.A.D.O. seen about training rifles and spare parts. ambulation preparing received and circulated to all companies and units. C.O. went to Salisbury important business.	
"	27/11/15		Brig. Gen. Coke came to inspect horses at 2 p.m. and cook to M.D. Routine.	
"	28/11/15		C.O. returned 11 a.m. O/c details from instruction in a.m. Vet. officer obtained & proceed with 331 Coy on leave Dec 1st.	

Army Form C. 2118

WAR DIARY
or
INTELLIGENCE SUMMARY
(Erase heading not required.)

Welsh Divisional Train. Page 4

Instructions regarding War Diaries and Intelligence Summaries are contained in F.S. Regs., Part II. and the Staff Manual respectively. Title Pages will be prepared in manuscript.

Place	Date	Hour	Summary of Events and Information	Remarks and references to Appendices
Warehall	29/11/15	a.m.	330 & 331 Coy. paraded and marched off 6.15 a.m., 332 Coy. 6.25 a.m. proceeded to CRAWLEY DOWN. took up billets in 2 companies. The Queen arrived part at 12 noon. C.O. attended at the dais. Reviewed three times watched them went into cots then feel. C.O. inspected each Coy. before return, 2.35 p.m. rations in camp 5.30 p.m. C.O. attended a Entertainment Conference at Grist fellows 6 p.m. Programme of marches to Southampton received.	
"	30/11/15	p.m.	Further instructions received to Coy. Commanders about embarkation, marking of animals & vehicles. Railhead left arrived from Bulford. A.D. of S.T. was ringing up about rations and blankets issues pay. C.O. sent Left than Office here suspended × Capt. R.S. Cranbrook *from Cardew Forster	
"	1/12/15	9 a.m.	330 Coy paraded 8.25 a.m. before marching off to Crawford. unspected (Col. 28 Dr. ?... then marched to SOUTHAMPTON in Special. 331 Coy. all rates..... Capt. & others where 9.15 a.m. armed a company of 331 Coy. War office orders received from Reserves Bajt Dx. N.C.O. Brits Brighton and brighton bin sepents futurcuded by C.O. in morning. Quarters were closed 5 p.m.	
"	2/12/15	8 p.m.	C.O. inspected 331st Coy. 7.15 a.m. before marching off to Crawlers. Barrack Rooms of 331 Coy. inspected and found left in disgraceful condition. R.Q.M. paraded his staff then 1 N.C.O. from Nidewship posted at W.O. Orderly Rooms. C.O. left for train or special care. Orderly Room closed & so far in hostile. Lieut. F.S. has to reported to duty and arrived duly upshot to War Office mobilisation and equipment of Reserve details hurried on so far as possible. Coys. had not got their free duty as to A.T.s. 64 and equipping mens.	

WAR DIARY or INTELLIGENCE SUMMARY

Army Form C. 2118

38th Welsh Divisional Train

December 1915

Place	Date	Hour	Summary of Events and Information	Remarks
WINCHESTER	1/12/15		331 Coy A.S.C. (No 2 Company Divisional Train) inspected by O.C. Train at 8.30 a.m., then marched to SOUTHAMPTON to Entrainment. Captain Iveluell reported 9.15 A.M. and took over Entrainment. Divisional HdQuarters closed Command of HdQuarters Company. Divisional HdQuarters closed at 6 p.m. C.O. proceeded to SOUTHAMPTON to inspect intrainment Mt.t	W.L.T.
	2/12		332nd Coy inspected by C.O. at 7.15 A.M. & then marched to SOUTHAMPTON to entrainment. Found that 332 Coy had left their Barrack Rooms in disgraceful condition. Called on O.C. Company to his reasons in writing	W.L.T.

Army Form C. 2118

Page 5

WAR DIARY or INTELLIGENCE SUMMARY
(Erase heading not required.)

Place	Date	Hour	Summary of Events and Information	Remarks and references to Appendices
Kendrick	3/12/15	6.45am	333 Coy marched off in morning. AD of S&T was very up as regards notifying RFA 24th in transport. He referred it to his office and telephoned up that it was to remain as already noted by Divisional Head Qrs. Lieut. Y.S. Rankin was left in charge and given instructions. 67 men; 134 horses; 67 vehicles.	
"	4/12/15	7.15 am	Head Quarters and 333 Coy went out of Arrington Park Camp at 7.15 am. Capt. Marley Lieut. Y.S. Rankin, Lieut & QM W. Murrell (acting) and C.Q.M.S. remained behind with surplus men and RFA 24th Coy transport details. Remainder of officers and Orderly Room personnel. Reports on details left behind rendered by C.O. to AD/S.T. Salisbury. C.O. & Adjt. proceeded later by car to Southampton. Col. Fisher was in charge of embarkation of Division for 4th day Dec 4, 1915.	
		12 noon		
		1.10 pm	Col Fisher arrived 1.10 pm. Reported to Embarkation Staff. Train disembarked. Adj. Qr. Cap. arrived at strength in Officers N.C.Os & men, horses and vehicles.	
		2 pm.	2 pm under Major Smallwell. Embarkation begun forthwith. All embarking arranged and worked by personally. 2 days rations drawn. Everything embarked by 2.50 pm. Officers & men all went by it pm. Meeting of all officers in saloon at 4.30 pm. Col Fisher gave his	
At sea		4 pm.	instructions as to discipline, routine, accommodation of officers, lights, fireplaces, serving of life of men asleep in life stalls. Senior officers of each unit on board will	
	4.12.15		All officers and men slept in life stalls. Col Fisher moved ship. Ship on board about 720 officers & men and about 200 horses. Details were of 16th Welch, 17/R.W.F also 4/9th Middx Veterinary Section and 338 Coy ASC - the Div. 39/15 by S.S. Huntscraft. S.S. Huntscraft sailed 5.30 pm. Officers of the unit detailed for 2 hr. watches from 9am evening. Several horses went down between 4pm – 10pm. Very rough evening. Men complained to little stuffy. Men behaved very well. However & gave it orders on clearing & I went lights. Sick call morning, by nile orderer walter 2.30 am. No casualties at all.	
		5.30 pm		
		2.30 am		

WAR DIARY or INTELLIGENCE SUMMARY

Army Form C. 21
Page 6

Place	Date	Hour	Summary of Events and Information	Remarks and references to Appendices
At Sea and Le Havre	5.12.15	11.15am	S.S. Hunscraft arrived at Havre at 7.15 am Sunday morning. A.R. Quay Disembarkation proceeded with at once. Landing return handed to A.M.L.O. also Nominal Roll of Officers. Coy again was confronted on speed of disembarking, working in and getting clear of sheds. Surplus rations landed over to Supply Depot by Q.M.S. held who was a/Ship Coy Q.M. Coy The wood off to No 5 Rest Camp. The lines were settled, men put in tents. Otherwise slow resumed to complete Coy. Was drawn in afternoon, including teams, shop, skid where horses had traces, rope harness and wagon covers.	
Le Havre	6.12.15	3.30am	Ration party marched off with guide. Coy paraded 4am and marched to Railway Station (but had traces efficiently) used as accoutred wagon. Contained many to unstick horses waited after packing wagons ready to put in trucks. Teas got ready for men while horses were entrained. Train started 8.30 am. 16th halt. Hqt. Vet Set. A.FS On and 330 Coy on board. Several horses very much frightened and so let-down and stuffing flying. Train went a long way round and Rouen to Sangnere to Sherbonlu Morgny to Abbeville e-St. Over when 2/4 Brigtn met C.O. train with detaining instructions at 2.45am.	
Aire LIGNE	7.12.15	5.15am	Arrived at Aire. Instructions received from R.T.O. as to unloading which was began at once. Such Unloaded and horses and harness entrained. S.S.D. came and left G.O. Wgt. and S.O. of Brig. Men to find billets in hamlet of LIGNE. Cooks wagons sent ahead of rest of Coy and got ready for men breakfasts. Remainder of Coy marched in about 9.30 am. Men seen wells. Wagons parked by vehicles and horses rested, fed. Men had breakfast. Return drawn at 11 am. Brit. Head Qu'rs went Nominal Roll of officers, landing stalt. Horse return and Field Stale. C.O. and O.C. went about 3pm. C.O. 330 again went Etxad Quarters S.S.O. and to find Quarters. Mail delivered about 3pm. Staff Capt. 113th Bde. wgn and about accommodation 6.30pm and also looked for other billets. Memery of LIGNE and adjoining farms occupied by a hospital. Billet not suitable. Brit. Hd. Qn. at Roquetoure. 330 Coy Rogue. 331 at Candre d'Cape Head Quarters and 330th Coy Aire. 332 at Sleunenghem. 333 at St. Quentin.	

WAR DIARY or INTELLIGENCE SUMMARY

Army Form C. 2118

Page 7

Place	Date	Hour	Summary of Events and Information	Remarks and references to Appendices
LIGNE	8.12.15		Routine arranged under which O.T. Train and J.S.O. report at Divisional HdQuarters daily at 9 A.M. for informal conference. Arranged certain number of billets including Officers in Orderly Room & J.S.O.	W.H.P.
do	9/12	—	Visited Corps Headquarters MERVILLE. Saw Lieut: Wright - adjt - to Lt. Corps Ammn: Parks - (lt. being away) - also saw Col: Greer A.M.H.S. - Went on to LESTREM & interviewed D.M. Johnson Commg 19th D.V. Train. Motored with him to St FLORIS which will be our Train HdQrs in Reserve Area. Here are stables, half built by Col: Johnson. Arranged to lend out horse to complete them - Col Johnson promising to erect Stables in the forward area (LESTREM) so that both Train could have good shelter. also discussed billets & canteen arrangements. Country under water	W.H.P.
	10/12		Went round Dumps. Subsequently issued "Dump Discipline Orders" — Train Corp experiencing difficulty in getting supply & baggage wagons returned from Units - reported same to M.G.O. In afternoon rode into AIRE & saw Maj. Gen: Hobbs.	
	11/12		Informed today by S.S.O. and verbally by Brig H.Q. (nothing in writing) that 4 Brigade of Artillery will arrive at Boeseghem (near AIRE) to be attached to 38th Division by tomorrow (12th inst). Went out with S.S.O. and	

WAR DIARY or INTELLIGENCE SUMMARY

Army Form C. 2118

Page 8

Place	Date	Hour	Summary of Events and Information	Remarks and references to Appendices
LIGNE	11/12 cont:		Selected Refilling Point (X roads BOESENGHEN) - also selected possible billets to transport - have not been asked to provide latter - Wrote to Div: HQrs (Quarter) (T.F.2.b) asking what was to be done - Strength of Artillery said to be 2,900 men and horses. Ordered Supply Officer & R.O. (Div: Troops) with Clerks & Orderlies to proceed to BOESENGHEN for duty.	W.H.t
do	12/12	AM	Proceeded by car with S.S.O. to inspect R.M. dump at BOESENGHEN. Found all correct - went on to STEENBECK Stn arranged details with Major Scott Commdg 38th Div Supply Column for taking up rations to forward area for 38th Div: Troops attached to this Division. On return reported at Army HQrs AIRE but Col: St John Parker D.D.a.V.T was not in - Tried again in afternoon without success - All horses of Train are now under cover.	
do	13/12	-	On hearing of 331 Coy: died of pneumonia - Proceeded to Gen: l HQrs STOMER with dicist; Maree. Saw General Laste Elliott & Col: Colin Campbell, gave orders that sent want to be provided for men in billets at night.	
do	14/12		Reported to D.D.a.V.T. 1st Army. (Col: St John Parker). Weather dry & frosty.	

Army Form C. 2118

WAR DIARY
or
INTELLIGENCE SUMMARY
(Erase heading not required.)

Place	Date	Hour	Summary of Events and Information	Remarks and references to Appendices
LIGNE.	15/12		To THIENNES to arrange Unloading of coal train from Canal barges to railway trucks. Thence to LESTREM to interview OC. 15th Divl Train re transport questions. Also as to billets in that area. On returning called on Col. Black Comnd. Divl Train Supply Divn. and called again at THIENNES on way in.	N.t.r.
"	16/12		To ST OMER. To interview Major of General Staff. Can from great trouble in return journey.	N.t.r.
"	17/12		Received letter from Div. HQrs Quarters to effect that the Division will move into Reserve Area on 20th inst.	N.t.r.
	18/12		Proceeded by car to select billets and Refilling points in Reserve area. Billeting areas allotted to Divl Train as follows:—	N.t.r.
	19/12		Train HQrs moved to ST FLORIS. Orders issued for Train Companies to follow on 20th with Brigades & Divl Troops. Billeting parties occupied prospective billets.	N.t.r.

WAR DIARY or INTELLIGENCE SUMMARY

Army Form C. 2118
Page 10.

Place	Date	Hour	Summary of Events and Information	Remarks and references to Appendices
ST FLORIS	20/12		HdQrs of Train and 330, 332 Coys billeted at ST FLORIS. As however the accommodation was limited, & 2nd HdQrs was at ST VENANT, leave was obtained to move Train HdQrs into ST VENANT, leaving Coys behind. N° 331 & 333 Coys billeted at MERVILLE and ROBECQ respectively. Personnel were in MERVILLE, ROBECQ, CALONNE.	N.t.r.
ST VENANT	21/12		Selected billets. HdQr Officers Mess. Orderly Room & Quarters. Gave instructions for billeting of horse shelters to be proceeded with. 113 horses & mules arrived MERVILLE. Having been rained by HdQuarters to take them over for distribution to Units, detailed Captain Templeton & Lieut. Davies to proceed to MERVILLE with 3 teamsters & 20 men to take them over.	
"	22/12		Attempted unsuccessfully to find Office for Post Office in ST VENANT. Held meeting with Coy Officers as to Xmas festivities for men. Decided nothing could be done by not having men at the rate of 2/- per head of all "Other ranks" to OC Coys to expend for the men for Xmas. Men to be consulted as to individual requirements and to be given more than 2 glasses of beer to be allowed to any individual. Building of shelters for horses progressing. Engaged as hairdresser & Canteen.	N.t.r.

1875 Wt. W593/826 1,000,000 4/15 J.B.C. & A. A.D.S.S./Forms/C. 2118.

WAR DIARY or INTELLIGENCE SUMMARY

Army Form C. 2118
Page 11.

Place	Date	Hour	Summary of Events and Information	Remarks and references to Appendices
ST VENANT	23/12		Visited Corp. H.Q.rs MERVILLE. Interviewed C.R.E. Brown. Also went to LA GORGUE & saw Ry Station which is to be head temporarily. Railed to the Division - Went to LAVENTIE & saw Capt. G.R. Marshall who has applied for a commission. Cannot recommend him as regards appearance - Intended to inspect 331 Coy. Horses of 332 Coy died - but was detained too long.	W.F.F.
	24/12		London R.A. left for GLOEMINGEN but continued to be rationed from the Division. Sent in supply of rum with Major Mirin. G.GLOEMINGEN to remain for duty into R.A. lines. The Div Artillery from WINCHESTER begin to arrive -	W.F.F.
	25/12		Xmas Day. Routine - nothing of importance.	W.F.F.
	26/12		Visited Robecq & inspected 333 Coy. Horses in open but standing are being made by Coy. Men in huts. Officers housed in farm. Great deal of typhoid but billets generally good.	W.F.F.
	27/12		Arranged with C.R.E. for 2 huts for Coy (30'×17') to be erected as temporary Recreation rooms - Horses returned from R.A. (from Ireland) in very bad state, also vehicles -	W.F.F.

WAR DIARY
or
INTELLIGENCE SUMMARY

Army Form C. 2118

Page 12

Place	Date	Hour	Summary of Events and Information	Remarks and references to Appendices
ST. VENANT	28/12		To LA GORGUE with S.S.O. to see Guards Division re loading Train Supply Section from Station. Not a success today, for several minor reasons. Discussed question of buying straw re: with Col. Green A.D.M.S. 11th Corps. Transport tolls employed on R.E. & Ordnance Services.	W.t.t.
"	29/12		2 huts arrived to 330 Coy. Arranged for 1st Div. Transport to bring in bricks for Stables for this Unit. 2 motor lorries. Upper village to Lacoutune & bricks.	11.t.t.
"	30/12		330 Coy started to erect huts. Visited Depots MERVILLE - also Capt Hall 12/1 May accompanied by Col. Green to interview Col. St John Parker. D.D.S.T. 1st Army. AIRE re buying of straw & potatoes. Intended to inspect 331 Coy but owing to having to ride (no car being available) could not get through in time. Arranged with A.D.P.D.M.S. for M.T. Supply Column to be put under me. The question was referred to Corps Headquarters and approved.	W.t.t.
"	31/12/15		To AIRE (under instructions of A.Q.M.G. Corps HQrs) to interview D.D.S.&T. re buying of straw & potatoes. Am personally of opinion that in these areas which are likely to be occupied for a long time, straw & potatoes should be bought up in towns & fetched as required. Buying to be done by Corps representatives rather than by Brigade Representation. Officers 2nd Lieut W.F.T. Fisher R.F.A. Commdg 38th Welsh Divl Train.	

1875 Wt.W593/826 1,000,000 4/15 J.B.C. & A. A.D.S.S./Forms/C. 2118.

38th Strh. Frani
tot: 2
Tanks

WAR DIARY or INTELLIGENCE SUMMARY

Army Form C. 2118

38th (Welsh) Divisional Train

Page I

Place	Date	Hour	Summary of Events and Information	Remarks and references to Appendices
ST VENANT	1/1/16		Rode to MERVILLE & inspected 331 Coy of this Train. Afterwards interviewed Major Scott commdg Divl Supply Column – Considers billets of 331 Coy has made the best of it. Attended Conference at 19th Divl HQ at PLESTREM to discuss question of tabulating & trying up supplies in District. A.Q.M.G., 11th Corps (Lt Col Green) and representatives of 38th Divisional HQrs Staff present. Resolved that each Divisional Train should Exhibit and tabulate its own area. A Corps representative to be appointed later, to collect reports & adjust needs of each area.	11.1.1
	2/1/16		Inspected 330 Coy in morning – huts now in course of erection – obtained permission from Divl HdQrs for 2 Armstrong Canvas huts per Coy in addition to the wooden "useful huts" provided by R.E. Rode to ROBECQ in afternoon & inspected 333 Coy.	1/1/1
	3/1		Informed by Divl HQ that 113th & 116th Infy Bdes would go in to the forward area on 5th & 7th instt (Lt Bdes on each day) changing places with 114th & 115th Divs & Guards Divisn respectively. Made necessary S. & T. arrangements.	11/1/1

WAR DIARY
or
INTELLIGENCE SUMMARY
(Erase heading not required.)

Army Form C. 2118

Page 2

Instructions regarding War Diaries and Intelligence Summaries are contained in F.S. Regs., Part II. and the Staff Manual respectively. Title Pages will be prepared in manuscript.

Place	Date	Hour	Summary of Events and Information	Remarks and references to Appendices
ST VENANT	4/1/16		Went to LESTREM in morning with Captain Killearn (332 Coy) to select billets for his Coy. In afternoon inspected 1st Line Transport of 10th Welch Regt at ST FLORIS. Transport in good order, but T.O. reports he has had great difficulty in obtaining clothing. Is evidently a keen officer. One mule suffering from lice.	N.P.T.
	5/1		Attended 4th move but to Companies. Coys going great deal to trouble owing to regrouping constant repairs. Inspected 1st Line Transport of 13th and 14th Welch Regts in afternoon. Starting Orders issued from HQrs Divn	N.P.T.
	6/1		To AIRE in afternoon—saw Genl Hobbs and Col. J. John Parker—the latter re system of estimating amount of supplies to the country & what amount an regimant to receive or ; also to roads to be used after frost.	10.1.4.
	7/1		Inspected 1st Line Transport of 19th Pioneers. Very bad turn out - harness neglected. bits & all metal work untouched. Animals dirty & so galled.	11.1.4.

Army Form C. 2118

Page 3

WAR DIARY
or
INTELLIGENCE SUMMARY
(Erase heading not required.)

Place	Date	Hour	Summary of Events and Information	Remarks and references to Appendices
ST VENANT	8/1		Inspected 1st Divn Tpt of 10th R.W.F. (115th Inf & 78th By) - Good turn out - Sent for Transport Officer of Brs. in car in afternoon to point beyond LESTREM to inspect billet of 331 Coy & the Train - in billet, just vacated by 156 Divisn Train - very filthy place - 131 Coy is being cleaning it.	W.H.
"	9/1		To point beyond LACOUTURE to inspect 1st Divn Transport of 13th Infy Bgde. The new Staff Captain (Cap't Campbell) attended - Transport in good order generally - Metal work needs attention - also some vehicles - Especially brakes - Gave instructions to the Train Coy of Bgde (331. Cap't Eng) to send all his Staff Sergt Artificers - Saddler, Farrier & Wheeler to inspect harness, shoeing & vehicles respectively. LACOUTURE was being shelled during inspection.	W.H.
	10/1		Inspected 16th Welsh Regt 1st Line Transport. Turn out fair - Also visited 333 Coy. M.T.C. Major Oates, R.E., Past. Called in here in afternoon re investigation of supplies available in District.	W.H.

WAR DIARY
or
INTELLIGENCE SUMMARY

Army Form C. 2118

Page 4

Place	Date	Hour	Summary of Events and Information	Remarks and references to Appendices
ST VENANT	11/1		Routine – Visited 333 Coy.	A.H.
"	12/1		G.O.C. inspected lines of H.Q. Coy. Handed over billets of 332 Company in ST FLORIS to 19th Div: Train – 332 Coy will take billets of 333 Coy at ROBECQ.	W.H.
"	13/1		To LIGNE on horseback – settled up outstanding claims – Collected forage depôt at AIRE.	W.H.
"	14/1		Made enquiries re Chaff cutting machines – knew of need to hand machines. They were known antiquated & worthless. No others available at AIRE. Returned ST VENANT. Reported made that motor lorries from driven chaff cutter sh'd be bought. Informed by H.Q. that Div: H.Q. would probably move into forward area (LESTREM) on 24th inst. Arranged Transport for Brigade moves with H.Q.	W.H.

Army Form C. 2118

Page 5

WAR DIARY
or
INTELLIGENCE SUMMARY
(Erase heading not required.)

Place	Date	Hour	Summary of Events and Information	Remarks and references to Appendices
STEENAM	15/1	A.M.	With Major Shadwell by car to visit railhead (LABOURGUS) and light railway with dumps of 19th Div¹ Amm. Good arrangements. To AIRE and BILLERS to inspect proposals for Chaff cutting. First van got chaff cutter with 2½ h.p. engine installed to £80. delivery and installation would probably take 6 weeks. Purchased no hand machine in MERVILLE for the use of Contingent point.	W.A.B.
		P.M.		
"	16/1		To LESTREM by car with Major Shadwell & Adjutant. Letter to take summary of evidence in the case of 1000 Saddles I dropt Palmer who was in want charged with drunkenness. Visited order Room of 15th Div¹ Train and went round two Train Co¹⁾ billets. On return went to H.Q. applicable for trial of J.S. Palmer. Strict order received from 1 A.H.Q. re case of motr cars which will in future be grouped under O.C. Div: Train in the case of the 5th Cav. of Train. Mallowring of horses proceeding.	W.A.B.
"	17/1		To LESTREM by car to select billets to following move. Dropped Adjutant at MERVILLE for Field Gen: C.M. on S.S. Palmer & another. (Cap¹: Templeton Master of C.M.) Selected billets. Drew up orders (on return) for Canteens & Motor Cars of Train.	W.A.B.

Army Form C. 2118

Page 6.

WAR DIARY
or
INTELLIGENCE SUMMARY
(Erase heading not required.)

Instructions regarding War Diaries and Intelligence Summaries are contained in F.S. Regs., Part II. and the Staff Manual respectively. Title Pages will be prepared in manuscript.

Place	Date	Hour	Summary of Events and Information	Remarks and references to Appendices
ST VENANT	18/1		March Tables to move HQ Dinon into area now occupied by 19th Div received from H.Q. worked out table for supply & Transport arrangements in consultation with S.S.O. Rode into MERVILLE and saw A.Q.M.G. 11th Corps (Lt Col Green) who consented to employment of tongues from 1st Army H.T. Coy now billeted near LA GORGUE.	11.1.t.
"	19/1		Revised tables after consulting A.Q.M.G. 11th Corps and having arranged details of transport required with Lt. Max H.T. Coy (train Reserve). Also visited LOCON and found place in vicinity (due W) to billet for 331 Coy to handle stores, Coy to be known the Dump and Brigade.	11.1.t.
"	20/1		Issued orders to all Officers Commanding Train Companies regarding moving into new area. Interviewed C.R.A. re detail of move of Artillery	11.1.t.

Army Form C. 2118

WAR DIARY
or
INTELLIGENCE SUMMARY
(Erase heading not required.)

Instructions regarding War Diaries and Intelligence Summaries are contained in F. S. Regs., Part II. and the Staff Manual respectively. Title Pages will be prepared in manuscript.

Place	Date	Hour	Summary of Events and Information	Remarks and references to Appendices
ST VENANT	21/1		Handed over motor Speers to Supply Column - worked Officer in morning. Went to LESTREM to arrange details with OC. 1st Div Train. Visited D Battery 121st Bde in neighbourhood of VIELLE CHAPPELLE.	H.H.
"	22/1		Brigade began moving into new area.	H.H.
"	23/1		Sunday. Visited 332 Coy at ROBECQ. Saw majority of Train Officers at my Quarters at ST VENANT in evening re payment of Mess Bills.	H.H.
LESTREM	24/1		Moved to LESTREM at same time as Div'l HQ. 336 (H.Q.) Coy left at ST FLORIS to bring on the R.A. on 30th.	H.H.
"	25/1		Inspected Drivers in morning - also new billets of 332 Coy. In afternoon inspected No 3 Section Reserve Park (17th) under Lieut. Keats A.S.C. In a disgraceful state - men & horses have been presented & are done up - harness & harness, arms &c neglected.	W.F.

1875 Wt. W593/826 1,000,000 4/15 J.B.C. & A. A.D.S.S./Forms/C. 2118.

Army Form C. 2118

Page 8

WAR DIARY
or
INTELLIGENCE SUMMARY
(Erase heading not required.)

Instructions regarding War Diaries and Intelligence Summaries are contained in F. S. Regs., Part II. and the Staff Manual respectively. Title Pages will be prepared in manuscript.

Place	Date	Hour	Summary of Events and Information	Remarks and references to Appendices
LESTREM	26/1		Sent report in to H.Q. re state of 17th Res. Park. Inspected dumps & billets of 333 Coy. In afternoon 2.O.C. inspected Res. Park. talked agreed with my report. Have decided not to work more than 20 pairs of the 67 pairs they have available, in order to give the rest a chance to recuperate. Asked for 20 Aux. H.T. wagons to Field Engineers to replace those of Res. Park. wanted back.	Nil.
"	27/1		Rode to LOCON in morning. In afternoon PARADIS.	W.S.F.
"	28/1		Routine.	W.F.F.
"	29/1		Routine.	W.F.F.
"	30/1		330 Coy with Divl R.A. marched into the area. Forming quarters at PARADIS. Walked out & inspected billets in afternoon.	W.F.F.

Army Form C. 2118

Page 4.

WAR DIARY
or
INTELLIGENCE SUMMARY
(Erase heading not required.)

Place	Date	Hour	Summary of Events and Information	Remarks and references to Appendices
LE STREM	31/1		Arranged for R.A to return all drivers, horses & supply wagons but to retain their baggage wagons to be manned by themselves. Also arranged with Brigade to furnish from 4 to 6 pairs of 1st line H.T. horses to their Train Co. at 1.30 P.M. daily to work into supply wagons on their return from delivering rations. D.A.C. arrived. They will be able to supplement Transport.	Wit.

W.F.F. Fisher Major
Comm'g 38th Welsh Div'l Train

1st Feb 1916.

WAR DIARY or INTELLIGENCE SUMMARY

Army Form C. 2118

February 1916.

38th Welsh Divisional Train – B.E.F.

Page I. Vol

Place	Date	Hour	Summary of Events and Information	Remarks and references to Appendices
LESTREM	1/2/16		Arranged with H.Q. for Div'l Amm'n Column to supply 30-2 horsed wagons daily to supplement transport. Colonel Comm'n Ellison A.Q.M.G. Arrived (on way home to look round in a 3 day staff tour – took him to visit 330 & 333 Coys.	M.T.T.
	2/2		Went round Heavy (Howitzer) Batteries with Col: Comm'n Ellison – 6", 8" & 9.2. All transport being fully employed.	M.T.T.
	3/2		Col: Comm'n Ellison left for England. Arranged with Infantry Bde to furnish H.Q. horses from 1st Line Transport for duty with supply wagons of Companies in afternoon work – principally carrying straw.	M.T.T.
	4/2		M.S.S.M. Daniel. 1st Field Ambulance reported by O.C. 7st Ambulance as incompetent. Saw S.S.M. Daniel at Orderly Room & referred case to Headquarters and to Base.	M.T.T.

Army Form C. 2118

WAR DIARY
or
INTELLIGENCE SUMMARY
(Erase heading not required.)

Page 2.

Instructions regarding War Diaries and Intelligence Summaries are contained in F. S. Regs., Part II. and the Staff Manual respectively. Title Pages will be prepared in manuscript.

Place	Date	Hour	Summary of Events and Information	Remarks and references to Appendices
LESTREM	5/2		Visited R.A. McMaster. arranged with R.A. Major for O.A.R. to draw all bricks for R.A. R.A. complained that supply section was insufficient to draw straw from dump. Inspected remedy.	W.H.H.
"	6/2		Went to VENDIN LES BETHUNES and arranged for supply? Said to horse standings at Pa'? for Cab: Mitre. Monthly. Rejected to have being drawn direct from rich to units or to units.	W.H.H.
"	7/2		Inspected Supply section of 332 Coy. Excellent turn out.	W.H.H.
"	8/2		To STOMER by car to interview L'Gen: Sir S. Lake-Elliot. Move of 113th & 114th Brigade carried out.	W.H.H.

1875 Wt. W593/826 1,000,000 4/15 J.B.C. & A. A.D.S.S./Forms/C. 2118.

Army Form C. 2118

WAR DIARY
or
INTELLIGENCE SUMMARY
(Erase heading not required.)

No 3.

Place	Date	Hour	Summary of Events and Information	Remarks and references to Appendices
LESTREM	9/2		Informed by Q. Div H.Q. that left section of Front would probably be given up to heart of Front at present occupied by 2nd Division later on.	H.H.
"	10/2		Reverted Cpl. Beeston 333 by to permanent guard (Private) for inefficiency. — Remanded Driver Owen for trial by F.G. Court Martial for drunkenness on duty. — To BETHUNE by car in afternoon to see O.C. 2nd Div. Train (Lt. Col. Wilmot Jones). Afterwards to AIRE where I visited Gen. L. Hobbs.	H.H.
"	11/2		Informed by H.Q. that BETHUNE would not be the Div H.Q. in morning. Probably LOCON. Reserve Park inspected by Major Oakden on behalf of Corps.	H.H.

WAR DIARY
— or —
INTELLIGENCE SUMMARY

(Erase heading not required.)

Army Form C. 2118

P 4

Place	Date	Hour	Summary of Events and Information	Remarks and references to Appendices
LESTREM	12/2		Prince Arthur of Connaught inspected the Supply dumps - Col J. John Parker & Major Lawrence in attendance - Major Southwell placed on sick list.	W.H.
"	13/2		Sunday. Visited TOMBE WILLOT - inspected road - Sent in report to C.R.E. requesting that it be repaired. Bicycle stolen from orderly orderly room - reported to A.P.M.	W.H.
	14/2		Inspected baggage section of 332 Coy at 6 a.m. Very good turnout 7th Gen. Court martial sat on D.R. Owen 17th Res; Park. Went to LOCON in afternoon to find billets. -	W.H.
	15/2		Inspected 1st Kens Transport & Pioneers. Indifferent turn out. Got transport in serviceable condition - All cars laid up for review repair -	W.H.

WAR DIARY or INTELLIGENCE SUMMARY

Army Form C. 2118

p 5

Place	Date	Hour	Summary of Events and Information	Remarks and references to Appendices
LESTREM	16/2		HQ 113th & 115th Infantry Brigades moved into their new areas — to complete on 17th	W.t.t.
"	17/2		Above Brigades completed move.	W.t.t.
"	18/2		35th Div Headquarters moved into LESTREM and 38th Division (less Train) moved to LOCON. Lt. Col. Johnson 35th Div Train arrived with his S.S.O. (in advance) & Adjt to take over our Train Headquarters.	W.t.t.
LOCON	19/2		moved to LOCON with HQ Train. Took up quarters in W 6 d Central (Map Ref. 36 A).	W.t.t.
"	20/2		331 Company moved from FOSSE to LOCON. O.C. 105th Bn (35th Div) applied to train occupied by 331 Company, who have consequently received orders from Divl HQ to move	W.t.t.

Army Form C. 2118

WAR DIARY
INTELLIGENCE SUMMARY
(Erase heading not required.)

p 6

Place	Date	Hour	Summary of Events and Information	Remarks and references to Appendices
LOCON	21/2		Found extellent billet for 331 Coy. who moved in at 11 A.M. Heavy bombardment all day. Germans attacking French front on our right.	11.t.t.
"	22/2		Snowfall of 2 inches. Nothing of importance.	11.t.t.
"	23/2		Snow continued - much thinner. Some frost - nothing serious. Transport as usual.	11.t.t.
"	24/2		Thawer & then Returns. Snow & frost continued. Transport in hand.	14.t.t.
"	25/2		Snow & frost continued. Transport in hand. Arranged for 113th Inf B.De to keep 4 bufferys began for night R.E. work.	14.t.t.

1875 Wt. W593/826 1,000,000 4/15 J.B.C. & A. A.D.S.S./Forms/C. 2118.

Army Form C. 2118

WAR DIARY
INTELLIGENCE SUMMARY
(Erase heading not required.)

p 7

Place	Date	Hour	Summary of Events and Information	Remarks and references to Appendices
LOCON	26/2		Thaw - but so gradual that Transport was able to run as usual. C.O.C. authorized battalion in trenches to retain one baggage wagon to R.E. Services to be horsed by 1st Line Transport with Infantry drivers.	H.T.T.
	27/2		"Thaw precautions" ordered from Corps Headquarters for 3 days commencing at 6 A.M. today. These precautions consist in restricting motor lorries to certain roads, and restricting the use of horse transport to supply duties with half loads.	H.T.T.
	28/2		Thaw precautions continued. Otherwise nothing of importance.	H.T.T.
	29/2		Last day of Thaw precautions. An "Albatros" aeroplane brought down practically undamaged by two of our planes. by rifle fire - mechanic wounded but Officer (German Lieutenant) uninjured.	H.T.T.

29/2/16

W. T. F. Aston, Lt Colonel
Commanding 3rd Bn. Div'l Train

38th Brit: Train
Vol: 3

38 Dw Iran Vol 4

WAR DIARY
or
INTELLIGENCE SUMMARY

Army Form C. 2118

38th Welsh Divisional Train Part I

March 1916

Place	Date	Hour	Summary of Events and Information	Remarks and references to Appendices
LOCON	1/3/16		Interviewed Col. Beck. St. Roy: Flying Corps. BETHUNE re transport of S/Lieut: Daughter of the "Train" as an Observer. Mon. of 1/14th Infantry Brigade into Reserve Area carried out. Visited 130th Field Ambulance. Capt. Green and Lieut. J.T. Jones went to 130th Fd Ambulance on sick list.	K.F.E.
	2/3		Went to see S.D. of S & T. 1st Army AIRE and went 9/Lieut Deighton to ST OMER to interview H.Q. R.F.C. 330 Coy changed billets from PARADIS to LES CHOQUAUX.	K.F.E.
	3/3		Inspection of 14th & 10th Welsh Regtal (1st Line) Transport. Horses turn out of 106 and very poor from 1/14th Regr. Also of 1/13th Regt. 1st Line Transport. Excellent turn out - best in the Division so far -	

WAR DIARY
INTELLIGENCE SUMMARY
(Erase heading not required.)

Welsh Divisional Train — Page 2

Army Form C. 2118

Place	Date	Hour	Summary of Events and Information	Remarks and references to Appendices
LOCON	4/3		Routine. Interviewed Staff Officer at HQ Flying Corps and recommended untidiness on road — S.O. promised to attend to it.	W.L.L.
"	5/3		Sunday. To STOMER by permission of Q.O.C. 38th Division to interview Major Sir E. Locke Elliot re question of transfer to Infantry.	W.L.L.
	6/3		3.32 coy moved into new billet W17C. Gen. Sir E. Locke Elliot arrived to inspect collapsible Cookers. Interesting report on same recommending that it should replace Infantry Field Kitchens.	W.L.L.
	7/3		Routine.	W.L.L.
	8/3		113th & 114th Infantry Brigades changed areas — Employed 94 wagons during both journeys. Corps granted leave & stores in front of pair to 9/11. Taken from 10th to 20th inst.	W.L.L.
	9/3		2nd Lt F.T. Fisher proceeded on special leave. Major R. S. Gradwell arrived & commenced of this Divisional Train. Routine.	R.L.

WAR DIARY
INTELLIGENCE SUMMARY
(Erase heading not required.) Welsh Divisional Train.

Army Form C. 2118

Page 3

Place	Date	Hour	Summary of Events and Information	Remarks and references to Appendices
LOCON	10/3/16		Orders to draw 12 H.D. horses from 19th D.A.C	R.H.
	11/3/16		Driver Webb's I.G.C.M. ADVS inspected 330 Company horses; reported very satisfactory	R.H.
	12/3/16		Interviewed Major Scott 35 D.S.C. regarding Train Water-lorries. Orders received from J.T.O. R.T.C. for L/Sergt. — to report here as cook on emergency and for 2 m/t Pickfords to report for an indiviser.	R.W.
	13/3/16		Inspected Dumps 8.30 – 9.30. Cost. Templeton granted 10 days special leave	R.H.
	14/3/16		Inspected Dumps 8.30 – 9.30 found all in good order. Inspected transport of the 130 F.A. which was very satisfactory	R.H.
	15/3/16		Inspected dumps 8.30 – 9.30 – all correct, wagon chains away by 9.35. Went to Duranmez Hea Swallino. Inspected 129th F.A. found all satisfactory except horses which were low in condition	R.H.
	16/3/16		Inspected all dumps 8.30 – 9.30 in turn all in correct order. Wagons dvn: at Q. Inspected 131st F.A. The horses were in very poor condition & the wagons & harness showed great neglect. There onward.	R.S.S.
	17/3/16		Inspected all dumps 8.30 – 9.30 all in good order. Went to Divisional H.Q. Cas-Ormstry — to know APD. Visited all Company — inspected 1984 — all correct.	R.H.

Army Form C. 2118

Page 4

WAR DIARY
or
INTELLIGENCE SUMMARY
(Erase heading not required.) Welsh Divisional Train

Place	Date	Hour	Summary of Events and Information	Remarks and references to Appendices
LOCON	18/3/16		Inspected all dumps 8.30 - 9.30. Orders from Divisional H.Q. to procure Sears for four dumps from this date inclusive - Carried out General routine work	R.H.P.
	19/3/16		Visited all dumps 8.30 - 9.30 am all in good order. Went to Bris: Headquarters	R.H.
	20/3/16		Inspected all dumps 8.30 - 9.30 am. Everything satisfactory except Oat sacks there were weak no undue current. Iwulage was taking place, reported. Inspected Transport 19th Welsh (Pioneers) & found 117 horses & mules in good & air condition. Wagons Harness in good repair & in air division.	R.H.
	21/3/16		Visited all dumps 8.30 - 9.30 am - all correct. Went to Divisional H.Q. Inspected horse transport of Headquarters Company, the horses, wagons, harness & lives were in most excellent condition -	R.J.S.
	22/3/16		Inspected all dumps 8.30 - 9.30 am - Satisfactory. Went to Divisional Headquarters. Inspected Transport of 19th Reserve Park & found workout provision but 67th in horses wagons, also Inspected Transport of 333 Company which was in good order.	R.H.
	22/3/16		Visited all dumps 8.30 - 9.30 am - all correct. Went to Divisional H.Q. Arranged hours of 7.15 P.M. and 11.15 P.M. R.S	R.H.
	24/3/16		Inspected all dumps 8.30 - 9.30 am. Went to Divisional H.Q. Major T.F. Bennall Arrived to take over Command of the Divisional Train	R.H.

WAR DIARY

INTELLIGENCE SUMMARY

(Erase heading not required.)

Army Form C. 2118

Page 5

Welsh Divisional Train.

Place	Date	Hour	Summary of Events and Information	Remarks and references to Appendices
LOCON.	25/3/16	—	Visited Nos 8 & 34 Divisional Trains. — Inspected 113 Brigade dump — Ordinary Routine.	T.B.
"	26/3/16	—	2'Lieut Affleck joined from No 8 Reserve Park for duty. — Ordinary routine & office work.	T.B.
"	27/3/16	—	Visited No 34 Divisional Train, & did a days work with O.C. Train. Ordinary routine in the Train.	T.B.
"	28/3/16	—	Conference with S.S.O on the subject of Divisional Supplies — Ordinary Routine.	T.B.
"	29/3/16	—	Visited number of Divisional Trains & spent the day investigating Train management. 2 Lt Rickham proceeded to H.Q.A.R.T.C. on Transport.	T.B.
	30/3/16	—	Ordinary Routine	T.B.

Army Form C. 2118

Page 6

WAR DIARY
INTELLIGENCE SUMMARY
(Erase heading not required.)

Welsh Divisional Train.

Place	Date	Hour	Summary of Events and Information	Remarks and references to Appendices
LOCON	31/8/16	—	Visited dumps with S.S.O. also went to Richebourg. Inspected 883 Company of the train in the afternoon. Brigade Relief (113-117) was carried out successfully.	W.

Th Bennett.
Major A.S.C.
O.C. 38. Divisional Train.

38 Div Incmn Kal... 2118
38th Welsh Divisional Train

APRIL 1916.

WAR DIARY
INTELLIGENCE SUMMARY
(Erase heading not required.)

Page 1
Army Form C. 2118

Welsh Divisional Train.

Place	Date	Hour	Summary of Events and Information	Remarks and references to Appendices
LOCON	1-4-16	—	113 & 114 Brigade Relief completed. Inspected 330 Co A.S.C.	T/3.
"	2-4-16	—	Inspected 332 Co A.S.C. O.C. 38 (Welsh) Divisional Supply Column came in for a consultation. Lieut T.P. Jones returned from duty with XI Corps Requisitioning Officer.	T/3.
"	3-4-16	—	Lieut T.T. Jones went on leave to 14 April inclusive. Inspected the 113 Bde First Line Transport. In the Afternoon inspected the 115 Bde First Line Transport.	T/3.
"	4-4-16	—	Went to Railhead. Inspected 114 Bde Transport in the afternoon. Refilling Time altered to 8 A.M. instead of 9 A.M.	T/3.
"	5-4-16	—	Office work — Sent in report to H.Q. on Bde First Line Transport. Adjutant sent round checking First Line Transport & Vehicles	T/3.

WAR DIARY

INTELLIGENCE SUMMARY

Welsh Divisional Train.
Page 2.

Army Form C. 2118

Place	Date	Hour	Summary of Events and Information	Remarks and references to Appendices
LOCON.	6/4/16	—	D.D.V.S. 1st Army inspected 331 Co. M.T.C. Lorries. — Ordinary Routine	
"	7/4/16	—	Interviewed the G.O.C. — Inspected No 3 Section 17 Reserve Park which is attached to the Train.	
"	8/4/16	—	D.D.V.S. 1st Army inspected 330, 332 & 333 M.T.C Co's horse - & 3rd Section Reserve Park — Was present at the inspection. Captain H.M. Hoare proceeded for Temporary to XI Corps H.Q. :: Captain Brace Browne A.S.C. reported from XI Corps to Train for Temporary duty. Ordinary Routine.	
"	9/4/16	—	Ordinary Routine. — Parade Church Service.	

WAR DIARY

INTELLIGENCE SUMMARY

Army Form C. 2118

Welsh Divisional Train.

Page 3

Place	Date	Hour	Summary of Events and Information	Remarks and references to Appendices
Locon	10/4/16		Office work in connection with "Next line of Transport." Informed this the Division would move on 14 – 15 – 16 – 17 – 18 April.	
Locon	11/4/16		Made arrangements for the move at H.Q. & for cars to new area in afternoon to try & arrange matters with the Division being relieved. 19th Pioneer Batt. Transport inspected by O.C. "A" & "C" Co in my absence. Two motor cars struck off-strength on proceeding to 1st Army, in accordance with D/of T's orders.	
Locon	12/4/16		All leave stopped. O.C. 39 Train, the Olympians S.S.O. Came down to make arrangements to Enquiries concerning this area – subs	

WAR DIARY or INTELLIGENCE SUMMARY

Army Form C. 2118

1st Welsh Divisional Train. Page 4

Place	Date	Hour	Summary of Events and Information	Remarks and references to Appendices
Locon	12/4/16		Whit Mon. Division is about to move, replacing this. Arrangements worked concerning move being made. 1 motor car broke down.	Ed.
"	13/4/16		Transport movements in connection with 115 Inf Bde. Office work in connection with the Divisional move. One car detached to 1/2 Army Workshops for 1 month.	Ed.
"	14/4/16		Office work in connection with the Divisional move – unable to proceed to Rail head & superintend matters generally because the one remaining motor car was very much required by S.S.O. for his duties. 24 wagons, 3 officers, 29 other ranks, 49 horses toned for duty this 6 Reserve Park – Walted to 331 M.T. Co. A.S.C. Transport.	
"	15/4/16		Move of Division proceeding – still only 1 motor car available in Train – so supervision impossible.	

Army Form C. 2118

1 Welsh Divisional Train.

Page 5

WAR DIARY
or
INTELLIGENCE SUMMARY

(Erase heading not required.)

Place	Date	Hour	Summary of Events and Information	Remarks and references to Appendices
LOCON.	16/4/16	—	Move of Division proceeding - There is a great deal of work in connection.	
LOCON.	17/4/16	—	H.Q. of Division H.Q. Coy & H.Q. of Train move to LA GORGUE.	
" "	18/4/16	—	Inspected the Refilling at Riez Bailleul with the A.A. & D.H.Q. Captain Hoare D.S.C. who had been detached for duty with Corps - returned for divisional duty & took over his position as S.S.O.	
" "	19/4/16	—	Inspected 331 Co. A.S.C. - Ordinary Routine.	
" "	20/4/16	—	Inspector of motor vehicles G.H.Q. inspected the Division motor cars. Very busy arranging for spare officer.	
" "	21/4/16	—	Flag System of Signalling at Riez Bailleul for Refilling wagon was adopted.	

Army Form C. 2118

WAR DIARY
INTELLIGENCE SUMMARY
(Erase heading not required.)

Welsh Divisional Train.

Page 6.

Place	Date	Hour	Summary of Events and Information	Remarks and references to Appendices
LA GORGUE	22nd	—	Very wet weather – Inspected Refilling at Rail head – Ordinary Routine.	
"	23rd	—	Lt Col T.E. Bennett Section of 1st Army A.H.T. Coy attached to T.B. 10 days' Special leave granted to Major R.S. Swalwell and Captain M. Williams. Austin car sent to Divisional Supply Column & Captain J. Templeton in command of Train. Ordinary Routine.	
"	24th	—	Relief of 113th Bde by 114th Bde. Carried out satisfactorily. Routine.	Capta
"	25th	—	Routine. Other car sent to repairs to Supply Column	Capta
"	26th	—	A.A. & Q.M.G. inspected Refilling Point. Very satisfactory. Capt. Templeton (on Adjutant) inspected 332 Coy. in afternoon. Leave re-opened.	
"	27th	—	Staff Captain R.A. interviewed about condition of wagons sent to a Bde. R.F.A. Gas alarm 11.30 P.M. Train did 2nd warned.	
"	28th	—	One water car returned from R.E. workshops 1st Army. One limber and 5 H.D remounts drawn from D.A.C. All transport fully occupied, moving to be cleaned by order of Head Qualies.	Capta

1875 Wt. W593/826 1,000,000 4/15 J.B.C. & A. A.D.S.S./Forms/C. 2118.

WAR DIARY
or
INTELLIGENCE SUMMARY

(Erase heading not required.)

Army Form C. 2118

Welsh Divisional Train.

Page 7.

Place	Date	Hour	Summary of Events and Information	Remarks and references to Appendices
LA GORGUE	29/4/16	—	113th Bde. refilled direct from Pack Train at Railhead. 40 minutes, including cutting up and issue. Supply Column.	C/We
— " —	30/4/16	—	G.O.C. 1st Army presented medal ribbons to 113 – 115th Bdes. A.S.C. not represented owing to 113 – 115th Bdes. relieving. Relief of half of 113th and half 115th Bdes carried out. Divisional troops refilled direct from Pack Train at Railhead.	C/We

In the field
1 – 5 – 16.

J. Templeton
Captain A.S.C.
Comdg. 38th Welsh Divisional Train.

38 Div Train
Army Form C. 2118
V516

WAR DIARY
INTELLIGENCE SUMMARY
(Erase heading not required.)

Page 1.

MAY. 1916.

Place	Date	Hour	Summary of Events and Information	Remarks and references to Appendices
LA GORGUE	1-5-16	—	114th and 115th Infantry Bdes' groups refilled direct from Pack Train at Railhead & trial of one occupied 50 minutes. Relief of 115th and 113th Bdes. satisfactorily completed.	
"	2/5/16.	—	Survival Troops and all three Brigade groups refilled direct from Pack train at Railhead. Time occupied 2hrs. 20 mins. Routine.	
"	3"	—	Refilling as on previous day. Routine. Captain Templeton and Adjutant visited 331-2-3 Coys. in morning. Lt. Norman granted leave from 4th to 14th inst. and two men one weeks leave each. S.S.O. went to D.D.S.T. 1st Army at AIRE. Lt Colonel T.E. Bennett returned	L.
	4/5/16	—	H leave Ordinary Routine.	DO
	5/5.	—	A great deal of office work. Ordinary Routine	DO
	6/5	—	Scheme for advance &c. being worked out. Ordinary Routine	L
	7/5	—	Scheme for advance continued. Ordinary Routine	DO
	8/5	—	Royal Welsh Yeomanry Transport to 4 Army. Arrangements made to take over their duties for 330 Co A.S.C. Scheme for advance still being continued	L.

Army Form C. 2118

WAR DIARY
INTELLIGENCE SUMMARY

(Erase heading not required.)

Instructions regarding War Diaries and Intelligence Summaries are contained in F.S. Regs., Part II. and the Staff Manual respectively. Title Pages will be prepared in manuscript.

Place	Date	Hour	Summary of Events and Information	Remarks and references to Appendices
LA.G.AG JE	9/5/16	—	Relief of "G" Brigade by 115 Brigade – H.Q of Royal Welsh Yeomanry moved to 4 Army. Advance scheme this being prepared.	W.
"	10/5/16	—	Ordinary Routine – Went round 333 C.M.A.C. Finishing Advance Scheme.	W.
"	11/5/16	—	The Cyclists proceeded from Division to X¹ Corps. Inspection of our own vehicle by J.O.H. X¹ Corps. Ordinary Routine.	W.
"	12/5/16	—	Day Advance Scheme finished. Rodis habitation of Artillery Brigades – R.E. Companies & Field Ambulances among the Companies.	W.
"	13/5/16	—	330 Co: moved to its new billets. Ordinary Routine.	W.
"	14/5/16	—	Visited Railhead – Ordinary Routine.	W.
"	15/5/16	—	Ordinary Routine.	W.
"	16/5/16	—	Brigade Relief between 113 & 114 Brigades. Ordinary Routine otherwise.	W.
"	17/5/16	—	Lieut Capt's Nash & Robertson & Lieut Nave sent on leave. Lieut Norman Sadlett 14 days extension on	W.

1875 Wt. W593/826 1,000,000 4/15 J.B.C. & A. A.D.S.S./Forms/C. 2118.

WAR DIARY

INTELLIGENCE SUMMARY

(Erase heading not required.)

Army Form C. 2118

Instructions regarding War Diaries and Intelligence Summaries are contained in F. S. Regs., Part II. and the Staff Manual respectively. Title Pages will be prepared in manuscript.

Place	Date	Hour	Summary of Events and Information	Remarks and references to Appendices
LA GORGUE	17/5/16	—	Medical ground. Was present at Pelletting.	H.
"	18/5/16	—	Lieut J.T. Jones appointed acting adjutant vice Lieut C.H. Mane - Conference re control of Traffic at Railhead. I.S.O. v Requisitioning officer 61 Division reported for instruction. Train orders for advance v Retirement in progress. Was present at Pelletting.	H.
"	19/5/16	—	The machine gun company arrived v posted to this division. London Gazette dated 18/5/16 rec'd this day v notifying the promotion of Captain H.N. Hoare to Major - Train orders for advance v Retirement in progress.	H.
"	20/5/16	—	London Gazette received showing the promotion of Lieut. E. Foster, J.T. Jones to Captain - 2 Lts R.B. Stratton W.S.S. Taylor, R.A. Jfleck to Lieut. Advance v Retirement Train orders still in progress - 8 motor cycles evacuated on behalf of the 3 Field Ambulances. Attacked at Railhead.	H.
"	21/5/16	—	3 Sergts v 1 driver reports from the Field ambulance for evacuation to Base on reduction of Establishment	H.

1875 Wt. W593/826 1,000,000 4/15 J.B.C. & A. A.D.S.S./Forms/C. 2118.

WAR DIARY
INTELLIGENCE SUMMARY

Army Form C. 2118

Place	Date	Hour	Summary of Events and Information	Remarks and references to Appendices
LA GORGUE	22/5/16	—	Was present at Rejilling - Went in to the question of the reorganization of the R.A. 2nd line vehicles. Ordinary Routine.	nil.
"	23/5/16	—	Was present at Railhead - Ordinary Routine	nil
"	24/5/16	—	A.A. v A.M.G. visited Railhead vn inspected everything. Also visited 331 Company A.S.C. in the afternoon. Artillery 2nd line Transport reorganized owing to change. Lieut J.E. Hughes proceeded on leave.	nil.
"	25/5/16	—	Was present at Railhead. A.A. v A.M.G. visited 332 Company A.S.C.	nil.
"	26/5/16	—	Was present at Railhead v Rejilling - 26 Limbers 98 mules v Lorries for 104 mules rec'd from Brigade for Evacuation - A.A. v A.M.G. visited 333 Company A.S.C.	nil.
"	27/5/16	—	Was present at Railway Rejilling - Considerable office work in progress owing to the Road up in of 1st Line Transport.	nil.

WAR DIARY
INTELLIGENCE SUMMARY
(Erase heading not required.)

Army Form C. 2118

Instructions regarding War Diaries and Intelligence Summaries are contained in F.S. Regs., Part II. and the Staff Manual respectively. Title Pages will be prepared in manuscript.

Place	Date	Hour	Summary of Events and Information	Remarks and references to Appendices
LA GORGUE	28/5/16	—	Inspection of surplus mules & horses by D.D.R. 1st Army. Was present with the A.A.V. & M.G. Captain Nash & Lieut Nairn arrived from leave.	69
"	29/5/16	—	More office work concerning surplus Brigade Turnout. Captain Robotham returned off leave. Was present at Richebois.	
"	30/5/16	—	Had a conference with O.C. 3rd Div: Train Res. Captain Cross & Jones - Lieuts Taylor & Isaac went on leave. Was present at Richebois.	
"	31/5/16	—	2/Lt Hodgson returned with cars from Corps Requisition up office whom he had been attached to duty. Went to MERVILLE to Reserve Supplies in Base. Was present at Richebois & Refilling.	70

W Bennett Lt Col.
O.C. 38 (Welsh) Divi Coal Train.

1875 Wt. W593/826 1,000,000 4/15 J.B.C. & A. A.D.S.S./Forms/C. 2118.

38 JUNE

Army Form C. 2118

WAR DIARY

INTELLIGENCE SUMMARY

(Erase heading not required.)

Instructions regarding War Diaries and Intelligence Summaries are contained in F.S. Regs., Part II. and the Staff Manual respectively. Title Pages will be prepared in manuscript.

Place	Date	Hour	Summary of Events and Information	Remarks and references to Appendices
LA GORGUE	1/6	—	Refilling much delayed at Railway station owing to slowness of 3rd Divisional Train.	
"	2/6	—	Very busy working on the advance Scheme. Surplus mules of the Brigades evacuated to GONNEHEM Remount Depôt	
"	3/6	—	Busy all day at the Advance Scheme — 2 Lt Hobson reported for duty & went to H. Q. Company Advance Scheme all day.	
"	4/6	—	Busy on Retreat Scheme — Major H. N. Hoare went on leave. Lieutenant Hug has returned from leave to.	
"	5/6	—	115 Inf Brigade relieved by 114 Infantry Brigade — Lieuts Davies, Affleck & Jones proceeded on leave Inspected 33. C.A.S.C.	
"	6/6	—	Visited Railhead & Refilling Point. Ordinary Routine	

Army Form C. 2118

WAR DIARY
INTELLIGENCE SUMMARY
(Erase heading not required.)

Place	Date	Hour	Summary of Events and Information	Remarks and references to Appendices
LA GORGUE	7/6	—	Visited Railhead & Refilling Point — Instruction in Musketry commenced in all Train Companies. Ordinary Routine.	
"	8/6	—	Visited Railhead & Refilling Point. Visited 332 Co. A.S.C.	
"	9/6	—	Preparing for Divisional move — very busy.	
"	10/6	—	332 Co A.S.C. moved to BUSNES — Busy trying to get information which was not forthcoming.	
"	11/6	—	Orders begun to come in — 333 Company M.C. moved to ROBECQ with 11th Infy. Brigade — Captain Templeton placed in charge of R.F.A. detachment proceeding to ST VENANT.	
"	12/6	—	Train H.Q. & Divisional H.Q. moved to ST VENANT. Advance party of R.F.A. to ST FLORIS.	

WAR DIARY

INTELLIGENCE SUMMARY

Army Form C. 2118

Place	Date	Hour	Summary of Events and Information	Remarks and references to Appendices
SIVENANT 13/6	13/6	—	332 Co A.S.C. proceeded to RAIMBERT. ROCHELLES. CAUCHY area. 330 Co. to ST FLORIS — Went round area that the Division is to proceed through, to select Refilling Points.	J.
"	14 6/76	—	Alteration in T.M.Bs going with Division. Time altered 1 hour. Brigade moving South. Went TO TINQUES to arrange matters. H.Q. Division proceeded to ROELLECOURT.	J.
"	15/6/26	—	H.Q. Train moved to TINQUES. Refilling delayed owing to mistake on the subject of which station the Pack Train was to go to. 330 Co arrived ROCOURT. 331 Co arrived ROCOURT 332 Co arrived VANDELICOURT. 333 Co arrived Chelers.	J.

WAR DIARY

INTELLIGENCE SUMMARY

(Erase heading not required.)

Army Form C. 2118

Place	Date	Hour	Summary of Events and Information	Remarks and references to Appendices
TINQUES	16/6	—	MAJOR R HOARE returned from leave — went round the A.S.C. Companies	
"	17/6	—	Certain batteries R.F.A. went up in to the Line — detached Captain Trupleton with part of 330 Co. A.S.C.	H.
"	18/6	—	Went to R.A. H.Q. to try & get information re Artillery move — Busy preparing transport notes for the A.S.C. Companies.	H.
"	19/6	—	Visited D.D.S.V.T. 3rd Army — Lieut Isaac made S.O. 114 2nd A.C. Busy in office all day.	dd.
"	20/6	—	Received application from 4 Officers in our Company to proceed to R.F.C. — ordered to Relief of the O.C. Company.	dd.

WAR DIARY
INTELLIGENCE SUMMARY

Army Form C. 2118

Place	Date	Hour	Summary of Events and Information	Remarks and references to Appendices
TINQUES	21/6	—	Captain Foster took over 332 Co R.E. from Captain Williams. Went to HERMANVILLE to interview 51 Divisional Train.	
"	22/6	—	Went out to prospect area through which Division is about to move.	
"	23/6	—	332 Co. ordered to move to CAMBIGNEUL. Lieut. Affleck removed from 332 Co to 330 Co. as R.O. Interviewed Captain Williams re his removal from his command of 332 Company. A.D.C.	
"	24/6	—	13 H.D. Horses & 3 Rviv arrived at Railhead for Train. Collected & distributed - Very wet morning - 3 complete Turnouts Demples To Potarliement wereted to 6.A.V.S. Highland. Had an interview with G.O.C. 2 Captain Williams.	

WAR DIARY

INTELLIGENCE SUMMARY

(Erase heading not required.)

Army Form C. 2118

Place	Date	Hour	Summary of Events and Information	Remarks and references to Appendices
TINQUES	25/6	—	Visited D.D.S.&T. 3rd Army. Very interesting orders for the Divisional move	td.
"	26/6	—	Left TINQUES for BONNIERES. Busy all day with the move orders & arrangements generally	td.
BONNIERES	27/6	—	Visited all Companies. Proceeded to VACQUERIE.	td.
VACQUERIE	28/6	—	Visited all Companies. Horses very done up as the country traversed was very hilly. Interviewed S.V.C. again re Captain Williams.	td.
"	29/6	—	Visited all Companies. H.Q. Train & Division moved out again.	
RUBEMPRE	30/6	—	RUBEMPRE. Companies moving are right.	td.

W. Kennedy Lt Col. A.S.C.
O.C. 38 (Welsh) Div. Train.

Army Form C. 2118

Vol 8

WAR DIARY
~~INTELLIGENCE SUMMARY~~ W3
(Erase heading not required.)

Instructions regarding War Diaries and Intelligence Summaries are contained in F. S. Regs., Part II. and the Staff Manual respectively. Title Pages will be prepared in manuscript.

Place	Date	Hour	Summary of Events and Information	Remarks and references to Appendices
From	1/1/16		Lieut Colonel F.E. Bennell A.S.C. Commanding 38 (Welsh) Divisional Train	To 31/7/16.

Army Form C. 2118

WAR DIARY
or
INTELLIGENCE SUMMARY
(Erase heading not required.)

Place	Date	Hour	Summary of Events and Information	Remarks and references to Appendices
RUSEMPRE	1/7/16		330 Co: A.S.C. & H.Q. of Train at CARNON FARM. - 331 Co: A.S.C. at HERISSART, 332 Co: at LE VAL DE MAISON, 333 Co: at TOUTENCOURT. - Horses very done up. at 7.P.M. received orders for Train to move with B— & Artillery groups - H.Q. Train arrived ACHEUX at 9.P.M.	U.
ACHEUX	2/7/16		At 1 A.M. informed that Train H.Q. should beat LEALVILLERS. Went there very early in morning. 330 Co: at TOUTENCOURT. 331 Co: at LEALVILLERS, 332 Co VAL DE MAISON, 333 Co: at ACHEUX all the Companies moved by night - very busy all day with Companies & Refilling Point.	U
TREUX	3/7/16		Arrived with Train H.Q. at about 7.P.M. - 330 Co: just outside TREUX - The others at HERICOURT & BUIRE.	U.
TREUX	4/7/16		Commenced the system of MEETING POINTS - ie. Units Representatives not coming to Refilling Points - but Guides from every unit attending at from "Points" to guide the Supply vehicle to wherever the Unit might be.	

WAR DIARY
INTELLIGENCE SUMMARY
(Erase heading not required.)

Army Form C. 2118

Place	Date	Hour	Summary of Events and Information	Remarks and references to Appendices
MORLANCOURT	5/7/16		T.H.Q. + the N.J.C. Companies except 330 Coy R.E. moved to near the place named. The Division relieved the 7 Division. Bombardment in front very heavy.	
"	6/7/16		Meeting Point system not particularly working owing to units not understanding it. Horses recovering but rather slow. Petrol Tins Lurched for 20 Hs men attacking in front could have had water sent up.	
"	7/7/16		Horses showing signs that the rest is doing them good. 4 favor Petrol Tins being given to Companies so that each vehicle should have Two. Always fallen in. Meeting Point system working well.	
"	8/7/16		Visited + inspected the Companies. Horses improving rapidly.	

Army Form C. 2118

WAR DIARY
INTELLIGENCE SUMMARY
(Erase heading not required.)

Place	Date	Hour	Summary of Events and Information	Remarks and references to Appendices
STAFF HOLLANCOURT	9/7/16	—	Went looking for positions for D.A.C. Companies. Stored an advance to ordered - woke the Chief Trouble.	W.
"	10/7/16	—	Again went to look for positions for D.A.C. Companies. Found suitable locations. Severe fighting by division in HAM E.T.Z wood. All the supply Column lorries being utilised for Collection of wounded - dumped replenishing delayed in consequence & dumped late at night - rewarding ammunition afterwards. Several dumps of Iron Rations left by 7 Division & 8th Division, which were much scattered - collected by trains transport into one big dump close by the Camp. Train wagons working up	

Army Form C. 2118

WAR DIARY
or
INTELLIGENCE SUMMARY
(Erase heading not required.)

Instructions regarding War Diaries and Intelligence Summaries are contained in F. S. Regs., Part II. and the Staff Manual respectively. Title Pages will be prepared in manuscript.

Place	Date	Hour	Summary of Events and Information	Remarks and references to Appendices
MORLANCOURT	10/7/16	—	At FRICOURT. Somewhat hazardous — more patrol this sent up to Brigades. Houses being worked rather hard — but am very fit — Informed that the Division was about to move — Attended D.H.Q. for a Conference at 9 P.M. — orders received about midnight.	
"	12/7/16	—	The 113 - 114 - 115 Infantry Brigades ordered to PONT REMY area. The Infantry by Lorry. The First Line Transport marched under the Train. 115 Inf W₁₁ Train & First Line Transport ordered to return to MORLANCOURT after it had started some time, as that Brigade was remaining behind.	

1875 Wt. W593/826 1,000,000 4/15 J.B.C. & A. A.D.S.S./Forms/C. 2118.

WAR DIARY
INTELLIGENCE SUMMARY

(Erase heading not required.)

Army Form C. 2118

Place	Date	Hour	Summary of Events and Information	Remarks and references to Appendices
MORLANCOURT	12/7/16	—	330 Coy. also did not move to the R.F.A. v D.A.C. were not moving.	W
BULAINVILLE	13/7/16	—	113 v 114 Infantry Brigade Groups with Train H.Q. arrived in this area about 12.30 A.M. Latter proceeded at 8 A.m. to PONT REMY and — Horses were very done up on arrival. The supply difficulties during this move from MORLANCOURT were very great - v the Transport difficulties also were considerable.	W
PONT REMY	14/7/16	—	113 v 114 Inf: Bde Groups moved again to another area - very small march - which is as well as the horses are very much done up - some of the front lines particularly so.	W

WAR DIARY
or
INTELLIGENCE SUMMARY
(Erase heading not required.)

Army Form C. 2118

Place	Date	Hour	Summary of Events and Information	Remarks and references to Appendices
PONT REMY Area.	15/7/16	—	113 & 114 Inf A.T. Coys moved to COUIN Area - The Train to FAMECHON. A very long & very hilly march of 27 miles - not so many casualties in spite of Horses as inspected. First line Tpt again under train.	W.
FAMECHON	16/7/16	—	48 Divisional Train moved out of FAMECHON. Took over a number of Horses mules water cart & stores from them. Also considerable amount of Reserve Rations - which were scattered all over the area.	W.
"	17/7/16	—	A very busy office day. Inspected the companies	W.
"	18/7/16	—	Reconnaissance of area with a view to picking fresh camps in case of advance.	W.

WAR DIARY or INTELLIGENCE SUMMARY

Army Form C. 2118

(Erase heading not required.)

Place	Date	Hour	Summary of Events and Information	Remarks and references to Appendices
FANECHON	19/7/16	—	Inspection of companies. — Horses beginning to recover again.	W.
"	20/7/16	—	Orders received for H.Q. Company to come up from HORLANCOURT. Had to send order by car as the distance is over 20 miles. Otherwise ordinary Routine.	W.
"	21/7/16	—	All Iron Rations collected from all over the District into 2 dumps — one at COUR. the other at CORBNEUX. 330 Co. arrived & put in Camp. Still collecting Iron Rations. Selvage — Ordinary Routine.	W.
"	22/7/16	—		W.
"	23/7/16	—	Office work nearly all day.	W.
"	24/7/16	—	Inspection of companies. Otherwise ordinary Routine.	W.

WAR DIARY / INTELLIGENCE SUMMARY

Army Form C. 2118

(Erase heading not required.)

Instructions regarding War Diaries and Intelligence Summaries are contained in F.S. Regs., Part II. and the Staff Manual respectively. Title Pages will be prepared in manuscript.

Place	Date	Hour	Summary of Events and Information	Remarks and references to Appendices
FAKECHON	25/7/16	—	Office work rang all day -	
"	26/7/16	—	The train line have almost recovered now from the recent severe Tackting. Ordinary Routine.	
"	27/7/16	—	Informed that the Division would shortly be moving north. Commenced making arrangements with 20 Divisional Train.	
"	28/7/16	—	Orders issued regarding Baggage Turnout, general arrangement in view of the move.	
"	29/7/16	—	H.Q. Co. H. R.F.A. & D.A.C. are 9/2 going behind - not moving with the remainder of the Division. Received 35 L.D. hour & sent away 27 H.D. hour in accordance with the scheme to keep L.D. hour in	

WAR DIARY

INTELLIGENCE SUMMARY

(Erase heading not required.)

Army Form C. 2118

Place	Date	Hour	Summary of Events and Information	Remarks and references to Appendices
FRANCTON	29/7/16	—	All entrained vehicles.	J.A.
"	30/7/16	—	331 Co: 332 Co & 333 Co: entrained for the North — All train transport arrested to units handed over to those units. There was a double shifting in the morning. Everything went very satisfactorily. J.A.O. proceeded ahead in his car to the new area to find billeting point. I also proceeded to the new area in the afternoon. The Adjutant remained behind.	
"	31/7/16	—	Visited the detraining stations & then the A.S.C. companies in their new area. Everything very satisfactory — Very hot weather — It has been	

WAR DIARY
INTELLIGENCE SUMMARY
(Erase heading not required.)

Army Form C. 2118

Place	Date	Hour	Summary of Events and Information	Remarks and references to Appendices
ESQUELBECQ	31/7/16	—	undoubted feeling the Effect of it. The Companies commenced collecting from vehicles from units that have arrived — detrainment still in progress. H.Q. train wagons arrived at midnight. This has been a very hard month for the train. M.	

T.W. Stewart Lt. Col. A.S.C.
O.C. 8 S/field/ Divisional Train

31/7/16.

Vol 9

WAR DIARY

INTELLIGENCE SUMMARY

Train

From 1/8/16 To 31/8/16

1.

Lieut Colonel T.E. BENNETT.
A.S.C.
Commanding.
38/Welsh/Divisional Train.

Army Form C. 2118

WAR DIARY

INTELLIGENCE SUMMARY

(Erase heading not required.)

Instructions regarding War Diaries and Intelligence Summaries are contained in F.S. Regs, Part II. and the Staff Manual respectively. Title Pages will be prepared in manuscript.

Place	Date	Hour	Summary of Events and Information	Remarks and references to Appendices
ESQUELBECQ	1/8/16	—	Visited 332 Co: A.S.C. & then out to POPERINGHE to find out about Pttrig bricks. Office work in the afternoon.	N.
"	2/8/16	—	Visited 331 Co A.S.C. at HOUTKERQUE. Ordinary routine.	N.
"	3/8/16	—	332 Co A.S.C. moved from BOLZEELE to WORMHOUDT — 333 Co A.S.C. from MILLAIN to BOLZEELE — 331 Co. A.S.C. from HOUTKERQUE to L. 4:a central (sheet 27). Busy in Office.	N.
"	4/8/16	—	Adjutant went to 2nd Army on the subject of returns (A.F. B.2.13a) Arrangement being made for various detachments & troops from the Division	N.

1875 Wt. W593/826 1,000,000 4/15 J.B.C. & A. A.D.S.S./Forms/C. 2118.

WAR DIARY

INTELLIGENCE SUMMARY

Army Form C. 2118

Place	Date	Hour	Summary of Events and Information	Remarks and references to Appendices
ESQUELBECQ	5/7/16	—	Busy over plans for horse standings. Visited 331 & 332 Companies.	J.B.
"	6/7/16	—	Visited 338 Company N.C. — and there visited BERGUES & its environs also DUNKERQUE to just cement. Lieut R. Affleck. left the train to go to the Royal Flying Corps. Lt E.E. Couch joined the train from the Supply School of Instruction BOULOGNE	J.S. J.S.
"	7/8/16	—	Visited 338 Co: N.C. Busy over horse standings & wrote accommodation. Also with locations for winter lines	J.S. J.S.

WAR DIARY

INTELLIGENCE SUMMARY

(Erase heading not required.)

Army Form C. 2118

Place	Date	Hour	Summary of Events and Information	Remarks and references to Appendices
ESQUELBECQ	8/10	—	Visited 332 Co A.D.C. when the forward area about the Brick Cues tion for winter standings — Sent the adjutant to visit 331 Co & 332 Co.	AL
"	9/10	—	I visited 331 – 332 & 339 Companies on the question of winter standings & horse lines. Very busy all day.	AL
"	10/10	—	24 Remounts arrived at ARNEKE — were distributed to the units of the division requiring them by 333 Co. A.D.C. — also 6 horses from the Field Remount Section — I went to POPERINGHE VELVERSINGHE & collection of bricks.	AL
"	11/10	—	Sent all Baggage Wagons from 332 Co to Tin 338 Co near POPERINGHE — in order to be near the area where broken bricks &c could be collected.	AL

Army Form C. 2118

WAR DIARY
INTELLIGENCE SUMMARY

(Erase heading not required.)

Place	Date	Hour	Summary of Events and Information	Remarks and references to Appendices
ESQUELBECQ	11/8/16 (cont:)		Lieut N.G.S. Hopson Transferred from 338 Co A.S.C. to 332 Co A.S.C.	
"	12/8/16	—	2/Lt B.H.H. Clark reported for duty. Is the Train & was posted to 333 Co: A.S.C. went to POPERINGHE in the collection of brick.	
"	13/8/16	—	330 Co: A.S.C. which had been left behind with the Reserve Army Area with the R.F.A. & A.C. came up from there to ESQUELBECQ.	
"	14/8/16	—	Visited O.C. 330 Co: A.S.C. to hear about 15 Areas re of Captain Templeton. 332 Company moved from WORMHOUDT to L.4: a Central with 331 Co: A.S.C. — Lieut E.E. Crouch Transferred from 330 Co: A.S.C. to 332 Co: A.S.C. & R.O.	

WAR DIARY
INTELLIGENCE SUMMARY

Place	Date	Hour	Summary of Events and Information	Remarks and references to Appendices
ESQUELBECQ (contd)	15/8/16	—	Lieut W. J. S. Taylor transferred from 332 Co. to 330 Co. A.D.C. a R.O.	A.
"	16/8/16	—	Again went to ELVERDINGHE - re trick for milk standings. The supply from POPERINGHE having been stopped. Visited POPERINGHE - 332 Co. A.D.C. moved to 331 Co. A.D.C. - 332 Co. A.D.C. moved to Standcamp south of POPERINGHE. Very busy with reference to the trick by F.B.C.H. of Captain Templeton. Very busy in office re complaint from 10 Welsh Regt. The collect con of Sec- from F L V E R D I N G H E. Milk from ELVERDINGHE stopped.	A3
"	17/8/16	—	Trick by F.G.C.M. of Captain Templeton of 330 Co. A.D.C. of four drivers	A

WAR DIARY

INTELLIGENCE SUMMARY

(Erase heading not required.)

Army Form C. 2118

Place	Date	Hour	Summary of Events and Information	Remarks and references to Appendices
ESQUELBECQ	8/7/16 (cont?)	—	as to Character. Ordinary Routine the usual.	H.
"	18/7/16	—	Captain Templeton Janus Swift of Drumkerass sentenced to take precedence in the O.S.C. rank of the Army as if his appointment to the rank of Temporary Captain bore date May 17 1916. I promulgated sentence – 7 days C.B. to 330 Coy R.S.C. about 10.30 A.m. O.C. Company was out at the time.	
"	19/7/16	—	Visited 333 Co M.T. – office work in the afternoon. Made arrangements re R.T.A. move.	H.
"	20/7/16	—	Advance party of R.T.A. & the Transport Henfords proceeded to forward area.	H.

Army Form C. 2118

Instructions regarding War Diaries and Intelligence
Summaries are contained in F. S. Regs, Part II.
and the Staff Manual respectively. Title Pages
will be prepared in manuscript.

WAR DIARY
INTELLIGENCE SUMMARY
(Erase heading not required.)

Place	Date	Hour	Summary of Events and Information	Remarks and references to Appendices
ESQUELBECQ	20/8/16	—	Under Captain Templeton. Went to visit 33 Co D.T.C. Joined Captain Templeton on the march.	H.
"	21/8/16	—	33 Co D.T.C. moved from ESQUELBECQ to near POPERINGHE. Divisional H.Q. to St SIXTE.	H.
"	22/8/16	—	Went to PESELHOEK to reconnoitre Railway station & roads for transport also to find the train officer of 4th Division who was securing the Canteens of that division	TF3 FP3.
"	23/8/16	—	Railhead changed to PESELHOEK —	FP3.
"	24/8/16	—	Train M.S. moved up to ST JEAN DER BIEZEN. Went to 2nd Army re Captain Templeton's transfer to 2nd Army — 2nd Army re A.F.B. 213 A — 2nd Army having issued circular with errors in it	T.8.

1875 Wt. W593/826 1,000,000 4/15 J.B.C. & A. A.D.S.S./Forms/C. 2118.

Army Form C. 2118

WAR DIARY
or
INTELLIGENCE SUMMARY
(Erase heading not required.)

Place	Date	Hour	Summary of Events and Information	Remarks and references to Appendices
ST JEAN DER.	25th	—	Been to Canteens of the Division. Visited Railhead.	A1
DIEZEN	26th	—	Report on Major Swanwell called for — Captain William warned by instructions of 2nd Army re his behaviour in the Templeton Case. Visited Railhead.	A1
"	27th	—	Ordinary routine. Much office work — especially with O.C.; 330 Co. M.P.s. Visited Railhead.	A1.
"	28th	—	Orders rec'd for Captain Templeton to proceed to Base. Captain Williams v Major Swanwell had interviews with the J.O.C.	A1. 763.
"	29th	—	Ordinary Routine. Visited Railhead.	A1. 763.

Army Form C. 2118

WAR DIARY
or
INTELLIGENCE SUMMARY
(Erase heading not required.)

Place	Date	Hour	Summary of Events and Information	Remarks and references to Appendices
ST JEAN DER BIEZEN	30/8/16	—	Went with the Adjutant to inspect 330 - 331 - 332 v 333 Companies A.S.C. — Very wet — v horse lines in bad condition in consequence. On reorganization of R.T.A. of wagon became impossible to establish.	W3.
"	31/8/16	—	Went to Railhead. A.S.M.G Corps visited Two Companies - v ST JEAN DER BIEZEN. Went to Divisional H.Q. twice	H.

W Bennett Lt. Col. D.S.C.
O.C. 38/Welsh/ Div: Train.

Army Form C. 2118

WAR DIARY
INTELLIGENCE SUMMARY.
(Erase heading not required.)

Instructions regarding War Diaries and Intelligence Summaries are contained in F.S. Regs., Part II. and the Staff Manual respectively. Title Pages will be prepared in manuscript.

Vol 10

Place	Date	Hour	Summary of Events and Information	Remarks and references to Appendices
From 2/16.			of Lieut Colonel T.E. Bennett A.D.C. Commanding 38/Welsh/Divisional Train.	10 / 30/9/16.

Army Form C. 2118

WAR DIARY

INTELLIGENCE SUMMARY

(Erase heading not required.)

Instructions regarding War Diaries and Intelligence Summaries are contained in F.S. Regs., Part II. and the Staff Manual respectively. Title Pages will be prepared in manuscript.

Place	Date	Hour	Summary of Events and Information	Remarks and references to Appendices
ST JEAN DE R. MEZEN.	1/2/16.	—	Toured round all Companies with the A.A. v Q.M.G. Worked in offices all the afternoon & evening.	A.
"	2/2/16.	—	Visited some 1st Line Transport lines with the A.A. v Q.M.G. — I also visited 333 Co. A.S.C. twice v 330 v 351 Companies once each — Went out looking for a Camping ground for 331 v 352 Companies — Office work all the evening.	A.
"	3/2/16.	—	Visited 333 Co. A.S.C. — Office work remainder of morning — Inspection by G.O.C. Division accompanied by A.A. v Q.M.G. of all 4 Companies.	A.

Army Form C. 2118

WAR DIARY
INTELLIGENCE SUMMARY
(Erase heading not required.)

Instructions regarding War Diaries and Intelligence Summaries are contained in F.S. Regs., Part II. and the Staff Manual respectively. Title Pages will be prepared in manuscript.

Place	Date	Hour	Summary of Events and Information	Remarks and references to Appendices
ST JEAN TER. DIEZ EN.	4/9/16	—	Very busy all the morning endeavouring to find Camping Ground for two Companies that have to move. Part of the afternoon also. Very busy in office.	
"	5/9/16	—	Very busy all the morning looking for Camping Grounds. Also very busy planning Camps.	
"	6/9/16	—	Routine work. Visited 333 Co about horse standings TOB. Also the new Camp of 331 Co to plan standings. Held a canteen meeting in the afternoon. Then did office work.	
"	7/9/16	—	Offr going to Div: H.Q. visited 2nd Army H.Q. Ordering Routine.	
"	8/9/16	—	D.A.D.S. & D.A.D.T. visited Refilling Point. Both visited 333 Co Camps & Tber S/.	

Army Form C. 2118

WAR DIARY
INTELLIGENCE SUMMARY
(Erase heading not required.)

Instructions regarding War Diaries and Intelligence Summaries are contained in F.S. Regs., Part II and the Staff Manual respectively. Title Pages will be prepared in manuscript.

Place	Date	Hour	Summary of Events and Information	Remarks and references to Appendices
ST JEAN DER BIEZEN	8/9/16	—	331 Co. with reference to Horse Standings.	H.
"	9/9/16	—	Attended Raid had after returning from D.W. H.Q. Ordinary Routine.	S.
"	10/9/16	—	After attending Divisional H.Q. I went to visit the new camps of 331 & 332 Companies. Then with the S.S.O. I went to 16 PROVEN & arranged for loading at this. Reached in the future. Inspected 330 Co. A.S.C. – The afternoon I inspected Horse standings are progressing well.	
"	11/9/16	—	After going to Divisional H.Q. – I went to the 1st Line Transport Lines of 11th D.W.B. To have see a new Reorganization of Train transport to allow S.P. loading at a new road head in the near future direct from the truck. The R.F.A. Brigade allotted to Brigade Conference r.c.	D.

Army Form C. 2118

WAR DIARY
INTELLIGENCE SUMMARY.

(Erase heading not required.)

Instructions regarding War Diaries and Intelligence Summaries are contained in F. S. Regs., Part II. and the Staff Manual respectively. Title Pages will be prepared in manuscript.

Place	Date	Hour	Summary of Events and Information	Remarks and references to Appendices
ST JEAN DEN. BIEZEN.	11/9/16	—	Went to the Supply Column at WORMHOUDT with reference to the car which is replacing that evacuated — also with reference to Dr. (acting Corporal) Clark the Chauffeur — who had been sent down with the evacuated car.	S.
"	12/9/16	—	Went to Div. H.Q. & then to Railhead — office work remainder of morning. The A.D.V.S. & I inspected the horses of all companies at the Companies in the afternoon.	S.
"	13/9/16	—	To Div: H.Q. & then to Raishead & Refixing Point — office work morning. In the afternoon I interviewed a C.S.M.S. of the D.A.C. for a commission in the A.S.C. ordinary Routine.	S.
"	14/9/16	—	The S.S.O. David Davies & I had a Conference this morning at Div. H.Q. with the A.A. & Q.M.G. over shipping Centre afterwards I went to Raihead & Refixing Point. This afternoon I did office work.	S.

Army Form C. 2118

WAR DIARY or INTELLIGENCE SUMMARY

(Erase heading not required.)

Instructions regarding War Diaries and Intelligence Summaries are contained in F. S. Regs., Part II. and the Staff Manual respectively. Title Pages will be prepared in manuscript.

Place	Date	Hour	Summary of Events and Information	Remarks and references to Appendices
ST JEAN TER. BIEZEN.	15/9/16	—	I attended Divisional H.Q. - here the Adjutant I had an inspection of all transport attending the Refilling Point. Later on I inspected 333 Co:- & also visited the new Camps of 331 & 332 Companies - Today I received instructions to send Major R.S. Swalwell to England to report on arrival to War Office in writing - also I was informed that Major H. Baker had been posted to this train. I issued instructions to Major Swalwell accordingly - & this office handed over his Company to Captain Williams.	s.d.
"	16/9/16	—	I went to Div: H.Q. & took the D.A.Q.M.G. to Reinbeck & afterwards to the Bomb Store (Divisional) - Ordinary Routine. Major R.S. Swalwell left for England.	s.d.
"	17/9/16	—	Went with the Adjutant to Div: H.Q. - then to Refilling Points where I inspected the transport - I next had to the new line of 331 & 332 Companies - inspecting the Books of 331 Co.	s.d.

Army Form C. 2118

WAR DIARY
INTELLIGENCE SUMMARY
(Erase heading not required.)

Instructions regarding War Diaries and Intelligence Summaries are contained in F. S. Regs., Part II. and the Staff Manual respectively. Title Pages will be prepared in manuscript.

Place	Date	Hour	Summary of Events and Information	Remarks and references to Appendices
St Jean Ter Biezen.	18/9/16	—	After reporting at Divisional Headquarters - I went to Office - Major H. Baker A.D.C reported for duty.	
	19/9/16	—	Captain Jones, the adjutant, & 2 Lt N Hodgson went on leave - I took Major Baker to Divisional H.Q. also to Railhead - Also visited the new O'archups of 331 & 332 Companies & the lines v.c of 333 Co. Reached the morning & until further notice is PROVEN instead of PESELHOEK - Major Baker took over the H.Q Company from Captain Williams.	
	20/9/16	—	After reporting at Div: H.Q. I went to Refilling point along the PESELHOEK - ST SIXTE Road - also to Railhead to see the R.T.O. v R.S.O. regarding loading in detail is the sand direct from trains instead of the present extremely cumbersome system of loading the wagons in bulk - proceeded to Refilling point along the PESELHOEK ST SIXTE Road.	

1875 Wt. W593/326 1,000,000 4/15 J.B.C. & A. A.D.S.S./(Forms/C. 2118.

Army Form C. 2118

WAR DIARY
or
INTELLIGENCE SUMMARY
(Erase heading not required.)

Instructions regarding War Diaries and Intelligence Summaries are contained in F.S. Regs., Part II. and the Staff Manual respectively. Title Pages will be prepared in manuscript.

Place	Date	Hour	Summary of Events and Information	Remarks and references to Appendices
ST JEAN TER. BEZEN.	20/9 (cont.)	—	dumping the supplies for the Supply details & told them in it detail — The Transport take returning to fetch up the supplies in detail for conveyance to units — Office work see the afternoon.	
"	21/9	—	Went to Divisional H.Q. v afterwards to Refilling Point. Office work v ordinary Routine	AS
"	22/9	—	Visited Divisional H.Q. v Refilling Point — also 330 Co: A.D.C. v the new Camps of 331 v 332 Companies. Office work.	TD.
"	23/9	—	After attending Divisional H.Q. I went with Major Baker 330 Co: A.S.C. to 115 Infantry Brigade H.Q. I returned to Div: H.Q. v then went along the Refilling Points — Office work.	TD.
"	24/9	—	We commenced Refilling direct from the Train at Radhead. I attended — Went to Divisional H.Q. — Visited the new Camps of 331 v 332 Companies — Office work	TD.
"	25/9	—	Went to Divisional H.Q. v then went with the A.D.V.S. To the "E" Camp — Visited 331 v 332 Companies new Camps v the Subject of Horse Standings v 200	

WAR DIARY
INTELLIGENCE SUMMARY

Army Form C. 2118

Place	Date	Hour	Summary of Events and Information	Remarks and references to Appendices
ST JEAN TER. (Cont.)	25/9/16	—	there are the afternoon in office.	
BIEZEN	26/9/16	—	The new lines are progressing very well. I went to Railhead. The acting A.A. & Q.M.G. was also there to see Offering cruet from the Train - I went to Div: H.Q. & then to 331 new standings - had a Talk with Captain Cross on the subject. - Office work. Tes.	
"	27/9/16	—	After Divisional H.Q. I went to 331 & 332 Co. Standings. I found the A.A. & Q.M.G. VIII Corps there - Office work.	
"	28/9/16	—	Went to Divisional H.Q. - Visited 333 C.A.S.C. - also 331 & 332 Companies new standings which had been rather affected by yesterdays rain - Went to brewery for again. I visited 330 Co A.S.C. - [crossed out]	
"	29/9/16	—	After attending at Divisional H.Q. - I went to Railhead to see the R.S.O. regarding the continuance of loading direct from Train when the 55th Division	

WAR DIARY

INTELLIGENCE SUMMARY

Army Form C. 2118

Place	Date	Hour	Summary of Events and Information	Remarks and references to Appendices
STAN. TER. BIEZEN.	29 2/76 (Cont)	-	arms early next month. Ordinary Routine. Lieut Hodgson reported back from leave.	
"	30/76	-	To Divisional H.Q. & then to new Standings of 331 & 332 Companies. Office work all afternoon on the subject of the Divisional Canteens. Captain J. T. Jones, the Adjutant, reported back from leave.	

10/1/16

TW Russell Lt Colonel
O.C. 38 Welsh Divisional Train.

Army Form C. 2118

WAR DIARY
INTELLIGENCE SUMMARY
(Erase heading not required.)

Vol II

Place	Date	Hour	Summary of Events and Information	Remarks and references to Appendices
From				10
1/10/16			Lieut Colonel T.E. Brunel A.S.C. Commanding 38 (Welsh) Divisional Train.	31/10/16

Army Form C. 2118

WAR DIARY
INTELLIGENCE SUMMARY.
(Erase heading not required.)

Instructions regarding War Diaries and Intelligence Summaries are contained in F. S. Regs., Part II. and the Staff Manual respectively. Title Pages will be prepared in manuscript.

Place	Date	Hour	Summary of Events and Information	Remarks and references to Appendices
ST JEAN TER. BIEZEN.	1/10/16	—	I took Isaac the manager of the Divisional Canteen to Divisional H.Q. at had a long interview with the acting A.A.& Q.M.G on Canteen Subject. Office work & ordinary Routine.	A.
"	2/10/16	—	I went to Divisional H.Q. & there found the Companies. I first to 333 — then the new standing of 331 & 332 Companies — afterwards to 330 Co. Very wet weather. Lt J.P. Jones sent to Hospital. Ordinary Routine.	"
"	3/10/16	—	I went with the adjutant to Divisional H.Q. & from there on to H.Q. 2nd Army, where I saw both the D.D.D.T. & D.A.D.S. Jagani went to Divisional the evening to interview the G.O.C. on the subject of the Divisional Canteens.	A.
"	4/10/16	—	I was in bed all day as clear it.. the D.D.O. went to Div: H.Q. for me.	A.
"	5/10/16	—	I went to Div H.Q. but otherwise ordinary Routine.	A.
"	6/10/16	—	I went to Div: H.Q. & afterwards to 333 Co. & the 2 nees Camps of 331 & 332 Companies. Office work.	A.

Army Form C. 2118

WAR DIARY

INTELLIGENCE SUMMARY

(Erase heading not required.)

Place	Date	Hour	Summary of Events and Information	Remarks and references to Appendices
ST JEAN TER BEZEN	7/10/16	—	Brigade. I sent the adjutant to H.Q. of the Division. Ordinary routine.	JS.
	8/10/16	—	Went to Division at H.Q. Major Baker took over the train or rather made arrangements to take it over on my departure on leave. I went on leave.	JS.
	9/10/16		O.C. proceeded on leave. Major H. Baker A.S.C. 15th command of the Train. Went to Div. H.Q., visited 333 Coy. New men strength of 331 & 332 Coys. Ordinary routine.	JS
"	10/10/16		O.C. and Adjutant to Div. H.Q. Saw C.R.E. & material to train Commanding. Visited all companies.	JS

Army Form C. 2118

Instructions regarding War Diaries and Intelligence Summaries are contained in F. S. Regs., Part II. and the Staff Manual respectively. Title Pages will be prepared in manuscript.

WAR DIARY
INTELLIGENCE SUMMARY

(Erase heading not required.)

Place	Date	Hour	Summary of Events and Information	Remarks and references to Appendices
ST JEAN, TER BIEZEN	11/10		O.b. and Adjt. to Div Hdqrs. Visited 331, 332 Bdes. men standing in trenches to be relieved by D.D.R. O.b. visited 331, 332 Bdes. In afternoon visited 332 Bde men many crews & gave instructions re drawing out the trenches.	R.
	12/10		At O.b. to Div. Hdqrs & visited new entrenchmt. Visited O.B. 332 Bdt (intrenchd) re manng entrench.	R.
	13/10		O.b. & Adjt. to Div. Hdqrs. Visited new trenches & entrenchmt of 331, 332 Bdes.	R.
	14/10		O.b. & Adjt. to Div. Hdqrs. Ordinary routine.	R.
	15/10		O.b., Adjt. to Div. Hdqrs. Visited 331, 332 Bds. Advance visited 332 Bds re men & hosp. for sick in F.	D
	16/10		M.O. & Interpret. forwarded on leave. O.b. Adjt. & Div. Hdqrs. Adjutant 15 332, 331 bcompanies. Ordinary routine. Reports re that se of strainer & water cart in 331 Bdes 332 Bds.	R.

WAR DIARY
INTELLIGENCE SUMMARY
(Erase heading not required.)

Army Form C. 2118

Place	Date	Hour	Summary of Events and Information	Remarks and references to Appendices
ST. JEAN TER BIEZEN	17/10/16		O.b. Adjt to Div. Hdqts. visited 332, 333 Companies. Adjt visited 332 in afternoon. Ordinary routine.	R.
"	18/10/16		O.b. Adjt to Div. Hdqts. L. R.E. + R.E. park on hits to 333 Co. Ordinary routine.	R.
"	19/10/16		O.b. Adjt to Div. Hdqts. Ordinary routine. Col. Bennett returned from leave	R.
"	20/10/16		Took over from Major Bakal who commanded in my absence — Went to Div. H.Q. will Lieut. Isaac re Companies — Ordinary Routine.	R.
"	21/10/16		Went to Divisional H.Q. also new Camp for 331 v 332 Companies. Office work.	R.
"	22/10/16		Went to Divisional H.Q. — I inspected 331 v 332 v 330 Company camps — vic. The adjutant visited	R.
"	23/10/16		331 v 332 Companies new standings. Tino T/ Rafinerie went to Divisional H.Q. visited at PROVEN where to 9. P.M. visited of 7.30. this	R.

WAR DIARY
INTELLIGENCE SUMMARY

Place	Date	Hour	Summary of Events and Information	Remarks and references to Appendices
ST JAN TER	23/10/14		being of great benefit to horses there.	N.
BIEZEN.	24/10/14		Went to Poperinghe this morning. The Director of Supplies & the D.D.S. v T. 2nd Army were also there. We loaded in detail a unit from Train in 4·3 minutes, a record. Both these officers were pleased with the everything. I then visited 331 & 332 Companies and also placed w.R. also 333 Companies Camp. Lines &c. in C. I went to Divisional H.Q. & was informed that the Acting Divisional Commander, Brigadier General Marden, Commanding 113 Infantry Brigade would not be found & inspect my horse standings at 2·30 P.M. — I then returned to Office. At 1·45 P.M. I went to D.v.H.Q. in a car taking the Adjutant — the horses had been taken up & orderlies — the G.O.C.	

Army Form C. 2118

WAR DIARY

INTELLIGENCE SUMMARY

(Erase heading not required.) W.

Instructions regarding War Diaries and Intelligence Summaries are contained in F. S. Regs., Part II. and the Staff Manual respectively. Title Pages will be prepared in manuscript.

Place	Date	Hour	Summary of Events and Information	Remarks and references to Appendices
ST JAN TER. BIEZEN.	24/10/16	—	however elected to go round in a Car — It chiefrues being past & the afternoon & wet one. Major Baker ✓Captain Robotham went on leave. The G.O.C. seemed very satisfied with his inspection.	
	25/10/16	—	I went to Railhead, & then to Divisional H.Q. In the afternoon I went with a Corps Staff Officer to inspect some Corps Troops Transport at WATTEAU. ✓ then did this work.	N.B.
	26/10/16	—	Went to Divisional H.Q. & thence to the New Hardinge of 331, ✓ 332 Companies, after visiting the R.E. dump at PESELHOEK Cor-cerning material. I had a long conference with Captains Cross Foster on the subject of their new Camps, & the provision of extra horse accommodation for the Baggage horses of the R.F.A. newly returned to the Train.	N.B.

WAR DIARY
INTELLIGENCE SUMMARY

Army Form C. 2118

Place	Date	Hour	Summary of Events and Information	Remarks and references to Appendices
ST JAN TER BIEZEN.	26/1/10	—	This afternoon the J.I.O. & I went to RENINGHELST for a conference with the D.D.S. & T. 2nd Army on the subject of the application of light railways for supply work direct to the trenches from Railhead or thereabouts.	
"	27/1/10	—	Went to Divisional H.Q. & then to the Corps Ammunition Dump. Ordinary Routine. Lieut Crouch went on leave.	#3.
"	28/1/10	—	Went to Divisional H.Q. – Had a lot of office work today. Leave was stopped.	U.
"	29/1/10	—	Went to Divisional H.Q. & then to 382 Company near Standing – where I had a conference with Captain Foster. Today I have had a lot of office work.	U.

WAR DIARY

INTELLIGENCE SUMMARY
(Erase heading not required.)

Army Form C. 2118

Place	Date	Hour	Summary of Events and Information	Remarks and references to Appendices
JAN TER. BIEZEN.	30/1/16	—	Went to Divisional H.Q. & then with the S.S.O. had a conference with the War Office Inspector of Catering. Office work all the afternoon.	W3
"	31/1/16	—	Went to Rachrod - then to 331 v 332 Companies headquarters; then to Divisional H.Q. - I took the A.D.V.S. round 333 Co: - Office work -	W3

W Beward Lt Col. A.D.C.

11/1/16

O.C. 38/W.Vet/Divisional Train

Army Form C. 2118

WAR DIARY
or
INTELLIGENCE SUMMARY
(Erase heading not required.)

Place	Date	Hour	Summary of Events and Information	Remarks and references to Appendices
From				To
	1.11.16		Lieut Colonel T.E. BENNETT A.S.C. Officer in command of the 38th (Welsh) Divisional Train.	30.11.16.

Army Form C. 2118

Instructions regarding War Diaries and Intelligence Summaries are contained in F. S. Regs., Part II. and the Staff Manual respectively. Title Pages will be prepared in manuscript.

WAR DIARY

INTELLIGENCE SUMMARY

(Erase heading not required.)

Place	Date	Hour	Summary of Events and Information	Remarks and references to Appendices
St JAN TER. BIEZEN	1/1/16	—	After going to Divisional H.Q. I went to 2nd Army to see the D.D.S.V.T. Ordinary routine	Tel.
"	2/1/16	—	To Divisional H.Q. – Went to a Lecture at 330 Co. by the War Off. Inspector of Catering – Representatives of all Companies were present – I also inspected the Horse standings.	Tel.
"	3/1/16	—	Went to Divisional H.Q. & then went to 353 Co – afterwards to the newly standings of 336 & 351 Companies – Effect work.	Tel.

1875 Wt. W593/826 1,000,000 4/15 J.B.C. & A. A.D.S.S./Forms/C. 2118.

Army Form C. 2118

WAR DIARY
INTELLIGENCE SUMMARY
(Erase heading not required.)

W3.

Place	Date	Hour	Summary of Events and Information	Remarks and references to Appendices
S? JAN TER. BIEZEN.	4/1/16	-	After attending at Divisional H.Q. I went over a number to a Cinematograph at "D" Camp. I was there all day.	11.
"	5/11/16	-	I went to Divisional H.Q. Office work - fine weather but very windy.	"
"	6/11/16	-	I went to Faithead - then to 331 & 332 Companies new camps - office work after Divisional H.Q. Very wet & windy weather	"
"	7/11/16	-	I went to Divisional H.Q. Major Hoare the S.J.O. on leave - office work. Captain L.C. Ing reported from the 32?? Train for duty - Lieut. B.H.H. Clarke ordered to report to the 60th Train.	"
"	8/11/16	-	I went to Divisional H.Q. - & there to 331 & 332 Companies new Hardings - Lieut. B.H.H. Clarke	"

WAR DIARY
INTELLIGENCE SUMMARY
(Erase heading not required.)

Army Form C. 2118

Place	Date	Hour	Summary of Events and Information	Remarks and references to Appendices
STJAN TER.	8/11/16	-	Proceeded to join the 60 Divisional Train. Office work.	U.
BIEZEN	9/11/16	-	I went to Divisional H.Q. – Office work.	U. 163.
"	10/11/16	-	I went to Divisional H.Q. & then to 330 Co R.E. this company is not well situated for access to main roads & its surroundings are very muddy – Office work.	U.
"	11/11/16	-	The adjutant distributes 18 personals this morning to the Companies – he then went with Lieut Davis to WORMHOUDT to arrange & bringing up chairs on rail – I went to Divisional H.Q. & then visited 338 Company. Office work all the afternoon.	
"	12/11/16	-	The Adjutant and I went to Raikhed – Senior to Divisional H.Q. & thence to 331 & 332 Companies.	

WAR DIARY
INTELLIGENCE SUMMARY

Place	Date	Hour	Summary of Events and Information	Remarks and references to Appendices
ST JAN. TER. BIEZEN	12/11/16	-	New standings - office work - Weather good - Crescents the camp are putting beds, also the Turnouts.	
"	13/11/16	-	Took Lieut Isaac the President 8th Division - at Canteens with me to H.Q. Division, & then went on to 332 Companies new standing, where I had a talk with the Train V.O. Office work - Weather very gen. Turnout very much improved.	
"	14/11/16	-	Took Lieut Isaac the President of the Division at Canteens with me to H.Q. Division, & had a long interview on Canteens with the A.A.v.Q.M.G. Afterwards I went to PESELH OEK railhead to see whether the Jeumbo Thus are all right & ready to see	

WAR DIARY
INTELLIGENCE SUMMARY.

Army Form C. 2118.

Place	Date	Hour	Summary of Events and Information	Remarks and references to Appendices
ST JAN TER	14/2	-	Approaching Change of Railhead — Office Work. Captain Nash went on leave.	773.
BIEZEN	15/2	-	Went to Divisional H.Q. re. interviews with superior R.A. H.Q. re. the unnecessarily large amount of damage being done to our baggage wagons by the R.F.A.. G.O.C. VIII Corps visited the new camps of 331 + 332 Companies yesterday + was very pleased with them. This afternoon the Adjutant + I paid a visit to 330 Company. afterwards we inspected the Shaw dump	773.
"	16/2	-	Visited 331 Company. Very Cold weather. Very Cold weather. At Divisional H.Q. this morning there was some discussion about effecting a reduction of the numbers + horses actively retained for Divisional use in the Divisional area — Suggested copies as to the basis was concerned — Office work all the afternoon.	773.
"	17/2	-	I was ill all day — The Adjutant went to Divisional H.Q. + also PESELHOEK railhead + R.E. Iron stores	

WAR DIARY
INTELLIGENCE SUMMARY.
(Erase heading not required.)

Army Form C. 2118.

Place	Date	Hour	Summary of Events and Information	Remarks and references to Appendices
STAN TER BIEZEN	JAN 17th	—	repairs to the dumps. All Transport had to be in camp early this morning owing to a road being carried out by the 114th Infantry Brigade 2.l.	
.	18th	—	Went to Divisional H.Q. v there with the Claims officer to see about starting a piece of land next PESEL HOEK railhead for a shelter, coal wood & coke dump. Orderage went to Railhead. The Train arrived late owing to a truck having been derailed en route - This delayed our Transport. Office work - see the afternoon. Yesterday's read was very successful. Major HOARE returned from leave.	T.B.
.	19th	—	Went to Railhead & then to Divisional H.Q. Much office work. Captain Lambert went on leave - Had a long interview with Major Baker at Orderly Room.	T.B.
.	20th	—	Went to Divisional H.Q. v to Railhead - Had a	

WAR DIARY
INTELLIGENCE SUMMARY.

Army Form C. 2118.

Place	Date	Hour	Summary of Events and Information	Remarks and references to Appendices
ST JAN TER.	20th	—	Great deal of office work to do – Busy all the afternoon & evening.	
BIEZEN	21/16	—	To Railhead – & then Divisional H.Q. with Lewis Isaac & the S.S.O.	21.
"	22nd	—	Afterwards to 332 Co A.S.C. – Office work. To Railhead & then to Divisional H.Q. I visited 331 Co A.S.C. This afternoon I inspected the First Line Transport of the 113 Infantry Brigade on the PESELHOEK – ST SIXTE Road.	703. 703.
"	23/16	—	Visited Railhead & inspected Transport – Then went on To Divisional H.Q. – In the afternoon visited 331, 332, & 333 Companies to interview Officers Commanding those Companies.	703.
"	24/16	—	Went to Railhead & Divisional H.Q. The Adjutant proceeded at a F.G.C.M. at "D" Camp. Office work – Had an interview with Major Baker	723.
"	25/16	—	Visited Railhead – then to Divisional H.Q. –	

WAR DIARY
INTELLIGENCE SUMMARY. 728.
(Erase heading not required.)

Army Form C. 2118.

Place	Date	Hour	Summary of Events and Information	Remarks and references to Appendices
ST JAN.	25th	—	Then went to 331 Co A.D.C. — Ordinary Routine.	Weather fine. Z1.
TER.	26th	—	To Divisional H.Q. Office work.	Weather fine. Z1.
BIEZEN.	27th	—	Jales went to Reigning Point. Went to Divisional H.Q. Taking Lieut Isaac the Canders officer with me. — Before going, Captain Williams came to T.H.Q. with reference to his application for transfer to the Heavy Machine Gun Corps. Jales had an interview with Captain Jotes on certain train matters. This afternoon the D.S.O. v.D. went to 333 v 331 Companys. Jales went to 332 Company. Office work.	Weather fine. Z1.
"	28th	—	To Railhead v Divisional H.Q. with the S.S.O. Afterwards to the Pres dumps at POPERINGHE. — Office work.	Weather fine. Z1.

Army Form C. 2118.

WAR DIARY
INTELLIGENCE SUMMARY.
(Erase heading not required.)

Instructions regarding War Diaries and Intelligence Summaries are contained in F. S. Regs., Part II. and the Staff Manual respectively. Title pages will be prepared in manuscript.

Place	Date	Hour	Summary of Events and Information	Remarks and references to Appendices
ST JAN. TER. BIEZEN.	29/16	—	Went to Rúeland & then to Divisional H.Q. The Adjutant attended at 333 Companies Enquiry as Prosecutor in a Court Martial. Captain Cross went on leave. Office work.	160.
	30/16	—	Went to Rúeland & then to Divisional H.Q. Busy in office all afternoon. Lieut Crouch Joined T.H.Q.	71.
	1/16 12/16			

T. Deverell Lieut. Col.
O.C. 38/Welsh/Div: Train.

T/134. Wt. W708—776. 50c000. 4/15. Sir J. C. & S.

Army Form C. 2118.

Vol 13

WAR DIARY
or
INTELLIGENCE SUMMARY.   TNB.

(Erase heading not required.)

Instructions regarding War Diaries and Intelligence Summaries are contained in F. S. Regs., Part II. and the Staff Manual respectively. Title pages will be prepared in manuscript.

Place	Date	Hour	Summary of Events and Information	Remarks and references to Appendices
From				73
	1.12.16.		of Lieut Colonel T.E. Bennett. A.I.C. Commanding the 38th (Welsh) Divisional Train.	01.12.16

T/134. Wt. W708—776. 50000. 4/15. Sir J. C. & S.

Army Form C. 2118.

WAR DIARY
or
INTELLIGENCE SUMMARY. ToS.
(Erase heading not required.)

Instructions regarding War Diaries and Intelligence Summaries are contained in F.S. Regs, Part II. and the Staff Manual respectively. Title pages will be prepared in manuscript.

Place	Date	Hour	Summary of Events and Information	Remarks and references to Appendices
ST JAN TER. BIEZEN	1/12/16	—	Went to Railhead & to Divisional H.Q. 151 Field Co R.E. left the Division to go to HOULE then Train Transport with them. Very cold weather today. I worked in office all the afternoon.	ToS.
"	2/12/16	—	Went to Railhead & inspected the Transport - the Turnouts were very good, especially those of 333 Pioneer Company. I then went with the D.A.D.O. 1st Divisional H.Q. & discussed the morning & the 19 Welsh Pioneers from this Division to HOULE. The weather has again been very cold. I have had a lot of office work today.	ToS.
"	3/12/16	—	I went to Divisional H.Q. & then to Railhead - The Transport Turnouts were very good. The whole afternoon I spent in office. The weather is again very cold	ToS.
"	4/12/16	—	Went to Divisional H.Q. & also to Railhead. Very busy in office all the afternoon. Lieut. Taylor & Isaac went on leave.	ToS.

T2134. Wt. W708–776. 50000. 4/15. Sir J. C. & S.

WAR DIARY
INTELLIGENCE SUMMARY

Army Form C. 2118.

Place	Date	Hour	Summary of Events and Information	Remarks and references to Appendices
ST JAN. TER. BIEZEN	5/12	—	Went to Divisional H.Q. with the D.D.O. after going to Railroad. Lieut. Oak. of the Army Privatisation Department also Captain Bowlgrove 2nd Army Delost were at the Refilling Office work this afternoon.	
"	6/12	—	Went to Railhead with Lt. Col. Provo the O.C. 39th Welsh Divisional Train. We then went to Divisional H.Q. Afterwards we went round 331, 332 & 333 Companies. This afternoon did a lot of office work.	
"	7/12	—	Went to Divisional H.Q. with the Train Doctor. I had a long discussion on Canteen matters with the A.A. & Q.M.G. who promised that the trains would not again be asked to run the Divisional Canteen. The S.S.O. also came to Divisional H.Q. The afternoon the D.O.C. visited 330, 331, 332 & 333 Companies & expressed his satisfaction, allowing me to inform the Companies is	

WAR DIARY

INTELLIGENCE SUMMARY.

(Erase heading not required.)

Army Form C. 2118.

Place	Date	Hour	Summary of Events and Information	Remarks and references to Appendices
ST JAN.	7/1/16	—	Train Orders.	Tel.
TER.	8/1/16	—	Lieut Gauch the Train Officer in charge of Divisional Canteens — I went to Divisional H.Q. this morning. Afterwards we went to 332 Company. The adjutant is ill & in bed. — Office work the afternoon.	
BIEZEN.				
"	9/1/16	—	I visited Railhead & Refilling Point, I also went to the Divisional brick dump at Railhead (POPERINGHE). The S.S.O. went to VIII Corps to a conference. Idid your out of office work this afternoon. Captain Lambert returned off its leave.	
—	10/1/16	—	The G.O.C. accompanied by the A.A. & Q.M.G. visited Railhead & Refilling Point. — Afterwards I went with the A.A. & Q.M.G. to Divisional H.Q. the D.A.Q. & Lieut Gauch followed. We had a discussion on the subject of the forthcoming move of the Division. I did a bit of office work this afternoon. Captain Foster went on leave yesterday — Captain Irby today.	Tel.

Army Form C. 2118.

WAR DIARY
INTELLIGENCE SUMMARY.
(Erase heading not required.)

Instructions regarding War Diaries and Intelligence Summaries are contained in F. S. Regs., Part II. and the Staff Manual respectively. Title pages will be prepared in manuscript.

Place	Date	Hour	Summary of Events and Information	Remarks and references to Appendices
ST JAN TER.	11/12/16	—	The car I use broke down this morning. Went to Div: H.Q. The S.S.O. found me there to go with the Scout for our visit to Corps H.Q. — I went to R.A. H.Q. to get information on the R.A. mov.	
BIEZEN.	12/12/16	—	This afternoon I was very busy writing orders for the mov — The Liaison Officer 39 Division came to T.H.Q. T.S a wet morning — Said not go to Div: H.Q. as I was sent. — Lieut Gamel & the D.O.O. went up. Did a lot of work in office. Captain Coss came down to T.H.Q. The S.I.O. went to VIII Corps H.Q. this morning & the mov Orders have been issued for Captain Williams to join Lt. Carrichion — Forwarded orders to Lennishoeck — to him to proceed tomorrow.	
	13/12/16	—	I had a lot of office work this morning — The Conv to Div H.Q. for T. of 113 Bn. & consequently 33/C.o M.C. is on the mov to the Bertena. Captain Coss came to H.Q. concerning	

WAR DIARY
INTELLIGENCE SUMMARY.
(Erase heading not required.)

Army Form C. 2118.

Place	Date	Hour	Summary of Events and Information	Remarks and references to Appendices
ST JAN TER BIEZEN	13/7/16		The moss J 331 Co: Owing to shortage of officers I instructed him to remain with 331 Co: until the moss was over. Captain Williams reported to T.H.Q. for his movement order. The S.O.O. Joined me at Div: H.Q. - I was very busy in office all the afternoon writing R.A. & T. orders for the moss which I sent up to Div. H.Q. this evening by the adjutant. I have instructed Lieut. Hazell to report for duty on the 14th & 15th to 330 Co: U. The remainder of 113 Infantry 18th also Div: H.Q. moved to the Rest Area - Lieut Couch & I went to Divisional H.Q. this morning - T.H.Q. moved to ESQUELBECQ this afternoon. The Coys and Lieut Couch & I went round the Companies with Ammunition & take orders	
"	14/7/16		This morning I visited 332 C with Lieut Couch. I had an interview with Lieut. Hobson. Captain Williams arrived his train yesterday - but did not report the fact	

WAR DIARY
or
INTELLIGENCE SUMMARY.

Army Form C. 2118.

(Erase heading not required.)

Instructions regarding War Diaries and Intelligence Summaries are contained in F.S. Regs., Part II. and the Staff Manual respectively. Title pages will be prepared in manuscript.

Place	Date	Hour	Summary of Events and Information	Remarks and references to Appendices
ST. JAN. TER. BIEZEN.	14/16		He left to join his unit today. The 39 T.H.Q. took over from this train at ST JAN TER BIEZEN. 20 did one J.S. to 39 Train companies from 331 Co. near PROVEN.	
ESAUGUBECK 15/76			The J.S.O. went away on duty this morning. I went to Reffilling at PROVEN. I also went to 332 C.D.S.C. v visited Railhead at HERZEELE. After lunch the Adjutant & I visited 331 Co. at Civ & Rjes. The adjutant went to Bde: HQ this morning for me. I also went to Railhead at BOLLEZEELE.	
	16/16		The P.S.O. v the Adjutant went to Railhead & the Companies respectively. The J.S.O.'s car has broken down - so they are again reduced to one car with the train. Lieut Isaac reported back to Hdquars also Lieut Taylor. Captain Goss handed over to Lieut Dalton. He was invalided to yesterday owing to Pressure of work. He apparently was unable to catch	

WAR DIARY

INTELLIGENCE SUMMARY

(Erase heading not required.)

Army Form C. 2118.

Place	Date	Hour	Summary of Events and Information	Remarks and references to Appendices
ESQUELBECQ	16/12	-	A Train today to join his unit - so although officially off the strength of the Train he remains with 331 Co. for the night. I went to Div: H.Q. & then had a lot of work in office.	
"	17/12	-	Went to Div: H.Q. - Office work all the morning - Owing to lack of a car I am unable to get up to the Companies in the forward area.	
"	18/12	-	Went to Div: H.Q. this morning also. Went to Div: H.Q. 119 Bth R.T.A. are moving thro' CALAIS. The S.S.O. went to Army re their supply. I made arrangements with the R.A.H.Q. Staff Officer were later altered, owing to Army making other arrangements. This afternoon I went with the Adjutant to 332 & 333 Companies. whilst at 332 Co: I sent the Adjutant round to 330 Co: as I was unable to go owing to certain matters requiring attention in 332 Co.	
"	19/12	-	Fine weather. Went to Div: H.Q. & then did office work.	

Army Form C. 2118.

WAR DIARY
of
INTELLIGENCE SUMMARY. 73.
(Erase heading not required.)

Instructions regarding War Diaries and Intelligence Summaries are contained in F. S. Regs., Part II. and the Staff Manual respectively. Title pages will be prepared in manuscript.

Place	Date	Hour	Summary of Events and Information	Remarks and references to Appendices
ESSUERBECQ	19/12/16		The G.O.C. in Chief B.E.F. this morning inspected 113 Inf Bde at DOULZEELE & then passed through ESQUELBECQ. 2nd Army rang up this morning concerning the supply arrangements for 119 R.F.A. Bde Office work all the afternoon.	73.
"	20/12/16		I did a lot of office work this morning - Went to Div: H.Q. I also worked in office this afternoon.	73.
"	21/12/16		Wet weather. Office work. I went to Div: H.Q. to arrange for movement of 11.S.W.B. Office work again this afternoon. I also went to Div: H.Q.	73.
"	22/12/16		I went to CASSEL as I was a member on a G.C.M. which was held there - I came back late in the afternoon. The Adjutant went to H.Q. for me.	74
"	23/12/16		I went to Div: H.Q. - The S.S.O. to HERVILLE - then I had office work to do. Captains Foster & Day came back off leave yesterday. Office work.	73.
"	24/12/16		Fine weather - Office work in the morning & afternoon	73.

WAR DIARY
or
INTELLIGENCE SUMMARY 763.
(Erase heading not required.)

Army Form C. 2118.

Place	Date	Hour	Summary of Events and Information	Remarks and references to Appendices
ESQUELBEQ	24/12	—	The W.O. v I went to 2nd Army H.Q. His Lordship	H.
"	25/12	"	Fine weather - Office work - Xmas day.	763.
"	26/12	"	I went to Div: H.Q. - Then to L.O. to Railhead - Captain E.N. Taylor v Lieut D.D. MacLean reported from Base H.T. Depôt for duty. Vice Captain M. Williams v Captain T.N. Cross Lieut MacLean posted at once to 331 Coy: Office work.	
"	27/12	"	Captain E.N. Taylor posted to 330 Co. also Lieut E.R. Crouch Transferred from 332 Co to 330 Co. I visited 330, 331 v 332 Companies - v Arranged the move of 121 B de R.F.A. as far as A.S.C. work is concerned. The Julian or Th.	763.
"	28/12	"	Office work all day arranging the move of 113 v 115 Infantry Brigades - Went to Div: H.Q. The W.O. to Corps H.Q. for a conference. Lean v Lieut Shallow commenced Tel.	
"	29/12	"	I went to Div: H.Q. the W.O. to PROVEN Received 2 Tel Cops. Purchasing Board. Office TOWORKHOUDT. took morning v afternoon - 122 B de R.F.A. moved Today.	

WAR DIARY

INTELLIGENCE SUMMARY.

Army Form C. 2118.

Place	Date	Hour	Summary of Events and Information	Remarks and references to Appendices
Esquelbecq	30/12/16	—	113 Inf Bde v 10 I.C. Co relieved the 1st Inf Bde v Company. Travel to Div H.Q. v then did office work. — Wet weather. 333 Co v now at C.N.R RUES v 331 Co at 7.27.6.6.5.	20.
	31/12/16	—	Went to Div H.Q. v then did office work. The S.O. to Div H.Q. v then did office work. The 119 R.F.A. Bde Raided. Weather bad. The move of the commenced today. The Inf Bde yesterday was carried out very satisfactorily.	20.

B. Truscott Lt. Col.
O.C. 38/Welsh Div. France.

Army Form C. 2118.

WAR DIARY
or
INTELLIGENCE SUMMARY. Vol 14
(Erase heading not required.)

Instructions regarding War Diaries and Intelligence Summaries are contained in F. S. Regs., Part II. and the Staff Manual respectively. Title pages will be prepared in manuscript.

Place	Date	Hour	Summary of Events and Information	Remarks and references to Appendices

From
1/6/16
to
1/7/17.

Lieut. Colonel T. E. Brush
A.D.C.
Commanding
38 (Welsh) Divisional Train.

10.
3009
DAK
31/7/17.

WAR DIARY
INTELLIGENCE SUMMARY.

Army Form C. 2118.

Place	Date	Hour	Summary of Events and Information	Remarks and references to Appendices
ESQUELBECQ	1/1/17	—	I went to Div: H.Q. the S.S.O. to railhead – Office work the Sunbeam car which has just come out of workshops broke down. Certain questions regarding the responsibility for the figures of the Corps Purchase Board on the Topic. Received information that the S.S.O. had been awarded a D.S.O. Sic. the New Years Honour list	
"	2/1/17	—	I went to Divisional H.Q. the S.S.O. attended at Referring – 119 Bde R.F.A. passed through on its return journey from WISSANT. Office work.	700.
"	3/1/17	—	I went to Divisional H.Q. – 1 Complete Turnout Transferred to the New Zealand Division. The T.O. to Railhead. Office work – 2 Lts Hazell reported off leave	703.
"	4/1/17	—	I went to Divisional H.Q. – Have a great clear up Office work this morning. The O.S.S.O. attended a Refitting. This afternoon I went to 333 Co at	

WAR DIARY

INTELLIGENCE SUMMARY

Place	Date	Hour	Summary of Events and Information	Remarks and references to Appendices
ESQUELBECQ	4/1/ 5/1/17	—	CINE R.E.S. The accommodation is very poor. I went to Divisional H.Q. where the running of the Canteens for the Division by the Train was raised. I pointed out to the A.A. & Q.M.G. that this was most impossible owing to a reduction in establishment of 2 R.O.'s & 2 other R.O.s being attached to Corps & Army respectively for duty. I visited 330 & 332 Companies in the forward area - 330 Company is very reduced in numbers at present owing to the absence of the R.F.A. v D.A.C.	783.
"	6/1/17	—	I went to Divisional H.Q. - & then had a lot of office work to do. The weather is very cold. The L.S.O. went to WISSANT & CALAIS on the output of supplies for the R.F.A. Training at former places.	783.
"	7/1/17	—	I visited 331 Co. the morning after going to Divisional H.Q. The Adjutant	783.

WAR DIARY

INTELLIGENCE SUMMARY
(Erase heading not required.)

Army Form C. 2118.

Place	Date	Hour	Summary of Events and Information	Remarks and references to Appendices
ESQUELBECQ	7/7	—	reported back off Leave, also Lieut Dralton.	U.
"	8/7	—	I went to Divisional H.Q. v then did office work. The Adjutant went on duty to 333 Co H.v.s. The D.S.O. reported back from WISSANT.	B.
"	9/7	—	I went to Divisional H.Q. v then did office work — the 14 R.W.T. on moving from HOUTKERQUE to rejoin the Division. The L.S.O. went to Railhead this afternoon. Had a busy time in office.	B.
"	10/7	—	Wet weather — the D.O.O. to PROVEN — I went to Divisional H.Q. v there was very busy in office over the forthcoming reorganization of the R.F.A. v D.A.C.	B.
"	11/7	—	Wet v snowy weather — The L.S.O. to PROVEN. Lieut Grauch posted temporarily to 333 Co: in relief of Lieut J.P. Jones who proceeds on leave today — Lieut Davies the O/C C/ps Purchase Board

Army Form C. 2118.

WAR DIARY
INTELLIGENCE SUMMARY. Zd.
(Erase heading not required.)

Place	Date	Hour	Summary of Events and Information	Remarks and references to Appendices
ESQUELBECQ	11/7	—	A Train R.O. also proceeded on leave today. Very busy in office winding crews for the forthcoming move of the Division from rest to the forward area &c.	DO.
"	12/7	—	Wet weather. I sent the adjutant up to the forward area this morning. The D.S.O. went to BOLLEZELLE. I went to Divisional H.Q. & then did office work.	Zd.
"	13/7	—	Wet weather. The D.S.O. both toward area. I went to Divisional H.Q. & then worked in office all the morning. The question raised as to whether the 39th Trans. H.Q. would move or not from ST JAN TER. BIEZEN. The adjutant to CINQ RUES to see Lieut Gauch in the 7/5 Bde. Lieu R.T.O.	
"	14/7	—	I went to Div. M.D. 333 Co. moved up to their old camp.	

WAR DIARY
INTELLIGENCE SUMMARY.
(Erase heading not required.)

Army Form C. 2118.

Place	Date	Hour	Summary of Events and Information	Remarks and references to Appendices
ESQUELBECQ	14/17	—	On the PROVEN road — Inspected the Parade through ESQUELBECQ. I then did Office work — afterwards going to see the D.D.S.V.T. 3rd Army at CASSEL. 331 Co. yesterday took over their old camp on the PROVEN road from the Company of the 39th Train which had been occupying it. The adjutant investigated the accident which happened this after- noon to the Supply Turnout of Div: H.Q. near HERZEELE Rd.	
"	15/17	—	Left JAN TER BIEZEN. T.H.Q. moved to Divisional H.Q. this afternoon with the adjutant, & then did Office work. S.S.O. to Railhead.	H.
"	16/17	—	I went to Divisional H.Q. then to 333 & 332 Companies. Afterwards to PROVEN re Canteen matters. Major Oakes went on leave. A.D.O. to Railhead & then with the adjutant to DUNKIRK re duties.	

Army Form C. 2118.

WAR DIARY
INTELLIGENCE SUMMARY.
(Erase heading not required.)

Instructions regarding War Diaries and Intelligence Summaries are contained in F. S. Regs., Part II. and the Staff Manual respectively. Title pages will be prepared in manuscript.

Place	Date	Hour	Summary of Events and Information	Remarks and references to Appendices
ST JAN TER. BIEZEN.	17/1/17	1	I was ill & stayed in all day. I.S.O. to Railhead - Adjutant & I.S.O. to Divisional H.Q.	H.
"	18/1/17	-	Still ill - but did Office work. Did not go to Divisional H.Q. The I.S.O. went for me.	H.
"	19/1/17	-	Railhead changed to PESELHOF. Went to Railhead & to Dis H.Q. - Captain Ory came to T.H.Q. at 7 am breakfast - I was sent for by the G.O.C. this evening on A.V.C. subject.	H.
"	20/1/17	-	I went to Div. H.Q. & to Railway at Railhead. Ordinary routine.	H.
"	21/1/17	-	I went to Divisional H.Q. & then to Railway - this work	H.
"	22/1/17	-	Transport - In the afternoon I was very busy in Office. I went to Divisional H.Q. & then to Railway Office. Work all the afternoon.	H.
"	23/1/17	-	Went to Div: H.Q. & then to Railhead to visit Transport	H.

WAR DIARY
INTELLIGENCE SUMMARY

Army Form C. 2118.

Place	Date	Hour	Summary of Events and Information	Remarks and references to Appendices
S. JAN TEN BIEZEN	23/17	—	Keen interested in Offic — Captain Nash came to T.H.Q in the afternoon to take over the a.s.c. duties while that officer is away on leave. I was very busy in Office all the afternoon.	T.S.
"	24/17	—	I went to Divisional H.Q. v to Raickad — Office Routine — Orders re an outbreak of mange issued again.	T.S.
"	25/17	—	I went to Divisional Head Quarters — v had an interview with the g.o.c. on the subject of mange. I visited 331, 332 v 333 Companies. Apparently the outbreak is due to taking our horse standing from a company of 59 Divisional Train. Office work in the afternoon.	T.S.
"	26/17	—	I went to Divisional H.Q. v to Raickad — Keen inspection Transport — Office work afterwards — with the O.C. v works Dept Office 38 Supply Column came afternoon	T.S.

WAR DIARY
INTELLIGENCE SUMMARY

Army Form C. 2118.

Place	Date	Hour	Summary of Events and Information	Remarks and references to Appendices
ST JAN TER BIEZEN	26/1/17	—	to Train Head Quarters on the subject of return of cars.	H.
	27/1/17	—	I went to Divisional H.Q. v to Raithud v then visited / 39' Company A.S.C. Office work in the afternoon.	T.B.
"	28/1/17	—	Went to Divisional H.Q. v was informed that a Brigade of the 21st Division was coming up. Went to Raithud v was rung up by D.A.D.S. 2nd Army on the subject of the supply of this Brigade - informed that it was returned up to v including 29/1/17 - wrote orders at Raithud. In the afternoon the Adjutant A.D.O. went to the Compo occupied by the Brigade - their return for 29.1.17 not yet arrived - arrangement made to see them.	
"	29/1/17	—	Went to Divisional H.Q. - the 21st Divisional B- had receive its rations few there we delivered. I went to Raithud v inspected Transport. Office work all the afternoon.	O.S. H.

WAR DIARY
INTELLIGENCE SUMMARY.

Army Form C. 2118.

Place	Date	Hour	Summary of Events and Information	Remarks and references to Appendices
ST JEAN TER. BIEZEN.	Jan 30/17	—	Went to Divisional H.Q. & to Railhead Office. A company of the 21 Divisional Train attached to 330 Company for accommodation. Going to 322 Company. Lieut Hobson left to proceed to G.H.Q. Jr. for the purpose of being interviewed by the Director of Transport. It was very cruel in spite of the afternoon thawing.	
,,	31/7	—	Went to Divisional H.Q. & to Railhead & inspected Transport. I worked in office all the afternoon. The adjutant went to Divisional H.Q. this afternoon & stays later. Appreciation for an extension of leave.	ad/

W Stevens Lt Col.
A C438 /W/ad/ Div: Train.

Army Form C. 2118

WAR DIARY

~~INTELLIGENCE SUMMARY~~ H.H.

(Erase heading not required.)

Instructions regarding War Diaries and Intelligence Summaries are contained in F.S. Regs., Part II. and the Staff Manual respectively. Title Pages will be prepared in manuscript.

Vol 15

From Feb 1st 1917
To Feb 28th 1917

of

Lt Col T. E. Bennett. A.S.C.
Commanding.
38th (Welsh) Divisional Train.

Place	Date	Hour	Summary of Events and Information	Remarks and references to Appendices
From Feb 1st	1917			To Feb 28th 1917

Army Form C. 2118.

WAR DIARY

INTELLIGENCE SUMMARY

(Erase heading not required.)

Instructions regarding War Diaries and Intelligence Summaries are contained in F.S. Regs., Part II. and the Staff Manual respectively. Title pages will be prepared in manuscript.

Place	Date	Hour	Summary of Events and Information	Remarks and references to Appendices
ST JAN. TER.	1/1/17	—	I went to Divisional H.Q. v Railhead. In the afternoon I did office work.	AS.
BIEZEN.	2/1/17	—	I went to Railhead v to Divisional H.Q. — This afternoon the Adjutant v I went to Railhead v to Div: H.Q. on the subject of iron rations. Office work in the evening.	AS.
"	3/1/17	—	I went to Army H.Q. this morning to interview the D.D.S. & T. I returned to train H.Q. in the afternoon. Major Baker reported from leave.	AS.
"	4/1/17	—	I went to Divisional H.Q. v to Railhead this morning. In the afternoon the Acting S.S.O went to Bac St Maur about the supply of Coke v Charcoal. Major Baker reported personally home at T.H.Q. about 2.P.M.	AS.
"	5/1/17	—	I went to Divisional H.Q. v to Railhead. This afternoon I had a lot of office work.	AS.
"	6/1/17	—	I went to Divisional H.Q. v Railhead. Office work.	AS.

WAR DIARY

INTELLIGENCE SUMMARY.

(Erase heading not required.)

Army Form C. 2118.

Place	Date	Hour	Summary of Events and Information	Remarks and references to Appendices
SISTAN TER. BIEZEN	Feb 6	—	Lt Hodgson proceeded on leave. Novice to 333 v 332 Companies.	X 3.
"	7	—	I went to Divisional H.Q. v to Railhead when I had a long inspection of Transport. Captain Robertson reported back from leave.	Zd.
"	8	—	I went to Divisional H.Q. to Railhead. Transport was very good. I interviewed Captain Lambert in the afternoon at Orderly Room. Office work	Zd.
"	9	—	I went to Divisional H.Q. v to Railhead - Lieut Crouch reported back from leave. Major Baker ill. Office work	Zd.
"	10	—	I went to Divisional H.Q. v to Railhead. 9 visited 333 - 332 v 331 Companies this afternoon. The Adjutant ill - Office work	Zd.
"	11	—	I went to Divisional H.Q. v to Railhead - This afternoon I inspected 330 v 331 Companies - Major	Zd.

WAR DIARY
INTELLIGENCE SUMMARY

Army Form C. 2118.

Place	Date	Hour	Summary of Events and Information	Remarks and references to Appendices
ST JAN TER.	1917 11th	—	Baker went to Hospital. Office work in the evening.	Tel.
BIEZEN.	12"	—	At about 4 A.M. I received a message from Captain Taylor acting O.C. H.Q. Company that a fire had occurred in his camp & that he feared that S.S.M. Brown had been burned to death. I at once instructed the Train Doctor to proceed to 330 Company Camp. I went to 330 Company Camp myself later & found that his fears were confirmed. I ordered a Court of Inquiry under the Presidency of Captain Lambert to assemble at 2 P.M. I then went to Divisional H.Q. v to Railhead. At 2 P.M. I attended at the Court of Inquiry, at about 7 P.M. I returned to train H.Q. v did office work.	
"	13"	—	I went to Divisional H.Q. v to Railhead. At 2 P.M. I attended the Court of Inquiry with the S.S.O.	Tel.

WAR DIARY
INTELLIGENCE SUMMARY.

Place	Date	Hour	Summary of Events and Information	Remarks and references to Appendices
ST JAN TER.	13/1/17	—	which had been telling twice 10 A.M. G.P.M. at 3 P.M. Denounced Lt. H. Brown's funeral.	
BIEZEN.	14/1/17	—	Went to Divl: H.Q. & to Railhead. The adjutant to the Court of Inquiry at 330 Company — a bomb was dropped by a German aeroplane in 330 Co: Camp about 12.50 P.M. 5 men were wounded one who belonged to that Company & one who belonged to the Company of the 21 Divisional Train which is sharing 330 Co: Camp. Captain Lambert was down at T.H.Q. all the afternoon in connection with the inquiry. 330 Co: Lories. Much office work today.	
	15/1/17	—	Am going on leave today. Major Hoare returns from leave today.	
	16/1/17	—	I (Major H. Noel Hoare) took over temporary command of the Train from Lt Col T.E. Bennett who is about to leave. I attended at Refilling Points & Divisional HQ with Capt Mark acting S.P.O.O. at	

Army Form C. 2118.

WAR DIARY
INTELLIGENCE SUMMARY. Kn.t
(Erase heading not required.)

Place	Date	Hour	Summary of Events and Information	Remarks and references to Appendices
5th Jan. To BIEREN.	16/2/17 12/2/17		Div HQ again in the afternoon. Orders were received to impose trace precautions and instructions given accordingly. I visited Railhead + afterwards attended a conference of quartermasters + staff captains - the AA+QMG + DAQMG were also present. In the afternoon I did a considerable amount of R office work.	K2.H Katt.
	18/2/17.		I visited Refilling Points + Div HQ in the morning + was in the office all the afternoon.	17Ktt
	19/2/17.		I visited Refilling Points + Div HQ in the morning. In the afternoon I attended a Court of Enquiry at 332 Coy ASC re the fire at Hôtel Company - afterwards I saw Major Baker in hospital at PROVEN + then went to 333 Coy. Captain Forbes came to the Orderly Room in the evening.	HAH
	20/2/17.		Visited Refilling Points + Div HQ in the morning + went to Army HQ in the afternoon when I saw the AQMG - DADS - DADT - the Purchase board + O/c Accounts on various matters.	K2.H

WAR DIARY

INTELLIGENCE SUMMARY. K. H.

(Erase heading not required.)

Army Form C. 2118.

Place	Date	Hour	Summary of Events and Information	Remarks and references to Appendices
ST JAN TER BIEZEN.	21/1/17		This morning I went to Divisional HQ + on to Railhead - In the afternoon I visited Capt Foster at 332 Coy & Capt Jung at 331 Coy. 2/Lt Hodgson returned from leave.	14½ H.
	22/1/17		I visited Divisional HQ + Railhead - Orderly Room in the afternoon & the evening I went to Corps HQ	14½ H.
	23/1/17		In the morning I went to Railhead - Orderly Room at 2 pm - afterwards visited 333 Coy + in the evening I interviewed Colonel Hesse - S.M.T.O. & Major Scott in reference to the working of Supply Columns.	12 H.
	24/1/17		I went to Divisional HQ & Railhead in the morning & S.S. Office - work in the afternoon.	14 H.
	25/1/17		I visited Railhead Divisional HQ + Headquarters VIII Corps + afterwards to the Losses of 332 Coy "dipped" in the VIII Corps disinfecting Dip.	14 M
	26/1/17		Divisional HQ & Railhead in the morning - In the afternoon, after Orderly Room I went round 333 Coy + afterwards to VIII Corps Supply Columns to arrange about fuel returned by SS Div Train.	14½ H.

Army Form C. 2118

WAR DIARY
~~INTELLIGENCE SUMMARY~~ 1914
(Erase heading not required.)

Instructions regarding War Diaries and Intelligence Summaries are contained in F. S. Regs., Part II and the Staff Manual respectively. Title Pages will be prepared in manuscript.

Place	Date	Hour	Summary of Events and Information	Remarks and references to Appendices
ST JEAN TER BIEZEN.	27/2/17.		I went to Refilling Point this morning & met the A.D.M.S. who inspected them at 10.30. The car broke down at PESELHOEK so I walked back. Orderly Room office work in the afternoon.	W.M.H.
	28/2/17.		I went to Railhead & Divisional H.Q. in the morning & did office work, including the regrouping of limits for supply purposes, in the afternoon & evening.	W.M.H.

Army Form C. 2118

WAR DIARY
INTELLIGENCE SUMMARY
(Erase heading not required.)

Vol 16

Place	Date	Hour	Summary of Events and Information	Remarks and references to Appendices
From				VO
1/3/17			of. Lieut Colonel T.E. Bennées Commanding. 38 /A.Bde./Divisional Train.	31/3/17

WAR DIARY

INTELLIGENCE SUMMARY

Army Form C. 2118

Place	Date	Hour	Summary of Events and Information	Remarks and references to Appendices
ST JEAN TER BIEZEN	1/3/17		In the morning I visited Railhead & Divisional HQ. Orderly Room & Office work in the afternoon	H.A.H.
	2/3/17		I went to Railhead & inspected the Dumps this morning & afterwards went to Div H.Q. Orderly Room at 2 pm & afterwards I visited DDSrT: Office at 2nd Army.	H.A.H.
	3/3/17		I saw the S.S.O. of the 55th Division this morning in connection with "Spills" poison & attended refilling later. The Corps Commander visited 331 & 332 Coys in the afternoon.	H.A.H.
	4/3/17		I visited Railhead & Div. H.Q. this morning. Orderly Room & Office work in the afternoon.	H.A.H.
	5/3/17		In the morning I attended at Refilling - in the afternoon Office work - in the evening I attended a lecture at 330 Coy on the use of the water cart.	H.A.H.
	6/3/17		I went to Divisional HQ & Railhead in the morning & inspected 332 Coy in the afternoon - Capt Nash went on leave. The turnout of the 122 Bde RFA were transferred from 330 Coy to 330 Coy & the turnout of the 119 Bde (Army) RFA were transferred from 330 Coy to 332 Coy.	H.A.H.

Army Form C. 2118

WAR DIARY

INTELLIGENCE SUMMARY

(Erase heading not required.)

Place	Date	Hour	Summary of Events and Information	Remarks and references to Appendices
ST JEAN TER BIEZEN.	7/3/17.		I attended at the H.Q. of 39th Divisional Train to give evidence with reference to the amount of Fuel handed over by the 38th Division to the 39th Division on December 14th 1916. In the afternoon I did office work on the Evening I gave a lecture on Supplies at the 38th Divisional school.	H.R.H.
	8/3/17.		The Divisional School came to Refilling Point to see the issues actually take place — I explained everything thoroughly to them afterwards went to Divisional H.Q. & in the afternoon did office work via the evening went to Div. H.Q. again in connection with the honours list.	H.R.H.
	9/3/17.		Went to Div H.Q. took the interpreter M. Kahn — with me — (Sauer) in my recommendations for our known two servants) afterwards returned to Railhead & Refilling Points. In the afternoon I Inspected 338 Coy was not altogether satisfied	H.R.H.
	10/3/17.		I attended at Refilling Point & Div. H.Q & afterwards did office work — It has been freezing hard running to the last two days. Let is warmer today.	H.R.H.
	11/3/17.		Divisional H.Q. & Refilling Points in the morning — Office work at 330 Coy in the afternoon — The Adjutant went on Special leave today.	H.R.H.

Army Form C. 2118

WAR DIARY or INTELLIGENCE SUMMARY

(Erase heading not required.)

Place	Date	Hour	Summary of Events and Information	Remarks and references to Appendices
ST JEAN TER BIEZEN	12/3/17		I went to Railhead Refilling Point & afterwards interviewed the Gas Officer about R.E. Gas Chemicals. In the afternoon I inspected 330 Coy again.	Hq. H
	13/3/17		I visited Refilling Point & Div HQ in the morning. Ostroj Room at 2 o'clock. The V.O. came at 2.30 & was sent to inspect the horses of 330 Coy which are in a poor condition. The V.O. made various suggestions which I instructed the O.C. to carry out at once — included the purchase of a new chaff cutter — later inspected 331 Coy which I found in an excellent condition in every way.	Hq. H
	14/3/17		I showed two officers from the Investigation department round Refilling Point this morning. They expressed themselves as very pleased with all they saw — including the supply rendez at 147 Train H.Q. O/Cs 330 – 332 + 333 Coys came to Ostroj Room in the afternoon.	Hq. H
	15/3/17		I went to Divisional H.Q. Refilling Point this morning. Captain Barton came with me to advise the Division about growing potatoes — In the afternoon I did office work.	1½/Patt.

Army Form C. 2118

WAR DIARY

~~INTELLIGENCE SUMMARY~~

(Erase heading not required.)

Instructions regarding War Diaries and Intelligence Summaries are contained in F.S. Regs., Part II. and the Staff Manual respectively. Title Pages will be prepared in manuscript.

Place	Date	Hour	Summary of Events and Information	Remarks and references to Appendices
ST JEAN TER BIEZEN.	16/3/17.	—	I went to Div H.Q. with Captain Foster again this morning & afterwards went to Raikhoek – I have been rated for C.S.M Thomas from 332 Coy shall appointed the Planting of the potatoes. C.S.M Davies from 333 Coy acting as C.S.M at 332 Coy temporarily. In the afternoon I inspected 336 Coy. Office work in the evening.	A.H.
"	17/3/17.	—	I rode to Raikhoek this morning as no car was available. In the afternoon I went to 333 Coy & in the evening to 331 Coy.	A.H.
"	18/3/17	—	Farriers back from Cassel also Captain Nash. Office work.	
"	19/3/17	—	I went to Raikhoek & Reviewing & then with the S.O. to Div: H.Q. This afternoon Captain Lambert attended Orderly Room with 2 men under arrest. Office work.	

WAR DIARY
INTELLIGENCE SUMMARY

Army Form C. 2118

(Erase heading not required.)

Place	Date	Hour	Summary of Events and Information	Remarks and references to Appendices
STJAN TER BIEZEN.	20/3/17	—	I attended Repairs & inspected Transport at Railhead. Jales went to Divisional H.Q. Office work.	W.
	21/3/17	—	I went to Railhead & inspected Transport & then went to Divisional H.Q. Office work.	W.
	22/3/17	—	Went to Railhead - inspected Transport & then went to Divisional Head Quarters. In the afternoon the D.A. & Q.M.G. VIII Corps inspected 333 & 330 Companies accompanied by me.	W.
	23/3/17	—	Captain Lambert proceeded on leave. I went to Railhead & inspected Transport, also to Divisional Head Quarters. In the afternoon I visited 330 Company with the Train S.O. Office work.	W.

Army Form C. 2118

WAR DIARY
INTELLIGENCE SUMMARY
(Erase heading not required.)

Instructions regarding War Diaries and Intelligence Summaries are contained in F.S. Regs., Part II. and the Staff Manual respectively. Title Pages will be prepared in manuscript.

Place	Date	Hour	Summary of Events and Information	Remarks and references to Appendices
ST JAN TER. BIEZEN.	24/3/17	—	I went to Railhead & inspected Transport & Kin went to Divisional Head Quarters — Office work in the afternoon.	
"	25/3/17	—	I went to Railhead & inspected Transport — then I went to PESELHOEK To Divisional Head Quarters — Office work. Again in the afternoon.	H.
"	26/3/17	—	I went to Repining & to Divisional Head Quarters — Office work in the afternoon.	H.
"	27/3/17	—	I went to Railhead & inspected Transport, then went to Divisional Head Quarters. I reported to Hospital in the afternoon for Dental Treatment. Office work	H.
"	28/3/17	—	I went to Repining & to Divisional Head Quarters — Office work	H.

WAR DIARY
INTELLIGENCE SUMMARY
(Erase heading not required.)

Army Form C. 2118

Place	Date	Hour	Summary of Events and Information	Remarks and references to Appendices
ST JAN. TER. BIEZEN.	29/3/17	—	Went to Reninghe & to Divisional H.Q. The adjutant went to BOLLEZEELE re the move of 113 Infantry Brigade. 114 Infantry Brigade is relieving 113 Infantry Brigade in the Potarzo.	
"	30/3/17	—	Went to Reninghe & to Divisional H.Q. In the afternoon I inspected 332 Co. A.S.C. Captain Foster returned from leave. Half of pack company 331 v 332, moved. Backing up places. Office work.	
"	31/3/17	—	Went to Reninghe & to Divisional H.Q. The remainder of pack of 331 v 332 Companies moved to our relieving the other. 331 Company to CINQ RUES. Brigade moves completed. 14 Div: Train is occupying the lines. Company Hqrs 23"	

Army Form C. 2118

WAR DIARY
INTELLIGENCE SUMMARY

(Erase heading not required.)

Instructions regarding War Diaries and Intelligence Summaries are contained in F.S. Regs., Part II. and the Staff Manual respectively. Title Pages will be prepared in manuscript.

Place	Date	Hour	Summary of Events and Information	Remarks and references to Appendices
ST JAN TER. BIEZEN	3/1/17		Area of 331 Company — OO 331 Company has been located in the lines vacated by 332 Company.	

W Brunner Lt. Col.
O.C. 38/IIIII Div. Train

1/1/17

Army Form C. 2118

WAR DIARY
INTELLIGENCE SUMMARY
(Erase heading not required.)

Vol 17

From 1/4/17. To 30/4/17.

Lieut Colonel T. E. Bennetts
A.S.C.
Commanding
38/Arld / Divisional Train.

Army Form C. 2118

WAR DIARY
INTELLIGENCE SUMMARY
(Erase heading not required.)

Instructions regarding War Diaries and Intelligence Summaries are contained in F.S. Regs., Part II. and the Staff Manual respectively. Title Pages will be prepared in manuscript.

Place	Date	Hour	Summary of Events and Information	Remarks and references to Appendices
ST. JAN TER. PIEZEN	14/1/17	—	Sunday – Went to Rifleking & then to Division at Head Quarters – Attended Church Parade in the afternoon at 3.31 Company's old Lines.	M.
"	2 4/1/17	—	Went to Rainham & to Divisional Head Office work & Orderly Room in the afternoon	M.
"	3 4/1/17	—	Snow fell during the night. Went to Rainham & to Divisional Head Quarters – Office work in the afternoon – Orders re move J 113 & 114 B⁰⁵ issued.	M.

WAR DIARY

INTELLIGENCE SUMMARY

Army Form C. 2118

Place	Date	Hour	Summary of Events and Information	Remarks and references to Appendices
ST JAN TER. BIEZEN.	4/4/17	—	Went to Divisional Head Quarters & Refilling Point. Office work. The adjudant went to see him to see the 23rd Divisional Train. 331 Company had vacated their billets for 331 Co. to move in. 331 Co moved to their own lines from 332 Co Lines. 332 Co came up from BOLLEZEELE with 114 Infantry Brigade.	W.
	5/4/17	—	Went to Railhead & to Divisional Head Quarters – Office work in the afternoon.	H
	6/4/17	—	No cars were available today. The S.O. was away on duty. Major Graham from 38 Divisional "Q" came down to T. H.Q. & we inspected 333 Company in the afternoon.	RS.
	7/4/17	—	Went to Railhead & inspected Transport also to Divisional Head Quarters. This afternoon after visiting	

WAR DIARY
INTELLIGENCE SUMMARY

(Erase heading not required.)

Army Form C. 2118

Instructions regarding War Diaries and Intelligence Summaries are contained in F.S. Regs., Part II. and the Staff Manual respectively. Title Pages will be prepared in manuscript.

Place	Date	Hour	Summary of Events and Information	Remarks and references to Appendices
ST JAN TER, BIEZEN (cont'd)	7/4/17	—	130 Field Ambulance — The Train Doctor & I went with Colonel Davies to Canal Bank. Captain Lambert returned from leave.	T.L.
"	8/4/17	—	I went to Reserve Division Head Quarters — Office work in the afternoon	T.L.
"	9/4/17	—	I went to Railhead, & to Divisional Head Quarters. Office work this afternoon.	T.L.
"	10/4/17	—	I went to Divisional H.Q. after inspecting Transport at Railhead. After orderly room this afternoon went with Major Graham of 38/Welsh/Divisional & I went round 331 Co: A.D.C.	T.L.
"	11/4/17	—	I went to Railhead & to Divisional Head Quarters. Office work. 331 Co: Lorries went through the town also for the 2nd time. Rather a bad day for it as it Wind has been high & cold	T.L.

Army Form C. 2118

Instructions regarding War Diaries and Intelligence Summaries are contained in F. S. Regs., Part II. and the Staff Manual respectively. Title Pages will be prepared in manuscript.

WAR DIARY
INTELLIGENCE SUMMARY
(Erase heading not required.)

Place	Date	Hour	Summary of Events and Information	Remarks and references to Appendices
ST JAN TER. BIEZEN.	12/4/17	—	I went to Railway & Divisional Head Quarters. Office work this afternoon.	
	13/4/17	—	I went to Railhead & 6-Divisional Head Quarters Captain W-S. Walton reported this morning for duty from the Base H.T. Depôt HAVRE. Office work.	
	14/4/17	—	I went to Railhead & to Divisional Head Quarters. Office work this afternoon.	
	15/4/17	—	I went to Railway & 6-Divisional Head Quarters. I attended Church parade after Office this afternoon.	
	16/4/17	—	I went to Army to see the D.D.S.T on several Train matters - such as the footing of Captain Walton in place of Major Baker. Returning I had a lot of Office work to do this afternoon.	

WAR DIARY
INTELLIGENCE SUMMARY

Army Form C. 2118

(Erase heading not required.)

Place	Date	Hour	Summary of Events and Information	Remarks and references to Appendices
ST JAN TER.	17/4/17	—	Went to Railhead & to Divisional Head Quarters. Office work afterwards — Ordinary Routine	A.
BIEZEN	18/4/17	—	Went to Railhead & Divisional Head Quarters. Lieut. F.P. Jones on being sent to England sick was struck off the train Sheerys/k 1st date - 8.4.17. I went with the P.M.O. to 330 C. & inspected it this afternoon.	A.
	19/4/17	—	I went to Railhead & Divisional Head Quarters. Office work & ordinary routine.	A.
	20/4/17	—	Went to Railhead & Divisional Head Quarters. 2 Lieut. J.J. Creswell reported for duty & posted to 332 Company A.S.C.	A.
	21/4/17	—	Went to Railhead & Divisional Head Quarters. Ordinary Routine	A.

WAR DIARY
INTELLIGENCE SUMMARY

Army Form C. 2118

Place	Date	Hour	Summary of Events and Information	Remarks and references to Appendices
ST JAN TER. BIEREN.	22/4/17	—	I went to Railhead & Divisional Head Quarters - There was a long conference at Q. a scheme for an offensive - This afternoon the V.S.O. & I went looking for Refilling Points in connection with the scheme. Office work on return.	H.
	23/4/17	—	I went to Railhead & to Divisional Head Quarters This afternoon the V.S.O. the D.A.Q.M.G. & I went looking for Refilling Points & inspecting Railhead in connection with the "Offensive" scheme - Busy all day at it.	H.
	24/4/17	—	I went to Railhead & Divisional H.Q. - Also again with the D.A.Q.M.G. & V.S.O. to find Refilling Points & dumps - Again busy all day.	H.

Army Form C. 2118

Instructions regarding War Diaries and Intelligence Summaries are contained in F. S. Regs., Part II. and the Staff Manual respectively. Title Pages will be prepared in manuscript.

WAR DIARY
or
INTELLIGENCE SUMMARY

(Erase heading not required.)

Place	Date	Hour	Summary of Events and Information	Remarks and references to Appendices
ST JAN TER. BIEZEN	25/4/17	—	I went to Railhead & Divisional Head Quarters. Office work. & then went to inspect Certain Railhead in connection with the Officers Scheme. All the evening until late at night I was busy in office writing a report on the subject.	
"	26/4/17	—	I went to Railhead & to Divisional Head Quarters. Much office work.	
"	27/4/17	—	I went to Railhead & to 6" Divisional Head Quarters. I went with I.S.O. & the Adjutant to "W" Camp this afternoon. This evening I went to 333 Co. A.S.C.	
"	28/4/17	—	I went to Railhead & Divisional Head Quarters. Captain Lunberry Foster came & Train Inspection. Some small Train Inspection.	

Army Form C. 2118

WAR DIARY
INTELLIGENCE SUMMARY
(Erase heading not required.)

Place	Date	Hour	Summary of Events and Information	Remarks and references to Appendices
ST JAN TER.	29/4/17	—	I went to Railhead & Division at Head Quarters - Ordinary Routine	
BIEZEN	30/4/17	—	I went to Railhead & Divisional Head Quarters. This afternoon Inspected 331, 332 & 333 Companies & went to see their Company Books. 331 & 332 leaves improving repair in Condition.	

Th Bruce Lt Col.
O.C. 38/Welsh/Div: Train.

1/5/17.

Army Form C. 2118

WAR DIARY
INTELLIGENCE SUMMARY
(Erase heading not required.)

Vol 18

of

Lieut Colonel T.E. Bevvely
R.A.C.
Commanding
38 (Welsh) Divisional Train.

From 1-5-17. To 31-5-17.

Army Form C. 2118

WAR DIARY
INTELLIGENCE SUMMARY.
(Erase heading not required.)

Instructions regarding War Diaries and Intelligence Summaries are contained in F. S. Regs., Part II. and the Staff Manual respectively. Title Pages will be prepared in manuscript.

Place	Date	Hour	Summary of Events and Information	Remarks and references to Appendices
ST JAN TER.	1/5/17	—	I went to Railhead & to Divisional Head Quarters - Office work this afternoon.	H.
BIEZEN.	2/5/17	—	Moved into the BOLLZEELE area. 115 Infantry & B'de & 333 Company A.C. Bain Rest Camp for horse lines & sick in the camp on the PROVEN road vacated by 333 Co: A.S.C. under the charge of Captain N. J. Watson. I went to Divisional Head Quarters after inspection to train transport at Railhead. This afternoon the adjutant & I went out to find forward camps for Divisional Train.	W. B.
"	3/5/17	—	Drove to Divisional Headquarters & to Poperinghe & Reselhoek ordinary routine.	H.
"	4/5/17	—	Went to Railhead & then to Divisional Head Quarters - Much office work today.	H.

Army Form C. 2118

WAR DIARY

INTELLIGENCE SUMMARY

(Erase heading not required.)

Place	Date	Hour	Summary of Events and Information	Remarks and references to Appendices
ST JAN TER. BIEZEN.	5/1/17	—	The adjutant & I went to Poperinge & then on to Divisional Head Quarters. This afternoon the adjutant & I visited the Troni Rest Camp for foot & sick horses & then 332 Co: A.S.C. Later on – I went to 330 Co: A.S.C.	W.
"	6/1/17	—	I went to Rickhall & then to Divisional Head Quarters. A detachment of 330 Co: went to WATOU for the 122 Bde R.F.A. Office work.	W.
"	7/1/17	—	I went to Poperinge & to Divisional Head Quarters.	W.
"	8/1/17	—	I went to Poperinge & to Divisional Head Quarters & to ordinary Routine. Office work & ordinary Routine. With the adjutant & I.I.O.	W.
"	9/1/17	—	The I.I.O. & I went to Poperinge – to Divisional Head Quarters & then on to VIII Corps H.Q. re supplies on the new forward scheme. This afternoon	W.

Army Form C. 2118

Instructions regarding War Diaries and Intelligence Summaries are contained in F. S. Regs., Part II. and the Staff Manual respectively. Title Pages will be prepared in manuscript.

WAR DIARY
or
INTELLIGENCE SUMMARY
(Erase heading not required.)

Place	Date	Hour	Summary of Events and Information	Remarks and references to Appendices
ST JAN TER BIEZEN.	9/5/17	—	I had to remand R.S.M. Lloyd for trial by F.G.C.M. We had a conference of Company Commanders this afternoon to discuss the coming Paris sports.	A.
"	10/5/17	—	Went to Railhead & to Divisional Head Quarters. Office work. The J.J.O. adjutant & I went to PROVEN this afternoon.	do.
"	11/5/17	—	I went to Poperinghe & to Divisional Head Quarters. Office work & ordinary routine.	A.
"	12/5/17	—	Went to Railhead & to Divisional Head Quarters. Ordinary Routine.	A.
"	13/5/17	—	Went to Poperinghe & then on to Divisional Head Quarters. Office work.	A.

Army Form C. 2118

WAR DIARY
~~INTELLIGENCE SUMMARY~~
(Erase heading not required.)

Place	Date	Hour	Summary of Events and Information	Remarks and references to Appendices
ST JAN TER.	14/5/17	—	Went to — Reviewing & to Divisional Head Quarters Office work this afternoon — I afterwards visited 330 Company.	ZI.
BIEZEN	15/5/17	—	D.S.O. went on leave — The adjutant went to BOLLEZEELE Nook assumed the duties of D.T.O. & Found Train Head Quarters. I was very busy in Office writing orders for the move of 333 Co: A.S.C. to this area & 113 Co to back area. Went to Railway Div: H.Q.	ZI.
	16/5/17	—	Went to Railhead & to Divisional Head Quarters. The adjutant went to 330 Co concerning the (drinking) water This on wagons. I was very busy in Opes all the afternoon & evening going through the Divisional Train A.T.G. 1028. 333 Co: moved up country and R 118-13 do	ZI.

WAR DIARY
INTELLIGENCE SUMMARY

Army Form C. 2118

Place	Date	Hour	Summary of Events and Information	Remarks and references to Appendices
ST JAN TER BIEZEN	17/5/17	—	Went to Railhead & to Divisional Head Quarters. Captain Ings reported back after his month's leave. I was busy with Ifees all the afternoon. 115 B.C^n v 333 Co. arrived in this area.	
"	18/5/17	—	Went to Reybury & to Divisional Head Quarters. Been very busy in Office today.	L.D.
"	19/5/17	—	Went to Railhead & to Divisional Head Quarters. 331. Co: moved to the back area. The Rest Camp moved from 333 Co. Camp to 331. Company Camp. Went D.C. 39 Divisional Train today with reference to the carriage of Petrol Tins for water on Train vehicle.	L.
"	20/5/17	—	Went to Reybury & then with the acting S.S.O. to Divisional Head Quarters. Ordinary Routine.	L.D.

Army Form C. 2118

WAR DIARY
or
INTELLIGENCE SUMMARY
(Erase heading not required.)

Place	Date	Hour	Summary of Events and Information	Remarks and references to Appendices
SI JAN TER	21/5/17	—	Went to Reytwig v/6 Divisional Head Quarters.	Z.
BIEZEN	22/5/17	—	Ordinary routine. Went to Railhead v 6- Divisional Head Quarters - Office work this afternoon	Z.
"	23/5/17	—	Went to Reytwig - v made a close inspection of Train Transport there - then went on to 6" Divisional Head Quarters - ordinary routine.	Z.
"	24/5/17	—	Went to Railhead v again made a close inspection of Train Transport. Then went with the Acting S.S.O. To Divisional H.Q. The Train doctor - Captain R.C. McMillan proceeded on leave - Office work this afternoon.	Z.

WAR DIARY
INTELLIGENCE SUMMARY
(Erase heading not required.)

Army Form C. 2118

Place	Date	Hour	Summary of Events and Information	Remarks and references to Appendices
ST JAN TER.	25/1/17	—	I went to HOUTKERQUE to sit as a member on a Court Martial. Office work this afternoon.	H.
BIEZEN.	26/1/17	—	I went to Divisional Head Quarters after attending Repldng Adjutant went to 332 & 333 Companies with reference to the medical inspection of boilers attached to the Train. Office work.	H.
	27/1/17	—	I went to Railhead & inspected Train Transport & then to Divisional Head Quarters. The V.S.O. returned from leave. Office work. Captain Nash returned to 330 Co M.G.H.	H.
	28/1/17	—	I went to Reflding & then to Divisional H.Q. — The Adjutant went on leave — owing to urgent illness in his family. I was very busy in office all the afternoon & evening doing the adjutants work as well as my own. 1st 2nd C.R.E. arrived from back area.	H.

WAR DIARY

INTELLIGENCE SUMMARY

(Erase heading not required.)

Army Form C. 2118

Place	Date	Hour	Summary of Events and Information	Remarks and references to Appendices
SIJAN TER. BIEZEN.	29/5/17	—	123 Field Co: R.E. proceeded to the Back area – Divnl Railhead & 38 Divisional Head Quarters. Orders issued to 331/Co: re supplies in the Back area. Very busy in Office all day.	L.
"	30/5/17	—	113 B⁴ & 331 C.R.⁵.C. moved from HERZEELE to QUELMES Area in two stages. I went to Divisional Head Quarters after attending at Railhead – Office work all day.	L.
"	31/5/17	—	Divns: made 6" & 10" Div: H.Q. – S.L.O. went to Reninny – very busy in Office all the morning. The Train Book occupied all afternoon & evening.	Teβ.

T. Bruce L. Col.
O.C. 38 (Welsh) Divisional Train.

Army Form C. 2118.

WAR DIARY
INTELLIGENCE SUMMARY.
(Erase heading not required.)

Instructions regarding War Diaries and Intelligence Summaries are contained in F. S. Regs., Part II. and the Staff Manual respectively. Title pages will be prepared in manuscript.

Vol 19

From 1/6/17. To 30/6/17.

Lieut Colonel T.E. Bennett A.S.C.
Commanding

38 (Welsh) Divisional Train.

Place	Date	Hour	Summary of Events and Information	Remarks and references to Appendices

Army Form C. 2118.

WAR DIARY
~~INTELLIGENCE SUMMARY~~
(Erase heading not required.)

W3/

Place	Date	Hour	Summary of Events and Information	Remarks and references to Appendices
ST JANTER BIEZEN	1/6/17	-	Went to Railhead & to Divisional Head Quarters - Divisional Transport Sports Today.	
"	2/6/17	-	Went to Railhead & to Divisional Head Quarters. Ordinary Routine - chiefly office work - owing to adjutant being on leave	D.
"	3/6/17	-	Lieut Shallis went on leave to-day. A great deal of office work to-day.	D.
"	4/6/17	-	Office work again to-day - ordinary routine	D.
"	5/6/17	-	Went to Rejilling & thence to Divisional Head Quarters - Office work & ordinary routine.	D.
"	7/6/17	-	Went to Railhead & to Divisional Head Quarters. G/O.R.M. Head awarded the D.C.M. Captain & adjutant V.T. Nopes	D.
"	8/6/17	-	returned from leave - office work. Went to Rejilling & to Divisional Head Quarters - ordinary routine.	D.
"	9/6/17	-	Went to Railhead & Divisional Head Quarters. 331 Co: A.T.C. moved with the 113 Infantry Brigade from the QUELMES area - transport half way & looked for the night.	D.

Army Form C. 2118.

WAR DIARY
INTELLIGENCE SUMMARY.
(Erase heading not required.)

Instructions regarding War Diaries and Intelligence Summaries are contained in F. S. Regs., Part II. and the Staff Manual respectively. Title pages will be prepared in manuscript.

Place	Date	Hour	Summary of Events and Information	Remarks and references to Appendices
ST JAN TER BIEZEN	10/6/17	—	Down to Divisional Head Quarters - Shore of the 113 Infantry B de Transport including 331 Company A.S.C. completed.	H.
"	11/6/17	—	Down to Railhead & to Divisional H.Q. office work all day. This Division today joined the XIV Corps Fifth Army. On Transfer from the VIII Corps Second Army. The question as to Baggage vehicles marching with unit faced by 113 Inf B de. This afternoon visited 333 Company A.S.C. & had a consultation on the subject of the fitting of Petrol Tin Carriers to all vehicles. Also visited H.Q. 55th & 39th Div^{nl} Train.	H
"	12/6/17	—	Proceeded as usual, the morning to Rysselwij from to Divisional Head Quarters - This afternoon Inspected the O.C. 39 Divisional Train on a question of Trans Police. 332 Company together with the Transport of the 114 B de Commenced	H

WAR DIARY
INTELLIGENCE SUMMARY

Army Form C. 2118.

Place	Date	Hour	Summary of Events and Information	Remarks and references to Appendices
ST JAN TER	12/6/17	—	In journey to the SUELMES area in Two Jasro - Lieut W.J.S. Taylor proceeds on leave.	J.
BIEZEN	13/6/17	—	I went to Railhead v to Divisional Head Quarters - The afternoon I went to 333 Company Camp - inspected it - Then again went on to the Guardian of Water Tin Carriers on the Train Vehicle. I handed over 332 B. Camp to no: 4 Company of the Guards Train - v abolished the Train Rar-Camp for poor sick horses.	T.S.
"	14/6/17	—	I went to Rejuring v to Divisional Head Quarters - The afternoon I went to 331 v 333 Companies of the Train. Also to Fifth Army Head Quarters again to Divisional H.Q.	T.S.
"	15/6/17	—	I went to Rejuring v to Divisional Head Quarters - The afternoon I met 330, 331 v 333 Company Commanders in 333 Company Area to discuss the subject of Water Tin Carriers v to see an experimental filling applied to a vehicle as an Example for the whole Train.	T.S.

Army Form C. 2118.

WAR DIARY
INTELLIGENCE SUMMARY.
(Erase heading not required.) BS.

Place	Date	Hour	Summary of Events and Information	Remarks and references to Appendices
ST JAN TER BIEZEN	16/6/17	—	Went to Rijsseling v to Divisional Head Quarters — Detached 10 complete turnouts under Lieut Hazell from various companies to attachment to Divisional H.Q. in connection with the carriage of ammunition to cover the D.A.C. who are being overworked. The afternoon I visited 330 Co: A.S.C. v took the A.D.V.S. with me. Condition of the horses very much improved — Recent Remounts of poor quality. Some suffering from otn disease.	
"	17/6/17	—	I did not go to Rijsseling v Divisional Head Quarters — instead I went to visit 302 Company in the DUELNES area. The horses were very fit.	
"	18/6/17	—	Went to Rijsseling v to Divisional Head Quarters — Ordinary routine v office work.	10
"	19/6/17	—	Went to Rijsseling v to Divisional Head Quarters — Office work. Captain Duffield proceeded on leave.	113

Army Form C. 2118.

WAR DIARY
INTELLIGENCE SUMMARY.
(Erase heading not required.)

Place	Date	Hour	Summary of Events and Information	Remarks and references to Appendices
ST JAN TER. BIEZEN.	20/6/17	—	Went to Reffling & to Divisional Head Quarters. Then proceeded to inspect the site allotted to the Divisional Train at or about INTERNATIONAL CORNER with the A.A. v A.H.G v A.A.G. In the afternoon Captain Taylor A.S.C. came to orders on bicycles - I took him to INTERNATIONAL CORNER to allot 330 Company their future Camp. The XIII Corps address in horse markerships called at Train H.Q.	U.
"	21/6/17	—	Went to Reffling & to Divisional Head Quarters - Ordinary routine.	U.
"	22/6/17	—	Went to Railhead & to Divisional Head Quarters 330 Company moved to its new camp at INTERNATIONAL CORNER Ordinary Routine & office work.	U.
"	23/6/17	—	Went to Railhead & to Divisional Head Quarters - Sent the adjutant to Railhead early - as it should have changed this morning from PESELHOEK to INTERNATIONAL CORNER. But an error was made by Traffic & the back train went to PESELHOEK.	

Army Form C. 2118.

WAR DIARY

INTELLIGENCE SUMMARY.

(Erase heading not required.)

Place	Date	Hour	Summary of Events and Information	Remarks and references to Appendices
ST. JAN TER BIEZEN.	23/6/17 (cont:)	—	This afternoon the Adjutant & Van Hector V.V. visited 330 Company's new lines to Test water. for horses — we did the same to 383 Company's new camp. He arranged parties of 331 V 383 Companies arrived at INTERNATIONAL CORNER Camp — Isolated their respective Camps — then proceeded with the S.C.S.O. to INTERNATIONAL Corner Railhead with reference to Railway in detail at Railhead Check Tuck — & also Railway in detail Permission from 5th Army to do this. Visited Divisional Head Quarters again.	
"	24/6/17	—	This division commenced Refilling at INTERNATIONAL Corner railhead in detail six Truck. Interference by XIV Corps A.P.M. V the fact that the Pack Train was placed in the wrong siding. Somewhat lengthened proceedings. H.Q. Train moved from ST JAN TER BIEZEN to INTERNATIONAL CORNER Camp. 331 V 383 Companies also completed their move — Apparently the neighbourhood	

WAR DIARY

INTELLIGENCE SUMMARY

(Erase heading not required.)

Army Form C. 2118.

Place	Date	Hour	Summary of Events and Information	Remarks and references to Appendices
INTERNATIONAL CORNER. ST JEAN FER AZEBEN	24/6/17	—	INTERNATIONAL CORNER is rather disturbed to-day by the enemy's heavy Artillery & hostile flying Corps. This morning intense artillery duel	
"	25/6/17	—	The Divisional Refilling only took 1 hour & 20 minutes this morning - as the Pack Train was placed in the correct decies & the XIV Corps A.P.M. did not interfere with proceedings. I was present as usual & then went to Divisional H.Q. This afternoon Japani visited Divisional Head Quarters.	M.
"	26/6/17	—	The Divisional Pack Train was asked to-day by Army in Corps - with the result that the Pack Train that arrived for no was short of all commodities for the units attached to us - the arrangement has been that the Pack Train should be altered Tomorrow 27/6/17. Supplies had to be collected from all over the place to complete the Pack. Visited to-night Refilling & 16 Divisional Head Quarters. Tonight I visited	

WAR DIARY or INTELLIGENCE SUMMARY

Army Form C. 2118.

Place	Date	Hour	Summary of Events and Information	Remarks and references to Appendices
INTERNATIONAL CORNER.	26/6/17	—	The S.M.T.O. XIV Corps to Try & get the necessary Supply Column lorries for the forthcoming move of the Division. Apparently the duty of the S.M.T.O. is to forward divisions lorries their Supply Column lorries for supplies. There has been much trouble all day over this matter.	
"	27/6/17	—	Went to Reninghelst & to Divisional Head Quarters — 333 Company moved to EECKE on its way into the 115 Infantry Bde to the training area — A.D.O. went to the Training area & Refilling Point & Supplies generally. This afternoon I visited 331 Company & 330 Company Lines & also went to Divisional Head Quarters — Today was the last Time I drew rising in the XIV Corps area. H.Q. Staff are now drawing from the Guards Division. Heavy shelling of the area round our Camps & Company this morning was on a piece of wood-land outside 330 Company's Camp — on Railhead	N.
"	28/6/17	—	Went to Divisional Head Quarters — Refilling for 331	N.

Army Form C. 2118.

WAR DIARY
INTELLIGENCE SUMMARY.
(Erase heading not required.)

Place	Date	Hour	Summary of Events and Information	Remarks and references to Appendices
INTERNATIONAL CORNER.	28/6/17	—	O.C. 29 Divisional Train visited Train H.Q. very busy today our orders for the move.	
"	29/6/17	—	331 Company entrained its Journey to the training area having completed the first part yesterday — 333 Co. completed its journey with 115 Infantry — B.E. yesterday — 9 trucks Divisional H.Q. & 330 Company. T.H.Q. moved to the training area — NORRENT FONTES. T.H.Q. Camp handed over to 29 Div: Train — Visited 332 Company at ROMLEY where it had arrived from the QUELMES area.	21.
"	30/6/17	—	331 Co. A.C. continued its journey to the training area arriving eventually AUCHY AU BOIS. — 333 Co: is now at WESTREHEM. V Train H.Q. at NORRENT FONTES. The Adjutant & I were very busy in Office until late night on the subject of the Rose baggage exchange paper the supply procedure to be adopted is a move forward.	70.

R Bruce Lt Col.
O.C. 38 (Welsh) Divisional Train

Army Form C. 2118.

WAR DIARY
INTELLIGENCE SUMMARY
(Erase heading not required.)

Summary of Events and Information

OF

Lieut. Colonel. T.E. BENNETT.
A.S.C.
Commanding.
38th (Welsh) Divisional Train.

31/7/7
1/7/17

Army Form C. 2118.

WAR DIARY
or
INTELLIGENCE SUMMARY
(Erase heading not required.)

Place	Date	Hour	Summary of Events and Information	Remarks and references to Appendices
NORRENT-FONTES.	1/7/17		I with the Adjutant visited 331, 332, & 333 Companies, IT also proceeded to Racked Aire.	21.
	2/7/17		I went to Dist H.Q. and afterwards was busy in Office. Adjt went to International Corner to 330 Co. and to O.C. 19 D.r Train re 330 Co. attachment.	21.
	3/7/17		I went to Dist H.R. afterwards Office hours & Ordinary routine.	21.
	4/7/17		I went to Dist H.R. and in the afternoon visited the three Companies and also their Refilling Points. Capt Duffield & Stratton returned from leave.	21.
	5/7/17		I went to Dist H.Q. and thus from there proceeded round Refilling Points with A.O. & A.M.G. afterwards Ordinary routine.	21.
	6/7/17		I visited Div H.Q. Ordinary Routine.	21.
	7/7/17		I went to Div H.Q. Ordinary Routine.	18.
	8/7/17		I went to Dist H.Q. & 2) Office hours all morning. In afternoon held Orderly Room at Avenny au Bois. 331 Company & visited the Company Lines.	20.

WAR DIARY
or
INTELLIGENCE SUMMARY

Army Form C. 2118.

Place	Date	Hour	Summary of Events and Information	Remarks and references to Appendices
Nœux-les-Fosses.	9/2/17		I went to Div. H.Q. from H.Q. to Railhead. Visited Div.H.Q. again in the evening. Ordinary Routine: Lt. Hopson & Lt. Hodgson proceeded on leave.	A.
	10/2/17		I visited Div. H.Q. afterwards did Office work.	A.
	11/2/17		I visited Div. H.Q. afterwards Ordinary Routine.	A.
	12/2/17		I went to Div. H.Q. & to 332 Company. Orders received to move G. Division to forward area. Commencing on 13th.	A.
	13/2/17		I went to Div. H.Q. & Office work. Orders to move on 13th cancelled.	A.S.
	14/2/17		I went to Div. H.Q. afterwards busy with Supply Transport arrangements for move of G. Division to forward area.	A.
	15/2/17		I visited Div. H.Q. Advance sections of 331 & 332 Companies moved from AUCHY-AU-BOIS and ROMLEY respectively with portions of their Brigades to CASTRE area. I went round to Companies with S.S.O. and we also selected Billeting Points.	A.

Army Form C. 2118.

WAR DIARY
or
INTELLIGENCE SUMMARY
(Erase heading not required.)

Instructions regarding War Diaries and Intelligence Summaries are contained in F.S. Regs., Part II. and the Staff Manual respectively. Title Pages will be prepared in manuscript.

Place	Date	Hour	Summary of Events and Information	Remarks and references to Appendices
NORRENT FONTES	16/7/7.		I visited Div. H.Q. The advanced section of 331 & 332 Companies moved from CASTRE area to their old lines on PROVEN ROAD. Rear sections of 331 & 332 Companies moved from AUCHY-AU-BOIS & ROMLEY respectively to THIENNES. 333 Company moved with 115 Infantry Brigade from WESTREHEM to MOLENGHEM. The Adjutant visited the Companies on the move. 331 & 332 Companies Advanced Sections arrived PROVEN.	H.
	17/7/17.		I visited Div. H.Q. and also visited 333 Company and the Rear Sections of 331 & 332 Companies - all on the move, and selected Refilling Points for them. Rear Sections 331 & 332 Companies moved from THIENNES to CASTRE area. 333 Company from MOLENGHEM to CASTRE area.	H.
	18/7/7		I again visited Companies moving to forward area. Busy in Office afternoon & evening.	H.
	19/7/7		Train H.Q. moved from NORRENT FONTES to PROVEN ROAD - Lines of 331 Company temporarily. Moves of Companies completed. Present locations:- 330 Company - INTERNATIONAL CORNER. 331 " - Old Huts. PROVEN. 332 " - Old Lines. PROVEN. 333 " - Part in 331 Co's & part in 332 Co's Lines.	H.

2449 Wt. W14957/M90 750,000 1/16 J.B.C. & A. Forms/C.2118/12.

WAR DIARY

Army Form C. 2118.

Place	Date	Hour	Summary of Events and Information	Remarks and references to Appendices
PROVEN	20/7/17		I visited HQ 5th Army re Transport to be attached to Div: Train during operations and also re Railhead being changed for 21st inst from PROVEN to INTERNATIONAL CORNER. I also went to 330 Company. T/Major C. WATT reported for duty from Base and took over Primary of HQ Company from T/Captain E.N. TAYLOR. I visited Div. HQ & at PROVEN & was busy re above arrangements.	U
	21/7.		Train HQ, 331, 332, & 333 Companies moved from PROVEN to INTERNATIONAL CORNER. Railhead changed from PROVEN to INTERNATIONAL CORNER. I also visited Div. HQ & several times during the day.	U
INTERNATIONAL CORNER	22/7/17		Gas alarm at 12.30 a.m. All Companies on Parade. Busy with orders re all day. Pack Train arrived very late today.	U
	23/7.		I went to Div. HQ. and arrangements for Supplies Transport completed. 2 Drivers killed & 1 Sergt. wounded. 7 & 29 Field Ambulance attached from Train. 1 G.S. Wagon rendered unserviceable & 1 Horse slightly grazed.	U
	24/7.		I went to Railhead & Div. HQ. Very busy all day. Lt Col: Standon 20 Div: Train called re 2 Battalions of his Division joining.	U
	25/7.		I went to Railhead & Div. HQ. Unit attached from 20 & 29 Divisions for Supplies.	U
	26/7/17.		I visited Div. HQ. Office hours all day.	U

Army Form C. 2118.

WAR DIARY
or
INTELLIGENCE SUMMARY

(Erase heading not required.)

Instructions regarding War Diaries and Intelligence Summaries are contained in F. S. Regs., Part II. and the Staff Manual respectively. Title Pages will be prepared in manuscript.

Place	Date	Hour	Summary of Events and Information	Remarks and references to Appendices
	27/2/17.		I visited Div.H.Q. Office work all day. Busy re attached Units.	N.
	28/2/17.		I went to Div.H.Q. Units of Division and majority of attached Units to have a Double refilling tomorrow. It's loads up second days supplies on Wagons at 6.30 p.m. ready to move off at 6 a.m. in the morning.	N
	29/2/17.		I went to Div H.Q. re Refilling. Units has two days supplies delivered to them. Busy with Orders and arrangements re attached Units.	N.
	30/2/17.		I went to Div H.Q. HQ Coy & No 3 Coy (148-149 Coy) 20 Div. Train cross roads 6 INTERNATIONAL CORNER attached to the Train for administration. Doubled up. (Capt. W.S. WATSON relieved from Train 332-333 (on consequently Doubled from 330 Coy & Lt McLEAN Transferred from and now Transferred from 331 Coy & 332 Coy.	N.
	31/2/17.		Battle of FLANDERS began. Our Division going to the attack first. I went up to superintend the 1st Line Transport and its getting up of Supplies etc to the men.	N.

8/1/17.

T.E. Burnell Lt-Col.
O.C. 38/Welsh Div. Train.

Army Form C. 2118.

WAR DIARY

~~INTELLIGENCE SUMMARY~~

(Erase heading not required.)

Instructions regarding War Diaries and Intelligence Summaries are contained in F. S. Regs., Part II. and the Staff Manual respectively. Title pages will be prepared in manuscript.

Place	Date	Hour	Summary of Events and Information	Remarks and references to Appendices

Vol 21

OF

Lieut Colonel T.E.Bennett D.S.O. A.S.C.

Commanding.

38th (Welsh) Divisional Train.

1/8/17.

31/8/17

WAR DIARY
INTELLIGENCE SUMMARY

(Erase heading not required.)

Army Form C. 2118.

Place	Date	Hour	Summary of Events and Information	Remarks and references to Appendices
INTERNATIONAL CORNER.	1/8/17		I went to Div. HQ. Very heavy rain which hampered operations very considerably. R.T.A. moto Transport Lies without informing us and thus supply Parties returned very late from Delivering Supplies. I went with Major Watt O.C. HQ Coy to an R.A at Advanced Div HQ.	W.S.
	2/8/17		I went to Div HQ and then with O.C. R&H.Q. to forward area. I collected 50 Airdromes for use in front line Trenches as Braziers.	W.
	3/8/17		I did not leave Camp to-day, being unwell. L.O. went to Div H.Q.	W.
	4/8/17		I visited Div H.Q and then Post Office HQR re Move of Division to rest area.	W.S.
	5/8/17		I went to Div.H.Q. 331 Company moved from INTERNATIONAL CORNER to their Old Lines on PROVEN ROAD. Baggage Section of 331 Company also moved from INTERNATIONAL CORNER to PROVEN ROAD. Busy in Office with Orders etc.	W.S.

Army Form C. 2118.

WAR DIARY
INTELLIGENCE SUMMARY
(Erase heading not required.)

Instructions regarding War Diaries and Intelligence Summaries are contained in F. S. Regs., Part II. and the Staff Manual respectively. Title Pages will be prepared in manuscript.

Place	Date	Hour	Summary of Events and Information	Remarks and references to Appendices
PROVEN.	6/8/17.		Remainder of 332 Company moved from INTERNATIONAL CORNER to Old Lines (on PROVEN ROAD). Train H.Q. moved also from INTERNATIONAL CORNER to PROVEN ROAD - 331 Co. Lines. I visited Div. H.Q. which had moved from Dragon Camp to PROVEN. Division resting.	T.d.s.
	7/8/17.		I was not H.d.s. today. A.A. & Q.M.G. visited from H.Q. in morning. 330 Company (H.Q.C.) was detached to 20 n Div. Train today. I visited Div. H.Q. in the evening.	T.d.s.
	8/8/17.		I went to Div. H.Q. Ordinary routine.	T.d.s.
	9/8/17.		I went to Div. H.Q. Office work & ordinary routine.	T.d.s.
	10/8/17.		I visited Div. H.Q. Busy in Office all day.	T.d.s.
	11/8/17.		I went to Div. H.Q. and to Railhead and inspected & Remounts received.	T.d.s

Army Form C. 2118.

WAR DIARY
INTELLIGENCE SUMMARY
(Erase heading not required.)

Instructions regarding War Diaries and Intelligence
Summaries are contained in F. S. Regs., Part II.
and the Staff Manual respectively. Title Pages
will be prepared in manuscript.

Place	Date	Hour	Summary of Events and Information	Remarks and references to Appendices
PROVEN.	12/8/17		I went to Div H.Q. & Ordinary routine afterwards.	W.
	13/8/17.		Visited Div H.Q. 333 Company moved from Corps Staging Area to new Old Lines on PROVEN Road. Ordinary routine.	W.
	14/8/17.		I went to Div H.Q. with Adjutant and afterwards visited Army H.Q. Also visited 330 Company at VOX VRIE FARM. Afternoon Office work.	W.
	15/8/17.		I went to Div H.Q. 333 Company moved from their old Lines on PROVEN Road and doubled up with 331 & 332 Companies also on PROVEN Road. 114 Infantry Brigade moved to forward area to support 20" Division. 332 Company remained on PROVEN Road.	W.
	16/8/17.		I visited Div H.Q., afterwards doing Office work.	W.
	17/8/17.		I went to Div H.Q. and to Railhead & thence to 5th Army. Coy 5 O.T. inspected the Lines of 331, 331 & 333 Companies. Orders received for Division to move up to forward area again.	W.

2449 Wt. W14957/M90 750,000 1/16 J.B.C. & A. Forms/C.2118/12.

Army Form C. 2118.

WAR DIARY
INTELLIGENCE SUMMARY
(Erase heading not required.)

Instructions regarding War Diaries and Intelligence Summaries are contained in F. S. Regs., Part II. and the Staff Manual respectively. Title Pages will be prepared in manuscript.

Place	Date	Hour	Summary of Events and Information	Remarks and references to Appendices
PROVEN	18/8/17		I visited Div H.Q. 331, 332, & 333 Companies moved from PROVEN ROAD to VOX VRIE FARM. Train H.Q. remained on Proven Road. Busy in Office all Day.	A.
DRAGON CAMP.	19/8/17.		Train H.Q. moved from PROVEN ROAD to DRAGON CAMP. Div H.Q. being at ELVERDINGHE. I visited all the Companies and also Div H.Q. I also inspected G. Camp with a view to putting Companies here & found it much more suitable.	A.S.
	20/8/17.		I visited Kirkland and also Div H.Q. He & Train Companies moved from VOX VRIE FARM to G Camp.	A.S.
	21/8/17.		I visited Div H.Q. and afterwards Div Office work. I was awarded D.S.O.	W.
	22/8/17.		I visited Railhead and inspected all the Supply Turnouts, afterward going to Div H.Q. Busy in Office all afternoon & evening. Lt. McCall & Hazell proceeded on Leave.	W.

2449 Wt. W14957/M90 750,000 1/16 J.B.C. & A. Forms/C.2118/12.

Army Form C. 2118.

WAR DIARY
INTELLIGENCE SUMMARY
(Erase heading not required.)

Place	Date	Hour	Summary of Events and Information	Remarks and references to Appendices
DRAGON CAMP.	23/8/17		I visited Div.H.Q. Repiling points. Ordinary Routine.	W.
	24/8/17		I went to Div.H.Q. Afterwards Office work. Capt Robertson proceeds on leave.	W.
	25/8/17		I went to Div.H.Q. & thence to 14 Welsh Transport Lines to inspect Experimental torpedoing in Trenches in place of Splashes Alcohol. In evening I again went to see 16 specimens well on way.	W.
	26/8/17		I went to Div.H.Q. Ordinary Routine. Visited Companies.	W.
	27/8/17		I visited Kitchens & Div.H.Q. afterwards Doing Office work.	W.
	28/8/17		I went to Div.H.Q. Ordinary routine.	W.

Army Form C. 2118.

WAR DIARY
or
INTELLIGENCE SUMMARY

(Erase heading not required.)

Instructions regarding War Diaries and Intelligence Summaries are contained in F. S. Regs., Part II. and the Staff Manual respectively. Title Pages will be prepared in manuscript.

Place	Date	Hour	Summary of Events and Information	Remarks and references to Appendices
DRAGON Camp	29/8/17.		I visited Railhead & Div H.Q. The Supply Column Loaders were taken away and the Loaders attached to Train together with Officers & Batmen were detailed to Off-load Pack Train.	Ts.
	30/8/17.		I did not go to Dart Q today. Busy in office. Lt. J.L. Cresswell moved to England to join Infantry School at BEDFORD. Major H.A. Noone D.S.O. (Ops) E.C. Noel proceeded on Leave.	Ts.
	31/8/17.		I went to Div H.Q. and also visited 880 Company. Afternoon & Evening Office work.	Ts.

TB Bowen
Lt Colonel.
O.C. 38 / Welsh / Div: Train.

9/1/17.

2449 Wt. W14957/M90 750,000 1/16 J.B.C. & A. Forms/C.2118/12.

Army Form C. 2118.

WAR DIARY
~~INTELLIGENCE SUMMARY.~~
(Erase heading not required.)

Instructions regarding War Diaries and Intelligence Summaries are contained in F. S. Regs., Part II. and the Staff Manual respectively. Title pages will be prepared in manuscript.

Place	Date	Hour	Summary of Events and Information	Remarks and references to Appendices
From 1/9/17			OF Lieut. Colonel. T. E. Bennett. D.S.O. A.S.C. Commanding 38th (Welsh) Divisional Train.	To 30/9/17

Vol 22

Army Form C. 2118.

WAR DIARY
INTELLIGENCE SUMMARY.
(Erase heading not required.)

Instructions regarding War Diaries and Intelligence Summaries are contained in F. S. Regs., Part II and the Staff Manual respectively. Title pages will be prepared in manuscript.

Place	Date	Hour	Summary of Events and Information	Remarks and references to Appendices
DRAGON CAMP.	1/9/17.		A.D.F.M.G. Division called this morning. I inspected 331, 332, 333 Companies this morning. Orderly Room and Office Work this afternoon and evening.	D.
	2/9/17.		I inspected 350 Company and proceeded with Major Nott to Div H.Q. Ordinary routine of Office Work.	D.
	3/9/17.		Visited Div: H.Q. and afterwards Lt: McCaw & Hazell returned from leave.	D.
	4/9/17.		Office work and afterwards 2d Office work all day.	D.
	5/9/17.		I visited the two Divisional Areas. O.C. J Div Train took me round Company Lines etc.	D.
			I went to Div H.Q. afterwards Ordinary routine. Adjt went to Div left in afternoon re Orders for Divisional Mots.	D.
	6/9/17.		Visited Div H.Q. in morning. Orderly Room & Office work re Mots in afternoon & evening.	D.
	7/9/17.		I visited Packhard and Army H.Q. and also went to 20th Div Train H.Q. re taking over from them at ROUEN	D.
	8/9/17.		I visited Div H.Q. in the morning. I visited Army in afternoon. I went to Div H.Q. in the morning. I visited Army in afternoon	

WAR DIARY or INTELLIGENCE SUMMARY

Army Form C. 2118.

Place	Date	Hour	Summary of Events and Information	Remarks and references to Appendices
DRAGON CAMP.	8/9/17	(contd)	to Railhead for trans of Division to new Area. Supply Section of 333 (Company) moved this afternoon from G Camp to PROVEN ROAD	
	9/9/17.		I visited Railhead and inspected all Trans Supply, Transport - then proceeded to Div. H.Q. An Baggage Section of 333 (Company) moves from G Camp to PROVEN ROAD. Capt. F. Grace reports from Base for duty. Supply Section 331 (Company) moved from G Camp to Corps Staging Area today.	
	10/9/17.		I visited Railhead & Div. H.Q. Busy in Office re Orders to moves. Baggage Section of 331 (Company) moved from G. Camp to Corps Staging Area. Went both Adjutant to Army re Railhead during movs.	
PROVEN ROAD.	11/9/17.		I went with Adjutant to GRUBBE'S Railhead and then to Div. H.Q. Train H.Q. moved from DRAGON CAMP to PROVEN ROAD. Major Moore & Capt. Nash returned from leave.	
	12/9/17		I went to Div. H.Q. 333 (Company with 1st Infantry Brigade moved from PROVEN ROAD to ZECKE Area.	

Army Form C. 2118.

WAR DIARY
INTELLIGENCE SUMMARY.
(Erase heading not required.)

Instructions regarding War Diaries and Intelligence Summaries are contained in F. S. Regs., Part II. and the Staff Manual respectively. Title pages will be prepared in manuscript.

Place	Date	Hour	Summary of Events and Information	Remarks and references to Appendices
PROVEN ROAD. ESTAIRES	13/9/17.		Train HQ moved from PROVEN ROAD to ESTAIRES. 333 Company moved from EECKE area to MORBECQUE area, refilled at EECKE. 332 Company moved from PROVEN ROAD to EECKE area. Arrived Div HQ as usual.	
	14/9/17.		333 Company moved from MORBECQUE area to ESTAIRES area. 332 Company moved from EECKE area to MORBECQUE area. 331 Company moved from CORPS STAGING area to EECKE area. Visited Div HQ and was busy in office all day.	
	15/9/17.		Visited Div HQ and did office work. 333 Company moved from ESTAIRES area to line at ERQUENGHEM. 332 Company moved from MORBECQUE to ESTAIRES area. 331 Company moved from EECKE area to MORBECQUE area. 330 Company with RA from G Camp to STEENVOORDE area. Adjutant went to 330 Company and 331 Company. Lt McLean returned from leave.	

WAR DIARY
INTELLIGENCE SUMMARY

Army Form C. 2118.

Place	Date	Hour	Summary of Events and Information	Remarks and references to Appendices
ESTAIRES.	16/9/17		I visited Div. H.Q. & 333 Company. 332 Company moved from ESTAIRES area to their lines at SAILLY. 331 Company moved from MORBECQUE area to ESTAIRES area. 330 Company moved from STEENVORDE area to MORBECQUE area.	
SAILLY-SUR-LA-LYS.	17/9/17		I visited Div. H.Q. and also 331 & 332 Companies. 331 Company moved from ESTAIRES to their lines Bac St MAUR. 330 Company moved from MORBECQUE area to THIENNES area. HQ Train moves from ESTAIRES to SAILLY-SUR-LA-LYS.	
	18/9/17		I visited Div. H.Q. and 2nd Army H.Q.	
	19/9/17		I went to Div. H.Q. and to ARMENTIERES. 330 Company moves from THIENNES to LA GORGUE. Adjutant, Capt Lawlor & Police Sergeant on leave.	
	20/9/17		I visited Div. H.Q. & went to ARMENTIERES. Afterwards Army routine.	
	21/9/17		I went to Div H.Q. & inspected 331 & 332 Companies. Army routine.	
	22/9/17		Inspected 331, 332 & 333 Companies with G.O.C. Division. Afternoon Office work.	

Army Form C. 2118.

WAR DIARY
INTELLIGENCE SUMMARY.
(Erase heading not required.)

Place	Date	Hour	Summary of Events and Information	Remarks and references to Appendices
SAILLY-SUR-LA-LYS.	23/9/17		I went to Div:HQ in morning. Ordinary routine.	
	24/9/17.		330 Company moved from LA GORGUE to SAILLY-SUR-LA-LYS. I visited Div:HQ, and also went to Railhead and to 330 & 331 Companies. 5 Category "A" Clerk proceeded to Base, having been replaced by Category "B" men.	W. W.
	25/9/17.		I went to Div:HQ. Ordinary routine.	W.
	26/9/17.		I visited Div:HQ & afterwards went with DAQMG to 331 Company re construction of new Camp.	W.
	27/9/17.		I went to Div:HQ in morning and again this afternoon: afterwards to Q's Office work.	W. W.
	28/9/17.		Office work this morning. Visited Div:HQ this afternoon.	W.
	29/9/17		I visited 330 & 331 Companies and also Div:HQ.	W.
	30/9/17		I went to Div:HQ and ordinary routine.	W.

B. Rumsen Lt.Col.
O.C. 38/W(elsh)Div: Train.

Army Form C. 2118

WA 23

WAR DIARY

~~or~~ INTELLIGENCE SUMMARY

(Erase heading not required.)

Instructions regarding War Diaries and Intelligence Summaries are contained in F. S. Regs., Part II. and the Staff Manual respectively. Title Pages will be prepared in manuscript.

Place	Date	Hour	Summary of Events and Information	Remarks and references to Appendices
1/10/19			OF Lieut Colonel T.L. Bennett DSO. ASC. Commanding 38th (Welsh) Divisional Train.	031/10/19

1875 Wt. W593/826 1,000,000 4/15 J.B.C. & A. A.D.S.S./Forms/C. 2118.

Army Form C. 2118.

WAR DIARY
of
INTELLIGENCE SUMMARY.
(Erase heading not required.)

Place	Date	Hour	Summary of Events and Information	Remarks and references to Appendices
Sailly-Sur-la-Lys	1/10/17		I visited Div. H.Q. Pack Trans arrived at LA Gorgue and visited J Bac. ST MAUR. Owing to a collision on the line. Adjt went with S.S.O. to La Gorgue Railhead.	W.D.
	2/10/17		I visited Div. H.Q. in the morning. Office Work remainder of the day.	W.
	3/10/17		I went to Div. H.Q. S.S.O. went to XI Corps today to be attached temporarily for duty. Capt E.C. Nash acting S.S.O.	W.D.
	4/10/17		I visited 330 & 332 Companies and inspected Camps and the work of Constructing new Standings etc. I returned to 330 Coy with A.D.V.R. & G. All Marcs nos sent to to be examined for brood purposes today.	W.S.
	5/10/17		I went with XI Corps Horse Adviser to 330, 332 & 333 Companies and inspected horses and stewards inspected horses of 130th Field Ambulance. Visited Div. H.Q. also.	W.
	6/10/17		I visited Div. H.Q. in the morning. Capt. Richards Welsh Regt attached to Train H.Q. as Staff Learner, for instructional office work.	W.
	7/10/17		I has not well and sent Adjutant to Div. H.Q. 2 Bombs dropped at Bac ST MAUR this morning, killing a loader attached to Train and wounding 2 H.D. Horses. One horse having to be destroyed.	W.

Army Form C. 2118.

WAR DIARY
or
INTELLIGENCE SUMMARY.
(Erase heading not required.)

Place	Date	Hour	Summary of Events and Information	Remarks and references to Appendices
SAILLY- SUR-LA-LYS.	8/10/17		I went to Div H.Q. Office work and ordinary routine.	H.
	9/10/17		I visited Div H.Q. in the morning. Orderly Room and ordinary routine.	H.
	10/10/17		Adjutant went to Div H.Q. Col: Birr A.D.S.T. 1st Army visited Train H.Q. Orderly Room and Office work afternoon & evening.	H.
	11/10/17		I went to Div H.Q. afterwards Office work.	H.
	12/10/17		I visited Div H.Q. twice to d/w Company. Orderly Room and Office work in afternoon & evening.	H.
	13/10/17		I was busy in Office all morning and visited Div H.Q. in afternoon.	H.S.
	14/10/17		I went to Div H.Q. and afterwards ordinary routine.	H.
	15/10/17		I was busy in Office all day today. Orderly Room in afternoon.	H.S.
	16/10/17		I went to Div H.Q. in morning. Ordinary routine.	H.
	17/10/17		I went to Div H.Q. Capt. V. Soues. R.W.F. attached to Train H.Q. as Staff Learner for instruction. I inspected 330 & 332 Companies in the morning and 330 & 333 Companies in the afternoon. 2 Horses wounded by Shell fire at Bac-St. Maur.	H.S.

Army Form C. 2118

WAR DIARY
or
INTELLIGENCE SUMMARY
(Erase heading not required.)

Instructions regarding War Diaries and Intelligence Summaries are contained in F.S. Regs., Part II. and the Staff Manual respectively. Title Pages will be prepared in manuscript.

Place	Date	Hour	Summary of Events and Information	Remarks and references to Appendices
SAILLY SUR-LA-LYS	18/10/17		I visited Divisional Headquarters, & was in Office all day	U.
	19/10/17		Divisional Headquarters as usual & there I went to 338 Company. I held Orderly Room in the afternoon and did Office work	U.
	20/10/17		I went to Divisional Headquarters - Ordinary routine.	U.
	21/10/17		Visited Divisional Headquarters. I had a lot of Office work in the afternoon and evening.	No.
	22/10/17		I visited Divisional Headquarters Orderly Room and usual routine.	No3.
	23/10/17		I went to Divisional Headquarters and afterwards was busy in Office.	No4.
	24/10/17		Reported as usual at Divisional Headquarters. Orderly Room and Office work afterwards.	No5.
	25/10/17		I went to Divisional Headquarters. A.D.M.S. XI Corps came with me and visited 330 & 331 Companies, which took up all the afternoon	No3.
	26/10/17		Very busy in Office all the morning. I went to Divisional Headquarters in the afternoon.	No5.

Army Form C. 2118

WAR DIARY
INTELLIGENCE SUMMARY
(Erase heading not required.)

Instructions regarding War Diaries and Intelligence Summaries are contained in F.S. Regs., Part II. and the Staff Manual respectively. Title Pages will be prepared in manuscript.

Place	Date	Hour	Summary of Events and Information	Remarks and references to Appendices
SAILLY Sur-la-Lys.	27/10/14		I visited Divisional Headquarters and was busy in Office all day.	T.B.
	28/10/14		Went to Divisional Headquarters as usual and afterward & did Office work.	T.B.
	29/10/14		I was a Member of F.G.C.M. at 114th Brigade Headquarters until late in the afternoon. I then visited Divisional Headquarters. Major A. Noad D.S.O. I.S.O. proceeded for duty to 23rd Divisional Train.	T.B.
	30/10/14		I went to Divisional Headquarters and was busy all day doing Office work.	T.B.
	31/10/14		I visited Divisional Headquarters and also 330 Company. Major Thomas reported for duty from 23rd Divisional Train vice Major A. Noad D.S.O.	T.B.

11/17.

B. Bennell Lt. Col.
O.C. 28/Welsh/Div: Train

WAR DIARY
INTELLIGENCE SUMMARY.
(Erase heading not required.)

Army Form C. 2118.

Vol 24

of

Lieut. Colonel T.E. BENNETT, D.S.O., A.S.C.

Commanding

38th (Welsh) Divisional Train.

1/10/17.

20/11/17

Army Form C. 2118.

WAR DIARY
INTELLIGENCE SUMMARY.
(Erase heading not required.)

Instructions regarding War Diaries and Intelligence Summaries are contained in F. S. Regs., Part II. and the Staff Manual respectively. Title pages will be prepared in manuscript.

Place	Date	Hour	Summary of Events and Information	Remarks and references to Appendices
Sailly-lez-Lannoy	1/11/17		I visited Divisional Headquarters in the morning and proceeded on leave in the afternoon. Major C. Watt. Headquarters Company acting as train.	
	2/11/17		I visited Railhead, Refilling Points and Divisional Headquarters and Adjutant and also inspected New Pattern Hay Rack at divisional Stables.	
	3/11/17		Went to Divisional Headquarters and also visited 331 Company. In the evening visited 11th Divisional Train re Section of HQ Coy of that Train coming for attachment. G.O.C. Division inspected 330 Coy Camp.	
	4/11/17		Saw Refilling P. Divisional Troops and inspected 330 Coy.	
	5/11/17		59. St. R.H.A. and Section of HQ Co. 11 Div. Train attached to Division	
	6/11/17		I visited Divisional Headquarters and 331 Company A.S.C. in the morning. Orderly Room and Office Work afternoon & evening. Went with Adjutant to Div. Troops Refilling Point. 330 Company and Divisional Headquarters. Held Orderly Room and did Office Work in afternoon.	
	7/11/17		Visited Divisional Headquarters, Refilling Points and also 331 Company. A A & Q M G inspected 332 Company's Lines.	

Army Form C. 2118.

WAR DIARY
or
INTELLIGENCE SUMMARY.
(Erase heading not required.)

Instructions regarding War Diaries and Intelligence Summaries are contained in F.S. Regs., Part II. and the Staff Manual respectively. Title pages will be prepared in manuscript.

Place	Date	Hour	Summary of Events and Information	Remarks and references to Appendices
SAILLY-LAB-LYS	8/1/17		I went to Divisional Headquarters and to Railhead in the morning and was busy in Office all afternoon. 1 H.O. Horse of 333 Company was wounded (slightly) today by stray fire. 59" Bde R.F.A and Section H.Q Coy 11 Divisional Train left to rejoin their own Division.	w.
	9/1/17		Visited Divisional Headquarters and Railhead. Sents in the morning afterwards Office work. 169th (Army) Bde R.F.A left the area.	w.
	10/1/17		Visited Divisional Headquarters and Railhead and 333 Company and in the afternoon inspected 330 Company Lines.	w.
	11/1/17		I went to Divisional Headquarters and to H.Q R.A. in the morning and in the afternoon inspected Baggage Wagons with A.T.C. Batteries 122 Bde R.F.A. also went to 333 Company Camp.	w.
	12/1/17		Went with Adjutant to Army School of Cookery to inspect Cooking Wines and afterwards proceeded to Divisional Headquarters. Orderly Room and Office work in the afternoon.	w.

Army Form C. 2118.

WAR DIARY
or
INTELLIGENCE SUMMARY.
(Erase heading not required.)

Place	Date	Hour	Summary of Events and Information	Remarks and references to Appendices
SALLY-SUR-LA-LYS.	13/4/17		I visited Regulus Posts and also Divisional Headquarters. Held Orderly Room in afternoon and was busy in Office.	
	14/4/17		G.O.C. Division inspected 555 Company lines. Went to Regulus Point & Air troops and to Divisional Headquarters afterwards. Orus Office work.	(2)
	15/4/17		To Divisional Headquarters in the morning and 330 Company afternoon.	(2)
	16/4/17		Went to Divisional Headquarters and Regulus and was busy in Office all the afternoon.	(2)
	17/4/17		Visited Divisional Headquarters and afterwards did Office work.	abs.
	18/4/17		Saw C.R.E. re Material for completing cages and afterwards proceeded to Divisional Headquarters. Ordinary routine. G.O.C. returned from leave.	(1)
	19/4/17		Went to Divisional Headquarters and was afterwards busy in Office all afternoon and Evening.	(2)

Army Form C. 2118.

WAR DIARY
INTELLIGENCE SUMMARY.
(Erase heading not required.)

Instructions regarding War Diaries and Intelligence Summaries are contained in F. S. Regs., Part II. and the Staff Manual respectively. Title pages will be prepared in manuscript.

Place	Date	Hour	Summary of Events and Information	Remarks and references to Appendices
S.P.14.4.S.a.v La-L.u.	20/4/17		I visited Divisional Headquarters in the morning and dis Office work afterward.	w.
	21/4/17		In the afternoon I inspected 330 Company. Went to Divisional Headquarters and afterwards inspected 331 Company Orderly Room and Ordinary routine Afternoon and Evening.	w.
	22/4/17		Visited Divisional Headquarters as usual and saw tray all Day with Office Work and Ordinary routine.	w.
	23/4/17		Proceeded to Divisional Headquarters in the morning and afterwards did Office Work.	w.
	24/4/17		I inspected 330 v 331 Companies and afterwards went to Divisional Headquarters. Major McS Nation proceeded to England for transfer to Infantry. 2/Lt. S. Biggs reported to 331 Company the Back and me noted to 331 Company.	w.
	25/4/17		I went to Divisional Headquarters in the morning and was afterwards busy with ordinary routine.	w.
	26/4/17		Proceeded to Divisional Headquarters as usual. Afterward Orderly Room and Ordinary routine.	w.

Army Form C. 2118.

WAR DIARY
or
INTELLIGENCE SUMMARY.
(Erase heading not required.)

Place	Date	Hour	Summary of Events and Information	Remarks and references to Appendices
SAILLY SUR LA LYS.	27/11/17		Went to Divisional Headquarters and C.R.E. re material for Tuilerie Camp. Ordinary Routine afterwards.	
	28/11/17		Visited Divisional Headquarters and was busy in Office all day. A.D.M.G. Corps visited 330 Company in the afternoon.	
	29/11/17		Went to Divisional Headquarters and inspected 333 Company. afterwards ordinary routine.	
	30/11/17		Proceeded to Divisional Headquarters and also in the afternoon took O.C. 333 Company with me to select a site for a new Camp for that Company. G.O.C. Division inspected 330 Company. I also inspected 330 Company.	

T. Bruce Jr Col. Train.
O.C. 38/Welsh Div. Train

1/12/17

… Army Form C. 2118.

WAR DIARY
INTELLIGENCE SUMMARY
(Erase heading not required.)

WA 25

Place	Date	Hour	Summary of Events and Information	Remarks and references to Appendices
From				From To
1/12/17			1. Lieut Colonel T.E. Bennett. D.S.O. Army Service Corps. Commanding 38/unit/ Divisional Train.	1/12/17 31/12/17

WAR DIARY

INTELLIGENCE SUMMARY

(Erase heading not required.)

Army Form C. 2118

Place	Date	Hour	Summary of Events and Information	Remarks and references to Appendices
SAILLY	1/12/17	—	Went to Divisional Head Quarters & then to the back area to select a site for a Field Ambulance Transport Lines also an A.S.C. Company Camp. In the afternoon the D.A.A.G. & I went to the back area to look at various camps with a view to bathing units to them — we also inspected several horse lines.	
"	2/12/17	—	Went to Divisional Head Quarters & was all the afternoon in Office.	
"	3/12/17	—	To Divisional Head Quarters — ordinary routine.	
"	4/12/17	—	After attending at Divisional Head Quarters — the D.D.S. & T. First Army came to Train Head Quarters & then inspected the Head Quarter Company. He	

Army Form C. 2118.

WAR DIARY
INTELLIGENCE SUMMARY.
(Erase heading not required.)

Instructions regarding War Diaries and Intelligence Summaries are contained in F. S. Regs., Part II. and the Staff Manual respectively. Title pages will be prepared in manuscript.

Place	Date	Hour	Summary of Events and Information	Remarks and references to Appendices
SAILLY	4/12/17	—	Expressed complete satisfaction. — The adjutant was away all day prosecuting at a Court Martial.	
"	5/12/17	—	Went to Divisional Head Quarters & was busy in office.	
"	6/12/17	—	After attending at Divisional Head Quarters — Ord. - inary routine office work	
"	7/12/17	—	Went to Divisional Head Quarters & then took the R.O. to MERVILLE to arrange about the Turkey & section for Christmas. Arrangements very satisfactory.	
"	8/12/17	—	To Divisional Head Quarters — ordinary routine	
"	9/12/17	—	Went to Divisional Head Quarters — Orderly Room at 2 P.M. — Office work & visit of Supply Officer instructions — G.O.C. Division visited Train Head Quarters this afternoon. Lt. McLean had a confidential interview with me in the	

WAR DIARY
INTELLIGENCE SUMMARY.

(Erase heading not required.)

Army Form C. 2118.

Place	Date	Hour	Summary of Events and Information	Remarks and references to Appendices
SAILLY	9/12/17 (cont?)	—	the presence of his Company Commander - 2 Lieut T.A. WALKER reported for duty & was posted to the Head Quarter Company for duty as a Transport Officer.	W.
"	10/12/17	—	Captain E.C. NASH now in Command of 331 Company vice Captain I.C. ING who was ordered to report to 5th Div? Train for duty. 332 Company proceeded to the back area to ESTAIRES from BAC ST MAUR. I went to 331 Company & also to Divisional Head Quarters.	W.
"	11/12/17	—	Ordinary Routine after visiting Divisional Head Quarters.	W.
"	12/12/17	—	I went to Gravières with the A.A. & Q.M.G. & then to Divisional Head Quarters - after Orderly Room I visited 332 Company in the back area.	W.
"	13/12/17	—	After visiting Divisional Head Quarters I did Officework	W.
"	14/12/17	—	Visited Divisional Head Quarters & this afternoon visited 332 Company at ESTAIRES.	W.

Army Form C. 2118.

WAR DIARY
of
INTELLIGENCE SUMMARY.

(Erase heading not required.)

Instructions regarding War Diaries and Intelligence Summaries are contained in F.S. Regs., Part II. and the Staff Manual respectively. Title pages will be prepared in manuscript.

Place	Date	Hour	Summary of Events and Information	Remarks and references to Appendices
SAILLY	15/12/17	-	Captain J.T. Jones the adjutant proceeded on leave owing to special death in his family. Went to Divisional Head Quarters as usual – Went again this afternoon with Major Wade the Head Quarter Company Commander.	M.
"	16/12/17	-	Went to Divisional Head Quarters – Office work & ordinary routine.	21.
"	17/12/17	-	Went to Divisional Head Quarters & visited 330 & 331 Companies – Office work.	21.
"	18/12/17	-	Went to Divisional Head Quarters & visited 332 Company – much Office work	21.
"	19/12/17	-	333 Company proceeded to the Rest Area & 332 Company returned to BAC ST MAUR – Went to Divisional Head Quarters – much office work	21.
"	20/12/17	-	To Divisional Head Quarters – ordinary routine	M.
"	21/12/17	-	To Divisional Head Quarters – ordinary routine & much Office work.	21.

Army Form C. 2118.

WAR DIARY
INTELLIGENCE SUMMARY.

(Erase heading not required.)

Instructions regarding War Diaries and Intelligence Summaries are contained in F. S. Regs., Part II. and the Staff Manual respectively. Title pages will be prepared in manuscript.

Place	Date	Hour	Summary of Events and Information	Remarks and references to Appendices
SAILLY	22/12/17	—	Went to Divisional Head Quarters – Office work.	H
"	23/12/17	—	Went to Divisional Head Quarters – Captain P.C. Nash went on leave – visited 333 Company in the back area to.	
"	24/12/17	—	To Divisional Head Quarters – Office work – ordinary routine	H
"	25/12/17	—	Went to Divisional Head Quarters – Visited 330 Company – Office work.	H
"	26/12/17	—	Thaw precautions adopted – all wagons carried only half loads – 20 wagons were lent by the D.A.C. to assist the Train Tunnels. Went to Divisional Head Quarters – Ordinary Routine.	H
"	27/12/17	—	To Divisional Head Quarters – ordinary routine Thaw precautions off – Visited 331 Company.	H
"	28/12/17	—	To Divisional Head Quarters – Office work	H
"	29/12/17	—	To Divisional Head Quarters – Office work – Visited 333 Company this afternoon in the back area.	B

Army Form C. 2118.

WAR DIARY
INTELLIGENCE SUMMARY.
(Erase heading not required.)

Instructions regarding War Diaries and Intelligence Summaries are contained in F. S. Regs., Part II. and the Staff Manual respectively. Title Pages will be prepared in manuscript.

Place	Date	Hour	Summary of Events and Information	Remarks and references to Appendices
SAILLY	30/12/17	—	Went to Divisional Head Quarters — Ordinary routine.	
	31/12/17	—	I went to Divisional Head Quarters & visited 333 Company in the back area	

1/1/18.

J. Bennett
Lt. Col.
O.C. 38/Welsh/Div: Train.

Army Form C. 2118.

WAR DIARY
~~INTELLIGENCE SUMMARY~~
(Erase heading not required.)

Vol 26

21/-/18

Instructions regarding War Diaries and Intelligence Summaries are contained in F. S. Regs., Part II. and the Staff Manual respectively. Title Pages will be prepared in manuscript.

Place	Date	Hour	Summary of Events and Information	Remarks and references to Appendices

1/1/18.

of

Lieut-Colonel T.E. BENNETT D.S.O.
Army Service Corps
Commanding
38th (Welsh) Divisional Train

Army Form C. 2118.

WAR DIARY
INTELLIGENCE SUMMARY
(Erase heading not required.)

Instructions regarding War Diaries and Intelligence Summaries are contained in F.S. Regs., Part II. and the Staff Manual respectively. Title Pages will be prepared in manuscript.

Place	Date	Hour	Summary of Events and Information	Remarks and references to Appendices
SAILLY SUR LA LYS.	1/1/18.		I went to Divisional Headquarters in the morning and Div Office went in the afternoon. Capt Isaac proceeded on leave.	
	2/1/18.		I was busy in Office all morning and visited Divisional Headquarters in the afternoon. S.S.O attended Conference at Div H.Q.	
	3/1/18.		Visited Divisional Headquarters as usual — Ordinary routine.	
	4/1/18.		Went to Divisional Headquarters in the morning and afterwards went again with OC 333 Company Coy re New Camp for that Company.	
	5/1/18.		After attending Divisional Headquarters I did Office work and ordinary routine. Adjutant awarded Military Cross.	
	6/1/18.		332 & 333 Companies RE moved to new Camps North of Rys. Divisional 1st Line Transport Lines also moved. I went to Divisional Headquarters as usual.	

Army Form C. 2118.

WAR DIARY
or
INTELLIGENCE SUMMARY
(Erase heading not required.)

Place	Date	Hour	Summary of Events and Information	Remarks and references to Appendices
SAILLY	7/1/18		I inspected Lines of 331 & 333 Companies and afterwards proceeded to Divisional Headquarters. Office work. Ordinary routine in the afternoon.	
	8/1/18		Ordinary routine o/c's attending Divisional Headquarters.	
	9/1/18		Capt. Foster proceeded on leave, Adjutant returned from leave. I went to Divisional Headquarters — Office all afternoon.	
	10/1/18		To Divisional Headquarters and Office work afterwards.	
	11/1/18		Inspected 330 Company accompanied by O.C. 1st Divisional Train, who will take over the Camp. I then visited Divisional Headquarters and afterwards ordinary work.	
	12/1/18		Busy with Orders for Divisional Move to Rest Area. Afterwards visited Divisional Headquarters as usual.	

Army Form C. 2118.

WAR DIARY
or
INTELLIGENCE SUMMARY

(Erase heading not required.)

Instructions regarding War Diaries and Intelligence Summaries are contained in F.S. Regs. Part II. and the Staff Manual respectively. Title Pages will be prepared in manuscript.

Place	Date	Hour	Summary of Events and Information	Remarks and references to Appendices
SAILLY	13/3/18		I was President of a Court of Enquiry re a Fire all day.	
	14/3/18		H.Q. Coy and Adjutant visited the Tram Companies on the Moor. 332 Company moved from Sailly area to BLEU. 333 Company moved from SAILLY to ESTAIRES.	
			Visited Divisional Headquarters and then proceeded with Offr. i/c 332 Company new Camp at BLEU, and then to H. & 1st Divisional Train at MERVILLE. 331 Company moved from BAC ST MAUR to Brigade RESERVE AREA to the lines vacated by 333 Company previous day. Major Noman proceeded away on Office afternoon Evening. Major Noman proceeded on Leave.	
MERVILLE	15/3/18		Train Headquarters moved from SAILLY to MERVILLE. I visited Divisional Headquarters. 331 Company moved from Brigade RESERVE AREA to ESTAIRES. Lieut J.D. Conner reported for duty from Investigation Department.	
	16/3/18		I visited Railhead and then rode to Divisional Headquarters. Adjutant went to 331 Company and to H.R.A. Ordnance railway.	

2449 Wt. W14957/M90 750,000 1/16 J.B.C. & A. Forms/C.2118/12.

Army Form C. 2118.

WAR DIARY
or
INTELLIGENCE SUMMARY
(Erase heading not required.)

Instructions regarding War Diaries and Intelligence Summaries are contained in F. S. Regs., Part II. and the Staff Manual respectively. Title Pages will be prepared in manuscript.

Place	Date	Hour	Summary of Events and Information	Remarks and references to Appendices
MERVILLE	17/1/18		Adjutant visited Railhead. I did Office work in morning and went to Divisional Headquarters in the afternoon.	
	18/1/18		I went to Railhead and then on to Divisional Headquarters - afterwards Ordinary routine. 335 Company moved from SAILLY to LE SART.	
	19/1/18		335 Company moved with Brigade from BLEU to LILLERS area. I attended Divisional Headquarters and afterwards did Office work.	
	20/1/18		Inspected Train Transport at Railhead with Adjutant and then proceeded to Divisional Headquarters. R.A. Brigade H.Q. and two Batteries moved to Training Area. Train Transport detached to 335 Company now in that Area.	
	21/1/18		I visited Divisional Headquarters - Ordinary routine.	

2449 Wt. W14957/M90 750,000 1/16 J.B.C. & A. Forms/C.2118/12.

Army Form C. 2118.

WAR DIARY
INTELLIGENCE SUMMARY
(Erase heading not required.)

Instructions regarding War Diaries and Intelligence Summaries are contained in F. S. Regs., Part II. and the Staff Manual respectively. Title Pages will be prepared in manuscript.

Place	Date	Hour	Summary of Events and Information	Remarks and references to Appendices
MERVILLE	22/1/18		Visited Railhead this morning and then went on to Divisional Headquarters. Orderly Room etc at 5pm and afterwards Office work.	
	23/1/18		Ordinary Routine after attending Divisional Headquarters.	
	24/1/18		I went to Divisional Headquarters and afterwards his Office work.	
	25/1/18		Office work and Ordinary routine in morning & visited Divisional Headquarters in afternoon.	
	26/1/18		Inspected 351 & 333 Companies Camps and Refilling. afterwards going to Divisional Headquarters. Office work afterwards.	
	27/1/18		Proceeded to Divisional Headquarters and his Orderly Room from - afterwards ordinary routine.	

WAR DIARY
INTELLIGENCE SUMMARY

Army Form C. 2118.

Place	Date	Hour	Summary of Events and Information	Remarks and references to Appendices
MERVILLE	28/1/18.		I visited 331 Company Reptileig Point this morning and then went to Divisional Headquarters - afterwards busy with 113 & 114 Brigades' work.	
	29/1/18.		Went to Divisional Headquarters as usual and Ordinary routine.	
	30/1/18.		Went to 333 Company Labo and also to Divisional Headquarters afterwards Office work.	
	31/1/18.		G.O.C. Division inspected Baux Party Toronto at Laithead and afterwards visited 113 Brigade Reptileig Point. afterwards went to Divisional Headquarters - Ordinary routine. Major Thomas returned from leave.	

F Bruce Lt Col
O.C. 38/Welsh/Div= Train

1 2/18.

Army Form C. 2118.

Vol 27

WAR DIARY
INTELLIGENCE SUMMARY
(Erase heading not required.)

Instructions regarding War Diaries and Intelligence Summaries are contained in F. S. Regs., Part II. and the Staff Manual respectively. Title Pages will be prepared in manuscript.

Place	Date	Hour	Summary of Events and Information	Remarks and references to Appendices
~~SEENING~~ From	1.2.18.		Lt Colonel T.E. BENNETT. 28.2.18. D.S.O. Commanding 38/(Welsh) Divisional Train.	10.

WAR DIARY
INTELLIGENCE SUMMARY 73.
(Erase heading not required.)

Army Form C. 2118.

Place	Date	Hour	Summary of Events and Information	Remarks and references to Appendices
MERVILLE	1/2/18	—	Went to Divisional Head Quarters & to 330 Co: at LE SARS. Watched the March of 331 Co: to ST HILAIRE area. In the afternoon I went to 115 Bde H.Q. at ESTAIRES v assisted in Judging Turnout in Bde Transport Competitions	73.
	2/2/18	—	I went to the 115 Infantry Bde Transport Competition. This took nearly all day. Busy in Office in evening over the Suggestion to use 1st Line Transport instead of Train Transport for drawing Rations at Railhead v Ripening the Liberating Train vehicles for Corps work.	73.
	3/2/18	—	Went to Divisional Head Quarters — Ordinary Routine.	73.
	4/2/18	—	Ordinary Routine — Visited Divisional Head Quarters — Office work.	73.

WAR DIARY
or
INTELLIGENCE SUMMARY
(Erase heading not required.)

Army Form C. 2118.

Place	Date	Hour	Summary of Events and Information	Remarks and references to Appendices
MERVILLE.	5/2/18	—	Went to Divisional Head Quarters — Office work. In afternoon to Forward area to reconnoitre lock round.	B.
,,	6/2/18	—	I went to Divisional Head Quarters — I watched the Transport of the 2nd Bn. R.W.F. which is Joining the Division. Pass through MERVILLE. Animals were in fair condition. Office work, arranging for 1st Line Transport to draw Supplies at Railhead.	
,,	7/2/18	—	First Line Transport of 114 & 115 Infantry Bdes. Commenced drawing supplies at Railhead & from Refilling Points under supervision of a Train Captain & 2 Transport Officers. S/Lt. Wesh assisted. 2 Transport Officers S. Hurbers per 2 G.S. wagons found to be 1 too many. Went to Divisional H.Q. after Railhead. Office work.	F.d.

Army Form C. 2118.

WAR DIARY
or
INTELLIGENCE SUMMARY

(Erase heading not required.)

Instructions regarding War Diaries and Intelligence Summaries are contained in F. S. Regs., Part II. and the Staff Manual respectively. Title Pages will be prepared in manuscript.

Place	Date	Hour	Summary of Events and Information	Remarks and references to Appendices
MERVILLE	8/2/18	—	Went to Divisional H.Q. - Ordinary Routine.	
"	9/2/18	—	Ordinary Routine. Went to Divisional Head Quarters. Orderly Room at 2 P.M. afterwards office work	
"	10/2/18	—	Busy in Office over forthcoming move of the Division - I went to Divisional Head quarters this afternoon.	
"	11/2/18	—	Was at XV Corps Head Quarters all the morning — on a Staff Exercise; returned in the middle of the afternoon. Office work on return.	

WAR DIARY
INTELLIGENCE SUMMARY

Army Form C. 2118.

Place	Date	Hour	Summary of Events and Information	Remarks and references to Appendices
MERVILLE	12/2/18	—	I was on the XV Corps Staff Exercise again all the morning. Office work on return.	
"	13/2/18	—	Went to Divisional Head Quarters – Bear over orders for the move of the Division to relieve the 57 Division. 333 Co & 115 Infantry Brigade moved to 57 Divisional Area. 331 Co & 113 Infantry Bde moved from ST HILAIRE Area to GUARBECQUE Area. Sent the adjutant to the GUARBECQUE area.	
"	14/2/18	—	Went to Divisional Head Quarters – then returned with the Adjutant to 57 Divisional Train Head Quarters to obtain information. The Adjutant & I then inspected all Repelling Points, Closes & all the Train Company Lines. Everything	

WAR DIARY
INTELLIGENCE SUMMARY

Army Form C. 2118.

Place	Date	Hour	Summary of Events and Information	Remarks and references to Appendices
MERVILLE	14/2/18	—	was in a very bad state & repair & upkeep, & the camps were exceedingly dirty & unsanitary. The H.&Co:Camp alone was a fairly good camp - Standings were fair in 3 companies - but very bad in the 4th. I gave immediate personal orders to work to be put in hand at once. 331 Co: moved from GARBECQUE area to ESTAIRES. S. with 113 Inf. Bde. 332 Co: moved from ESTAIRES.S. to 57 Divisional area. with 114 Infantry Bde.	
	15/2/18	—	331 Co: moved from ESTAIRES.S. to STEENWERKE area with 113 Infantry Bde. Moved to Divisional Head Quarters. Railhead changed to STEENWERKE. The Artillery group drawing from 57 Division Railhead. At MERVILLE 2/L Beal Jones for duty.	A.W.

Army Form C. 2118.

WAR DIARY
INTELLIGENCE SUMMARY
(Erase heading not required.)

Place	Date	Hour	Summary of Events and Information	Remarks and references to Appendices
STEENWERCK	16/2/18	—	Divisional Head Quarters & Train H.Q. moved to STEENWERCK from MERVILLE. I went to Divisional Head Quarters in the afternoon.	
	17/2/18	—	I went to Divisional Head Quarters - Then to S. Railhead & inspected Transport. I took the Adjutant & visited H.A. Co. Camp of 57 Divi: Train to see if arrangements had been made for part of my Train H.A. Co. which is coming. I saw Lt. McLean in Charge of everything satisfactory. I up to day - Every thing satisfactory. I my advance section. Visited 332 Co Camp in connection with planning a new camp &c. I visited Refilling Point of all companies except 333. I inspected Transport of W 19 Divi: Train for duty. W.	

Captain R.B. Mallon Etait Forms/C.2118/17

WAR DIARY

INTELLIGENCE SUMMARY

(Erase heading not required.)

Army Form C. 2118.

Place	Date	Hour	Summary of Events and Information	Remarks and references to Appendices
STEENWERCK	18/2/18	—	G.O.C. Division visited all the Company Lines. H.Q. Company moved from LE SART to this area with the R.A. Major E.N. Taylor proceeded to join the 2nd Division for duty. Captain Rogahan took Temporary Command of H.Q. Company. Lt. Cowan from 331 to 330 Co as Supply Officer temporarily. I went to Divisional Head Quarters - Office work. G.O.C. called at Train H.Q. & companies.	H.
	19/2/18	—	Went to Divisional Head Quarters. I went to Refilling Point - inspected Transport. Then with the I.S.O. prospected for a new Refilling Point for 114 Bde Group. Found one & gave instructions for a change. In the afternoon with the Adjutant visited 331 - 332 ~ 333 Company re alteration v.c.vc.	H.

Army Form C. 2118.

WAR DIARY
INTELLIGENCE SUMMARY
(Erase heading not required.)

Place	Date	Hour	Summary of Events and Information	Remarks and references to Appendices
STEENWERCK.	20/2/18	—	Went to Divisional Head Quarters. Ordinary Routine.	W.
"	21/2/18	—	Went to Divisional Head Quarters — The Adjutant & I visited 330 Company Camp re improvements &c. Captain Lambert returned from leave.	W.
"	22/2/18	—	Went to First Army Head Quarters for a Conference — Went to Divisional H.Q. on return in the afternoon. Major Watt returned from leave. 2/Lt Howson reported for duty from Base. Office work in evening.	W.
"	23/2/18	—	Went to Divisional Head Quarters & to find a new Refilling Point for 115-13th Group. Found one & wished for change to take effect immediately.	W.

Army Form C. 2118.

WAR DIARY
INTELLIGENCE SUMMARY
(Erase heading not required.)

Instructions regarding War Diaries and Intelligence Summaries are contained in F.S. Regs., Part II. and the Staff Manual respectively. Title Pages will be prepared in manuscript.

Place	Date	Hour	Summary of Events and Information	Remarks and references to Appendices
STEENWERCKE	23/2/18	—	Visited 331 Reficing Point.	
	24/2/18	—	I visited Divisional Head Quarters & the 115 Refilling Point to see if the new site was really suitable in working. Finding it was not. Moved it further along the same road. Also visited 113 B at Refilling Point. Office work in the afternoon.	
	25/2/18	—	Went to Rail head & inspected Transport then to 330 Co Refilling Point & to Fuel Dumps.	13.
	26/2/18	—	I went to Divisional Head Quarters - Inspected 330 Company Camp. Office work.	N.
	27/2/18	—	Went to Divisional Head Quarters. Very busy in office over Honours List. Recommend a Loos V orders.	N.

Army Form C. 2118.

WAR DIARY
INTELLIGENCE SUMMARY
(Erase heading not required.)

Place	Date	Hour	Summary of Events and Information	Remarks and references to Appendices
STEENWERK	28/2/18	—	I went to Divisional Head Quarters. was very busy in Office - Took Honours List recommendations to Divisional Head Quarters	

1/3/18.

A Bruno Lt Col.
O.C. 38 /Welsh/ Divisional Train.

Army Form C. 2118.

Vol 28

WAR DIARY
— or —
INTELLIGENCE SUMMARY.
(Erase heading not required.)

Instructions regarding War Diaries and Intelligence Summaries are contained in F. S. Regs., Part II. and the Staff Manual respectively. Title pages will be prepared in manuscript.

Place	Date	Hour	Summary of Events and Information	Remarks and references to Appendices
From 1/3/18			Lieut Colonel J. E. Bennett D.S.O Army Service Corps Commanding 38th (Welsh) Divisional Train.	To 31/3/18

Army Form C. 2118.

WAR DIARY
or
INTELLIGENCE SUMMARY.
(Erase heading not required.)

Instructions regarding War Diaries and Intelligence Summaries are contained in F. S. Regs., Part II. and the Staff Manual respectively. Title pages will be prepared in manuscript.

Place	Date	Hour	Summary of Events and Information	Remarks and references to Appendices
STEENWERCK	1/3/18	—	To Divisional Head Quarters — Office and orderly room work.	
"	2/3/18		To Divisional Head Quarters — Office routine work in the morning. In the afternoon visited the Camps & Coy of Capt. J. H. Davies of Nos. 331, 332 & 333 Cos.	
"	3/3/18		To Divisional Head Quarters. Office & orderly routine work.	
"	4/3/18		To Divisional Head Quarters — Visited cycling parts of 331, 332 & 333 Cos & inspected their Transport — Orderly Room in the afternoon — Office routine work.	

WAR DIARY

INTELLIGENCE SUMMARY

(Erase heading not required.)

Army Form C. 2118.

Instructions regarding War Diaries and Intelligence Summaries are contained in F. S. Regs., Part II. and the Staff Manual respectively. Title pages will be prepared in manuscript.

Place	Date	Hour	Summary of Events and Information	Remarks and references to Appendices
STEENWERCK SALLY	5/3/15		To Divisional Head Quarters — ordinary routine work	—
"	6/3/15		To Divisional Head Quarters — ordinary routine work	—
"	7/3/15		To Divisional Head Quarters — to 113 Brigade Head Quarters re Canopy Corporation inspection. Office routine work.	—
"	8/3/15		To Divisional Head Quarters — Office routine work	—
"	9/3/15		To Divisional Head Quarters — In the afternoon, accompanied by the Adj't, to forward areas re Observation Posts.	—
"	10/3/15		To Divisional Head Quarters — ordinary routine work	—

Army Form C. 2118.

WAR DIARY
INTELLIGENCE SUMMARY.
(Erase heading not required.)

Instructions regarding War Diaries and Intelligence Summaries are contained in F. S. Regs., Part II. and the Staff Manual respectively. Title pages will be prepared in manuscript.

Place	Date	Hour	Summary of Events and Information	Remarks and references to Appendices
STEENWERCK	11/3/15		To Divisional Head Quarters — Took several M.P's round to inspect C° Camps — In the afternoon, accompanied by the S.S.O. went round to look out Refilling Points — afterwards, accompanied by the D.A.A.G. to look out suitable Camps.	D
"	12/3/15		To Divisional Head Quarters — Went round with D.A.A.G. to look for Refilling Points & Camps.	D
"	13/3/15		To Divisional Head Quarters — Capt" & Adj" I.L.T. lines proceeded on Special leave — Visited Refilling Points of 331, 332 & 333 C°s	D
"	14/3/15		To Divisional Head Quarters — Engaged selecting sites for Refilling Points in case of Divisional Area being made into two Divisional Areas — Capt" W.E. Suffell proceeded on leave.	D

A5834 Wt. W4973/M687 750,000 8/16 D. D. & L. Ltd. Forms/C.2118/13.

Army Form C. 2118.

WAR DIARY
INTELLIGENCE SUMMARY.
(Erase heading not required.)

Instructions regarding War Diaries and Intelligence Summaries are contained in F.S. Regs., Part II. and the Staff Manual respectively. Title pages will be prepared in manuscript.

Place	Date	Hour	Summary of Events and Information	Remarks and references to Appendices
STEENWERCK	15/3/18		To Divisional Head Quarters - Office routine work	W
"	16/3/18		To Divisional Head Quarters - Office routine work	W
"	17/3/18		To Divisional Head Quarters - 330 Co saw it's Camp sites - Accompanied by Major Wall Inspector sites for new Camps - later I visited HAVERSKERQUE to see Head Quarters of Divisions leave centre & to Transport returning to New	W
"	18/3/18		To Divisional Head Quarters - 332 Co wagons stampeded at ARMENTIERES through shell fire, two wagons damaged, no casualties to horses or men - Visited 113 Brigade Replying point & also 330 Co Camp.	W
"	19/3/18		To Divisional Head Quarters - Visited ARMENTIERES - STEENWERCK selected for the to see Transport working - first time.	W

A5834 Wt. W4973/M687 750,000 8/16 D. D. & L. Ltd. Forms/C.2118/13.

Army Form C. 2118.

WAR DIARY
— or —
INTELLIGENCE SUMMARY.
(Erase heading not required.)

Instructions regarding War Diaries and Intelligence Summaries are contained in F. S. Regs., Part II. and the Staff Manual respectively. Title pages will be prepared in manuscript.

Place	Date	Hour	Summary of Events and Information	Remarks and references to Appendices
STEENWERCK	20/3/18		To Divisional Head Quarters —	
			6th Bat: Buffs 6th R.W. Kents } attached from 12th Div. 87 Field C.R.E. 2/4 L.N. Lancs 1/5 " " 502 Field C.R.E. } returned to 37th Div. 507 Field C.R.E.	
"	21/3/18		Accompanied by D.A.A.G. visiting Reinforcement Camps & Inspecting surplus Transport with D.D.S.T. 1st Army.	I.
"	22/3/18		To Divisional Head Quarters — Visited 115 Brigade Group. Lieut. I. O. Cowan proceeded on leave.	II.
ERQUINHEM	23/3/18		To Divisional Head Quarters — Office routine. To Divisional Head Quarters — Visited 330 Co. Camp and Repling point of 114 Brigade — office routine	III. IV.

A5834 Wt. W4973/M687 750,000 8/16 D. D. & L. Ltd. Forms/C.2118/13.

Army Form C. 2118.

WAR DIARY
INTELLIGENCE SUMMARY.
(Erase heading not required.)

Instructions regarding War Diaries and Intelligence Summaries are contained in F. S. Regs., Part II and the Staff Manual respectively. Title pages will be prepared in manuscript.

Place	Date	Hour	Summary of Events and Information	Remarks and references to Appendices
STEENWERCK	24/3/18		To Divisional Head Quarters - Office routine.	R
"	25/3/18		To Divisional Head Quarters - Visited 331, 332 + 333 Coys. Office routine.	R
"	26/3/18		To Divisional Head Quarters - Office routine.	R.
"	27/3/18		To Divisional Head Quarters - Office routine.	R
"	28/3/18		To Divisional Head Quarters - Preparing to move. The Division - Office routine - Capt. & Adj. I. J. Jones M.C. reported to have died today.	R
"	29/3/18		Death of Capt. I. J. Jones on the 28th officially reported today. - To Divisional Head Quarters - Issuing Orders for move - Starting new Reference Books - Office routine. 2nd Lt. W. H. Hogan reported to Turn Head Quarters for duty as Temporary Acting Adj.	R

Army Form C. 2118.

WAR DIARY
INTELLIGENCE SUMMARY.
(Erase heading not required.)

Place	Date	Hour	Summary of Events and Information	Remarks and references to Appendices
STEENWERCK	30/3/18		331 Co. with Brigade Group move to STEENBECQUE	
			332 Co. with Brigade Group move to MERVILLE	
			333 Co. with Brigade Group move to CALONNE	
			Proceeded to entraining area selecting Rallying Points & arranging dumps for reserve supplies	A
	31/3/18		Final Head Quarters moved from STEENWERCK to MERVILLE	
			Visited new Rallying Points & inspecting Rallying — Office routine	
			to Divisional Head Quarters	A

B. Pennie
Lt-Col.
O.C. 38/Welsh/Div. Train

Army Form C. 2118.

WAR DIARY
INTELLIGENCE SUMMARY
(Erase heading not required.)

Vol 29

Place	Date	Hour	Summary of Events and Information	Remarks and references to Appendices
From 1/4/18			of Lieut. Col. J.E. Bennett A.S.O. Army Service Corps Commanding 38th (Welsh) Divisional Train	To 30/4/18

Army Form C. 2118.

WAR DIARY
INTELLIGENCE SUMMARY.
(Erase heading not required.)

Instructions regarding War Diaries and Intelligence Summaries are contained in F.S. Regs., Part II. and the Staff Manual respectively. Title pages will be prepared in manuscript.

Place	Date	Hour	Summary of Events and Information	Remarks and references to Appendices
TOUTENCOURT	1/8		H.Q. marched from MERVILLE to STEENBECQUE. Entrained at STEENBECQUE for DOULLENS. Marched from DOULLENS to TOUTENCOURT. Motored round looking out & fixing suitable Refilling points in new area. Visited Railhead at DOULLENS & MERVILLE to inspect entraining & detraining. Visited D.H.Q. Offre Toulme.	D
"	2/8		Visited Refilling Points of 113, 114 & 115 Brigades. Also motored round Brigade areas to discover A.S.C. Cos former No. 331. 9 Aug. also located & visited the Cumps of No. 332 & 333 Cos. Motored round looking out suitable new Refilling points.	

A5834 Wt.W4973/M687 750,000 8/16 D.D.&L. Ltd. Forms/C.2118/13.

Army Form C. 2118.

WAR DIARY
INTELLIGENCE SUMMARY.
(Erase heading not required.)

Place	Date	Hour	Summary of Events and Information	Remarks and references to Appendices
TOUTENCOURT	2/4/18		Visited D.H.Q. Issuing orders at 12 mid-night. Office routine.	A
"	3/4/18		Visited D.H.Q. "all Brigades Refilling Points inspected Refilling the Camp of 332 C." Office routine.	A
"	4/4/18		Visited D.H.Q. "Refilling Points of 113 & 114 Brigades" "A.H.Q. & supervised D.O of S & T." Office routine.	A
HERISSART	5/4/18		Visited D.H.Q. Issuing orders relative to move of 113 & 114 Brigades, the former to between WARLOY & VARDENCOURT, the latter to	

Army Form C. 2118.

WAR DIARY
INTELLIGENCE SUMMARY.
(Erase heading not required.)

Instructions regarding War Diaries and Intelligence Summaries are contained in F.S. Regs, Part II. and the Staff Manual respectively. Title pages will be prepared in manuscript.

Place	Date	Hour	Summary of Events and Information	Remarks and references to Appendices
TOUTENCOURT	5/4/18		The following movements were carried out hereby:-	
			113 Bde H.Q. ⎫	
			3 Bats. ⎪	
			113 T.M.B. ⎪ Between WARLOY	
			"A" Co. X. H.Q ⎬ and	
			"A" Co. 38 M.G. Bat⁰ ⎪ VADENCOURT.	
			114 Bde H.Q. ⎫	
			3 Bats. ⎪	
			332 C⁰ A.S.C ⎪ To	
			114 T.M.B. ⎬ HERISSART	
			"B" C⁰ M.G. Bat⁰ ⎪	
			331 C⁰ A.S.C. returned to TOUTENCOURT.	
			Looking out & fixing suitable new Refilling Points.	
"	6/4/18		Visited D.H.Q.	M
			Issuing orders relative to move of 113 & 114 Brigade Groups	
			the former to RUBEMPRE, PIERREGOT & MIRVAUX, the latter	
			to TALMAS & LA VICOGNE.	

Army Form C. 2118.

WAR DIARY

INTELLIGENCE SUMMARY

(Erase heading not required.)

Place	Date	Hour	Summary of Events and Information	Remarks and references to Appendices
TOUTENCOURT	6/4/18		The following movements were carried out after 5 p.m.:— 113 Bde H.Q. 3 Bns 113 T.M.B. 331 Co A.S.C. 129 F.A. "A" Co. 38 M.G. Bat". 113 Bde Div. Sniping Section } To RUBEMPRE, PIERREGOT and MIRVAUX. 3 Sec. O.A.C. 114 Bde H.Q. 3 Bns 332 Co A.S.C. 114 T.M.B. "B" Co. 38 M.G. Bat". 114 Bde Div. Sniping Section } To TALMAS and LA VICOGNE. Visited Refilling Points of 113, 114 & 115 Brigades " Supply Column (M.T.) " 332 Co Corps Office routine	15.

Army Form C. 2118.

WAR DIARY
— or —
INTELLIGENCE SUMMARY.
(Erase heading not required.)

Place	Date	Hour	Summary of Events and Information	Remarks and references to Appendices
TOUTENCOURT	7/4/18		Visited D.H.Q. The following units of 115th Bde returned to TOUTENCOURT from HEDAUVILLE:- 115 B.H.Q. 3 Bdes 115 T.M.B. Issuing orders to 333 Coy. relative thereto. Visited 331 Coy Camp & also Refilling Point of 115 Bde.	U
"	8/4/18		Visited D.H.Q. 38th M.G. Batt (less "C" Coy) moved from PUCHEVILLERS to RUBEMPRE & were attached to 115 Bde for feeding purposes only. Issuing orders relative thereto. H.Q.Coy moved from STEENWERCK to HAVERSKERQUE. Lt. J.D.COWAN reported to T.H.Q from leave. 2nd Lt. J.A.WALKER returned to H.Q.Cº for duty. Office routine & general work.	

Army Form C. 2118.

WAR DIARY
INTELLIGENCE SUMMARY
(Erase heading not required.)

Place	Date	Hour	Summary of Events and Information	Remarks and references to Appendices
TOUTENCOURT	9/4/18		Visited D.H.Q. Issuing Orders relative to move of 331 & 333 Co⁶ to SEPTENVILLE. 331 Co moved from MIRVAUX to SEPTENVILLE. 333 Co " " " " TOUTENCOURT " Visited SEPTENVILLE inspecting new Camps of 331 & 333 Co⁶ & selecting new Repelling Points for 113 & 115 Brigades. Lt. J.D. COWAN sent on to 330 Co at HAVERSKERQUE offre routine. Issuing Orders relative to move (tomorrow) of 113 Bde to HARPONVILLE & of 331 Co to TOUTENCOURT. Issuing Orders relative to move (tomorrow) of 10 S.W.B. & one Co. M.G. Bat⁶. (115 Bde) to WARLOY & VADENCOURT respectively.	
"	10/4/18		Visited D.H.Q. 113 Bde H.Q. 3 Bat⁶⁰⁵ Bde Signals Sec. 113 T.M.B. Engineer Sec⁶. } moved from RUBEMPRE &c. to HARPONVILLE.	

WAR DIARY
or
INTELLIGENCE SUMMARY.
(Erase heading not required.)

Place	Date	Hour	Summary of Events and Information	Remarks and references to Appendices
TOUTENCOURT	10/4/18		331 Cº returned to TOUTENCOURT.	
		10	S.W.B. & "C" & "D" Cos M.G. Bat'; moved the former to WARLOY & the latter to VADENCOURT. Army orders for move of 114 Bde from TALMAS. The following units of 114 Bde moved from TALMAS to HENENCOURT.	
			114 Bde H.Q. 3 Batt.s Bde Signal Sec. 114 T.M.B. Bde Sniping Sec.	
			332 Cº moved to TOUTENCOURT. Lorry Paris returns to move (tomorrow) of 115 Bde to forward area.	
"	11/4/18		The following units of 115 Bde moved to the forward area today :—	

Army Form C. 2118.

WAR DIARY
INTELLIGENCE SUMMARY.
(Erase heading not required.)

Instructions regarding War Diaries and Intelligence Summaries are contained in F. S. Regs., Part II. and the Staff Manual respectively. Title pages will be prepared in manuscript.

Place	Date	Hour	Summary of Events and Information	Remarks and references to Appendices
TOUTENCOURT	4/11/18		115 Bde H.Q. ⎫ 2 Bn.s ⎪ Bde Signal Sec. ⎬ to FORWARD AREA 115 T.M.B. ⎪ Signal Sec. ⎪ 129 F.A. ⎪ H.Q & "A" & "B" Co.s ⎪ 38 M.G. Bn. ⎭ 333 C° returned to TOUTENCOURT. Visited D.H.Q. " Refilling Points " HARPONVILLE inspecting Camps to be taken over from 12th Division & making the necessary arrangements. 	
		10⁴⁵	Iss 3 Sec. D.A.C. ⎫ H.Q. Div. Signal C° ⎬ moved to FORWARD AREA Visited Brigade Refilling Points N.Q. Div. Train moved today to CONTAY	

Army Form C. 2118.

WAR DIARY
~~INTELLIGENCE SUMMARY~~
(Erase heading not required.)

Instructions regarding War Diaries and Intelligence Summaries are contained in F. S. Regs., Part II. and the Staff Manual respectively. Title pages will be prepared in manuscript.

Place	Date	Hour	Summary of Events and Information	Remarks and references to Appendices
CONTAY	12/4/18		114 Bde H.Q. 3 Bns. } moved to FORWARD AREA. 114 T.M.B. Snipping Sec. Visited D.H.Q	
"	13/4/18		" Camps of 331. 332 & 333 Co.s Visited D.H.Q " Reporting points of 113. 114 & 115 Bdes " Camps of 331. 332 & 333 Co.s Office routine.	K
"	14/4/18		Visited D.H.Q " camps of 332 & 333 Co.s Office routine	K
"	15/4/18		Visited D.H.Q Office routine	K

Army Form C. 2118.

WAR DIARY
INTELLIGENCE SUMMARY
(Erase heading not required.)

Place	Date	Hour	Summary of Events and Information	Remarks and references to Appendices
CONTAY	16/4/18		Visited D.H.Q. Orderly Room. Ceremony today Supplies were drawn from Racekeen by M.T. Visited Refilling Points of 113, 114 & 115 Bdes Racekeen	M
"	17/4/18		Office routine Visited D.H.Q. Office routine	M
"	18/4/18		Visited D.H.Q. Racekeen Visiting & selecting new Refilling Points for 113, 114 & 115 Bdes 113 Bde today relieved 115 Bde in the line Office routine	M
"	19/4/18		Visited D.H.Q. Office routine	M

Army Form C. 2118.

WAR DIARY
~~INTELLIGENCE SUMMARY.~~
(Erase heading not required.)

Place	Date	Hour	Summary of Events and Information	Remarks and references to Appendices
CONTAY	20/4/18		Visited D.H.Q. Selecting new Refilling Points for 113, 114 & 115 Bdes reviews necessary by the congestion of the road whereon the present Refilling Points are. Wire routine.	
"	21/4/18		Visited D.H.Q. " Railhead. " 332 & 333 Co.s. " Refilling Points & Camps reconnaissance in Back area suggested by V CORPS. Wire routine.	
"	22/4/18		Visited D.H.Q. Selecting new Refilling Points for all Brigades & new sites for encampments in reserve for move of Division. Visited Camps of 332 & 333 Co.s. Wire routine.	
"	23/4/18		Visited D.H.Q. Issuing Orders relative to move of 113 & 114 Bdes. Wire routine.	

Army Form C. 2118.

WAR DIARY
INTELLIGENCE SUMMARY.
(Erase heading not required.)

Place	Date	Hour	Summary of Events and Information	Remarks and references to Appendices
CONTAY	24/4/18		Visited D.N.Q. "Site of new camps of 331 C° with O.C. 331 C°. Selecting new repairing points for 113 & 114 Bdes. Lorry Orders necessitated by postponement of move for 24 hours. Office routine.	U
"	25/4/18		Visited D.H.Q. "Raisthered Repairing Points of all 3 Bdes & camps of 332 & 333 C.s. Lorry Orders necessitated by cancellation of movement order. Office routine.	U
"	26/4/18		Visited D.H.Q. Lorry Orders relative to divisional move. Office routine.	U
"	27/4/18		Visited D.H.Q. " new camps of 332 & 333 C.s	U

WAR DIARY
INTELLIGENCE SUMMARY
(Erase heading not required.)

Army Form C. 2118.

Place	Date	Hour	Summary of Events and Information	Remarks and references to Appendices
CONTAY	27/4/18		123 & 151 F. Cos R.E. today moved to TOUTENCOURT	I
			19 Welsh moved to HERISSART.	
			114 Bde " " TOUTENCOURT	
			113 " " HERISSART & MIRVAUX	
			331/332 Cos A.S.C. moved to M 36 d.	
			38 M.G. Batt (except "C" Co) moved to TOUTENCOURT	II
			115 Bde moved to Bivouacs of 113 Bde	
			Office routine.	
"	28/4/18		Visited D.H.Q.	
			129 F.A moved to VADENCOURT	III
			Office routine	
"	29/4/18		Visited D.H.Q.	
			Office routine	IV
"	30/4/18		Visited D.H.Q	
			Issuing Orders relative to move of 113 & 114 Bdes	V
			Office routine	

R. Purcell
Lt. Col.
Comdg 38 (Welsh) Div: Train.

War Diary

Army Form C. 2118.

WAR DIARY
INTELLIGENCE SUMMARY.
(Erase heading not required.)

Nov 30

From 1/5/18 to 31/5/18

of

Lt. Col. T. E. Bennell D.S.O.
Army Service Corps
Commanding
38th (Welsh) Divisional Train.

Army Form C. 2118.

WAR DIARY
INTELLIGENCE SUMMARY.
(Erase heading not required.)

Instructions regarding War Diaries and Intelligence Summaries are contained in F. S. Regs., Part II. and the Staff Manual respectively. Title pages will be prepared in manuscript.

Place	Date	Hour	Summary of Events and Information	Remarks and references to Appendices
CONTAY	1/5/18		Visited D.H.Q. Issuing Orders relative to move of 113 & 114 Brigades 113 Bde (less 13 R.W.F.) moved to Bivouacs near HEDAUVILLE 331 Coy A.S.C. returned from Back area to TOUTENCOURT Officers routine	D.
"	2/5/18		Visited D.H.Q. 113 Bde (less 13 R.W.F) went into the Line. 114 Bde (less 13 Welsh) moved to Bivouacs near HEDAUVILLE 332 Coy A.S.C. returned from Back area to TOUTENCOURT Saw TOWN MAJOR TOUTENCOURT arranging the question of Camp site for 331 Coy Visited Camps of 331, 332 & 333 Coys	D.

Army Form C. 2118.

WAR DIARY
INTELLIGENCE SUMMARY.
(Erase heading not required.)

Instructions regarding War Diaries and Intelligence Summaries are contained in F.S. Regs., Part II. and the Staff Manual respectively. Title pages will be prepared in manuscript.

Place	Date	Hour	Summary of Events and Information	Remarks and references to Appendices
CONTAY	3/5/18		Visited D.H.Q	
			114 Bde (less 13 Welsh) moved into the Line	
			Visited 330 Co. A.S.C at POPERINGHE	Td
"	4/5/18		Visited D.H.Q	
			Office routine	H
"	5/5/18		Visited D.H.Q	
			Office routine	Td.
	6/5/18		Visited D.H.Q	
			H.Q. Train moved to TOUTENCOURT	
			Office routine	
			2nd Lt L. JEFFERIES reported for duty & was posted to 333 Co.	Td.
TOUTENCOURT	7/5/18		Visited D.H.Q	
			" 333, 332 & 331 Co's	
			Orderly Room	
			Office routine	Td

Army Form C. 2118.

WAR DIARY
INTELLIGENCE SUMMARY.
(Erase heading not required.)

Instructions regarding War Diaries and Intelligence Summaries are contained in F. S. Regs., Part II. and the Staff Manual respectively. Title pages will be prepared in manuscript.

Place	Date	Hour	Summary of Events and Information	Remarks and references to Appendices
TOUTENCOURT	8/5/18		Visited D.H.Q	71.
			Orderly Room	
			Office routine	
"	9/5/18		Visited D.H.Q	71.
			Office routine	
			Visited 332 & 333 Co's	
"	10/5/18		Visited D.H.Q	71.
			Office routine	
"	11/5/18		Visited D.H.Q	71.
			Orderly Room	
			Visited 331, 332 & 333 Co's	
			Office routine	
"	12/5/18		Visited D.H.Q	71.
			Office routine	
"	13/5/18		Visited D.H.Q	71.
			Capt. E. FOSTER went on 1 month's Special Leave	
			Visited 331, 332 & 333 Co's	
			Office routine	

Army Form C. 2118.

WAR DIARY
INTELLIGENCE SUMMARY.
(Erase heading not required.)

Place	Date	Hour	Summary of Events and Information	Remarks and references to Appendices
TOUTENCOURT	14/5/18		Visited D.H.Q	
"	15/5/18		Inspecting Emergency Transport tracks selected by CORPS	H
			Office routine	
"	16/5/18		Visited D.H.Q	H
			Office routine	
"	17/5/18		Visited D.H.Q	H
			Visited 35th Divisional Train H.Q	
			Office routine	
"	18/5/18		Visited D.H.Q	
			Issuing Orders relative to Divisional move	
			Orderly room	
			Office routine	H
"			Visited D.H.Q	
			Office routine	
			Visited HERISSART selecting site for Camp of T.H.Q	
"	19/5/18		Visited D.H.Q	H
			Office routine	H

WAR DIARY
INTELLIGENCE SUMMARY

Army Form C. 2118.

Place	Date	Hour	Summary of Events and Information	Remarks and references to Appendices
TOUTENCOURT	20/5/18		Visited D.H.Q	
			113 Bde moved out of the line to RUBEMPRE	
			331 C° moved to VAL DE MAISON	
			T.H.Q moved to HERISSART	J.S.
			Office routine	
HERISSART	21/5/18		Visited D.H.Q	
			114 Bde moved out of the line to TOUTENCOURT	
			115 Bde moved out of the line to HERISSART	
			331 C° moved to VAL DE MAISON	
			Visited 331 & 333 C°s	
			Office routine	
"	22/5/18		Visited D.H.Q	A.
			Office routine	
"	23/5/18		Visited D.H.Q	A.
			Visited 331, 332 & 333 C°s	
			Office routine	
			130 Field Amb. (less detachment) rejoined the Divisional area	A.

Army Form C. 2118.

WAR DIARY
INTELLIGENCE SUMMARY.
(Erase heading not required.)

Instructions regarding War Diaries and Intelligence Summaries are contained in F. S. Regs., Part II. and the Staff Manual respectively. Title pages will be prepared in manuscript.

Place	Date	Hour	Summary of Events and Information	Remarks and references to Appendices
HERISSART	24/5/18		Visited D.H.Q. Office routine. 2nd Lt. J. BEAL admitted to Hospital today	H.
"	25/5/18		Visited D.H.Q. " 331, 332 & 333 Cos. Office routine	H.
"	26/5/18		332 Co. Camp was shelled & has to be temporarily evacuated. Visited 331, 332 & 333 Cos. D.H.Q. Orderly room at 333 Co. Camp. Office routine.	H.
"	27/5/18		Visited D.H.Q. V.K. Corps Horse Master visited 331 & 333 Co. Camps & inspected horses. Visited 331 & 332 Cos. Attended rehearsal parade of 114 Bde Group Office routine	H.S.

Army Form C. 2118.

WAR DIARY
or
INTELLIGENCE SUMMARY.
(Erase heading not required.)

Instructions regarding War Diaries and Intelligence Summaries are contained in F. S. Regs., Part II. and the Staff Manual respectively. Title pages will be prepared in manuscript.

Place	Date	Hour	Summary of Events and Information	Remarks and references to Appendices
HERISSART	28/5/18		Visited & inspected 332 C°. D.H.Q. Office routine.	W.
"	29/5/18		Vth CORPS COMMANDER inspected 114 Bde Group including 332 C°. Visited D.H.Q. Office routine.	W.
"	30/5/18		Visited D.H.Q. Office routine. CAPTn. H.F. LAMBERT admitted to 131 F. Amb: & evacuated	
"	31/5/18		Visited D.H.Q. Inspected Transport of 38th M.G. Batn. Office routine.	W.

R Bowen Lt Col.
O.C. 38/Welsh/Divisional Train

A5834 Wt. W4973/M687 750,000 8/16 D.D. & L. Ltd. Forms/C.2118/13

Army Form C. 2118.

WAR DIARY
INTELLIGENCE SUMMARY.
(Erase heading not required.)

Vol 31

To 6
30/6

of

Lt. Col. L. E. Bennett D.S.O.

Army Service Corps

Commanding

38th (Welsh) Divisional Train

From 1/5 to 6/18

Army Form C. 2118.

WAR DIARY
— of —
INTELLIGENCE SUMMARY.
(Erase heading not required).

Instructions regarding War Diaries and Intelligence Summaries are contained in F. S. Regs., Part II. and the Staff Manual respectively. Title pages will be prepared in manuscript.

Place	Date	Hour	Summary of Events and Information	Remarks and references to Appendices
HERISSART	1/8		Visited D.H.Q. 331 Co. Inspected Transport of 38th Divl. Signal Co. R.E. Office routine	W.
	2/8		Visited D.H.Q. Issuing Orders relative to move of 115th Bde Group. Office routine.	W.
	3/8		Visited D.H.Q. Issuing Orders relative to move of 113 Bde Group. Visited Camps of No. 2 & 4 Co's 63 Divl. Train to be taken over by No. 2 & 3 Co's 38 Divl. Train. 115 Bde moved to forward area. 333 Co. moved to TOUTENCOURT.	
	4/8		Visited D.H.Q. Issuing Orders relative to move of remainder of Division (less artillery)	W.

Army Form C. 2118.

WAR DIARY
INTELLIGENCE SUMMARY.
(Erase heading not required.)

Instructions regarding War Diaries and Intelligence Summaries are contained in F. S. Regs., Part II. and the Staff Manual respectively. Title pages will be prepared in manuscript.

Place	Date	Hour	Summary of Events and Information	Remarks and references to Appendices
HERISSART	4/5/18		113 Bde moved to forward area	
			331 Co moved to ARQUEVES	
			2nd Lt. G.E.H NINNIS invalided to ENGLAND 24/5/18 1 Struck off Strength of 38 Divl. Train	Tel.
			Inspected first line Transport of 113 Bde	
			Office routine	
	5/5/18		Visited D.N.O	
			114th Bde moved to forward area	
			332 Co moved to ARQUEVES	
			Train H.Q moved to neighbourhood of LEALVILLERS	
			Office routine	
LEALVILLERS	6/5/18		Visited D.N.O	D.
			331, 332 & 333 Co's	
			2nd Lt. S.H. DEAN reported for duty & was posted to 330 Co. he	
			Marched to 332 Co: temporarily	
			Office routine	Tel.

Army Form C. 2118.

WAR DIARY
INTELLIGENCE SUMMARY.
(Erase heading not required.)

Place	Date	Hour	Summary of Events and Information	Remarks and references to Appendices
LEALVILLERS	7/6/15		Visited D.N.Q	
			2nd Lt W.H. HOOPER appointed Adjutant & of Captain WELLS as	W
			employer	
	8/6/15		Visited 331 & 332 Co's	W
			Office routine	W
	9/6/15		Visited D.N.Q	
			Office routine	
	10/6/15		Visited D.N.Q	W
			Office routine	
			Visited 331, 332 & 333 Co's	
			D.N.Q	
			Orderly Room	
			Office routine	
	11/6/15		Visited D.N.Q	W
			Office routine	W

Army Form C. 2118.

WAR DIARY
INTELLIGENCE SUMMARY.
(Erase heading not required.)

Instructions regarding War Diaries and Intelligence Summaries are contained in F. S. Regs., Part II. and the Staff Manual respectively. Title pages will be prepared in manuscript.

Place	Date	Hour	Summary of Events and Information	Remarks and references to Appendices
LEALVILLERS	12/6/15		Visited D.H.Q. Office routine	H.
"	13/6/15		Visited D.N.Q. Office routine	H.
	14/6/15		CAPTⁿ E. FOSTER returned from leave. Visited D.N.Q. A.A.+Q.M.G. 35ᵗʰ Dⁿ: visited 331 Co⁵ Lines & camps Office routine	H.
	15/6/15		Visited D.N.Q. Office routine	H.
	16/6/15		Visited D.N.Q. Office routine	H.
	17/6/15		Visited D.N.Q. Office routine	H.
	18/6/15		Visited D.N.Q. 331 & 332 Co⁵ Office routine	H.

Army Form C. 2118.

WAR DIARY
~~INTELLIGENCE SUMMARY.~~
(Erase heading not required.)

Instructions regarding War Diaries and Intelligence Summaries are contained in F. S. Regs., Part II. and the Staff Manual respectively. Title pages will be prepared in manuscript.

Place	Date	Hour	Summary of Events and Information	Remarks and references to Appendices
LEALVILLERS	19/6/15		Visited D.H.Q. Office routine	R.
	20/6/15		Visited D.H.Q. " 330 C⁰. Office routine	R.
	21/6/15		Visited D.H.Q. 36th Div. A. A. & Q.M.G. 36th Div. accompanied by me visited Repealing Point of att 3 Brigades 1 of Div. troops and Repealing & afterwards inspected Camp & lines of 330 C⁰. Office routine	R.
	22/6/15		Orderly Room Office routine	R.
	23/6/15		Visited D.H.Q. Orderly Room Office routine	R.

A5834 Wt. W4973/M687 750,000 8/16 D. D. & L. Ltd. Forms/C.2118/13

Army Form C. 2118.

WAR DIARY
or
INTELLIGENCE SUMMARY.

(Erase heading not required.)

Instructions regarding War Diaries and Intelligence Summaries are contained in F. S. Regs., Part II. and the Staff Manual respectively. Title pages will be prepared in manuscript.

Place	Date	Hour	Summary of Events and Information	Remarks and references to Appendices
LEALVILLERS	24/6/18		LT. COL. T. E. BENNETT went on 10 days French Leave. MAJOR C. WATT took temporary command of the Team. Visited Rifling Butts of 113.114 & 115 Bdes & of Div. Hqrs. Camp of 330 C.S. Office routine.	W.
	25/6/18		Visited 330. 331. 332 & 333 C.S. Camps of 35th Div. Train H.Q. Office routine.	W.
	26/6/18		Visited 35th Div. Train H.Q. Office routine.	W.
	27/6/18		Visited D.H.Q. Office routine.	W.
	28/6/18		Visited D.H.Q. Office routine.	W.
	29/6/18		Visited D.H.Q. 330. 331. 332 & 333 C.S. Office routine.	W.

Army Form C. 2118.

WAR DIARY
or
INTELLIGENCE SUMMARY.
(Erase heading not required.)

Instructions regarding War Diaries and Intelligence Summaries are contained in F. S. Regs., Part II. and the Staff Manual respectively. Title pages will be prepared in manuscript.

Place	Date	Hour	Summary of Events and Information	Remarks and references to Appendices
LEALVILLERS	30/8		Visited D.H.Q. Ypres routine	(w)

Van Dam hw:
T/ Command Sing Div Siam R.E.
38th (65/5A)

Army Form C. 2118.

WAR DIARY
or
INTELLIGENCE SUMMARY.
(Erase heading not required.)

Vol 32

To
31/7/8

of

Lt. Col. T. E. Bennett D.S.O.

Army Service Corps

Commanding

38th (Welsh) Divisional Train

From
1/7/8

Army Form C. 2118.

WAR DIARY
or
INTELLIGENCE SUMMARY.
(Erase heading not required.)

Instructions regarding War Diaries and Intelligence Summaries are contained in F. S. Regs., Part II. and the Staff Manual respectively. Title pages will be prepared in manuscript.

Place	Date	Hour	Summary of Events and Information	Remarks and references to Appendices
LEALVILLERS	1/7/18		Visited D.N.Q.	P.W.
			Office routine	
	2/7/18		Visited D.N.Q.	P.W.
			" 330. 331. 332 & 333 Co's	
			Office routine	
"	3/7/18		Visited O.N.Q.	P.W.
			Office routine	
			LT. COL. T. E. BENNETT returned from French Leave	
			MAJOR C. WATT returned to 330 Co.	
"	4/7/18		Visited O.N.Q.	ZA
			" Refilling Points of 113, 114 & 115 Bdes & of Div. Troops respectively	
			" Train Transport	
			" 330 Coy Camp	
			Office routine	
"	5/7/18		Visited D.N.Q.	W.
			Orderly Room	
			Office routine	

Army Form C. 2118.

WAR DIARY
INTELLIGENCE SUMMARY.
(Erase heading not required.)

Instructions regarding War Diaries and Intelligence Summaries are contained in F. S. Regs., Part II. and the Staff Manual respectively. Title pages will be prepared in manuscript.

Place	Date	Hour	Summary of Events and Information	Remarks and references to Appendices
LEALVILLERS	6/7/16		G.O.C. 38th Div: accompanied by A.A & Q.M.G & myself inspected Camps of 330, 331, 332 & 333 Co's	W.
			Office routine.	
	7/7/16		Visited D.H.Q	W.
			Orderly Room	
			Office routine	
	8/7/16		Visited D.H.Q	W.
			Orderly Room	
			MAJOR C. WATT admitted to hospital & evacuated to Officers Rest Station CEZAINCOURT	
			CAPTN F.P. ROBATHAN assumes temporary command of 330 Co.	
			Office routine	
	9/7/16		Visited D.H.Q	W.
			Office routine	
	10/7/16		Visited D.H.Q	W.
			Attended field General Court Martial at LEALVILLERS	
			Office routine	

Army Form C. 2118.

WAR DIARY
INTELLIGENCE SUMMARY
(Erase heading not required.)

Instructions regarding War Diaries and Intelligence Summaries are contained in F. S. Regs., Part II. and the Staff Manual respectively. Title pages will be prepared in manuscript.

Place	Date	Hour	Summary of Events and Information	Remarks and references to Appendices
LEALVILLERS	11/2/15		Visited D.H.Q	W.
			Office routine	
	12/2/15		Visited D.H.Q	W.
			Office routine	
	13/2/15		Visited D.H.Q Office routine	W.
			MAJOR C. WATT returned from Officers Rest Station	
	14/2/15		Visited D.H.Q	W.
			Office routine	
	15/2/15		Visited D.H.Q	W.
			Allowed Lt. J.C.N. of LEALVILLERS in Respect of Case	
			Office routine	
	16/2/15		Visited D.H.Q	W.
			2nd Lt. J. BEAL invalided to ENGLAND Shock of Shell	
			Office routine	

Army Form C. 2118.

WAR DIARY
—or—
INTELLIGENCE SUMMARY.
(Erase heading not required.)

Instructions regarding War Diaries and Intelligence
Summaries are contained in F. S. Regs., Part II.
and the Staff Manual respectively. Title pages
will be prepared in manuscript.

Place	Date	Hour	Summary of Events and Information	Remarks and references to Appendices
LEALVILLERS	1/7/15		Issuing Orders relates to Divisional leave	A
	17/7/15		Office routine	
	18/7/15		C.O.C. Division inspected by A.A. & Q.M.G. inspected replying parts of 113, 114, 115 Bns & transport of 331, 332 & 333 Cos	N.
			En route	
	19/7/15		113 Bn Coy went into Reserve	
			114 " " to TOUTENCOURT	
			332 Co.	
			115 Bn to front	
			333 Co. HERISSART	
			Office routine	
	20/7/15		2ⁿᵈ Lt C.F.H. MOORE reported for duty. Divn posted to 331 Co.	N.
			Office routine	N.
	21/7/15		Office routine	N.
	22/7/15		CAPTN E.C. NASH went on 10 days special leave. Lt D.D. MACLEAN took over temporary command of 331 Co.	
			Visited D.H.Q.	
			Office routine	N.

A5834 Wt.W4973/M687 750,000 8/16 D.D. & L. Ltd. Forms/C.2118/13.

Army Form C. 2118.

WAR DIARY
of
INTELLIGENCE SUMMARY.
(Erase heading not required.)

Instructions regarding War Diaries and Intelligence Summaries are contained in F. S. Regs., Part II. and the Staff Manual respectively. Title pages will be prepared in manuscript.

Place	Date	Hour	Summary of Events and Information	Remarks and references to Appendices
LEALVILLERS	23/2/15		Office routine	W.
	24/2/15		Orderly Room	
			Visited D.H.Q	W.
			" 331, 332 & 333 Co's	
			One of Reserve	
			Office routine	
	25/2/15		Visited D.N.Q	W.
			Office routine	
	26/2/15		Visited D.N.Q	W.
			Office routine	
	27/2/15		Office routine	W.
	28/2/15		Office routine	
	29/2/15		Visited D.N.O	W.
			MAJOR C. WATT went on 30 days special leave	
			CAPTN F.P. ROBATHAN 13th on temporary command of 330 Co.	

A 5834 Wt. W4973/M687 750,000 8/16 D. D. & L. Ltd. Forms/C.2118/13

Army Form C. 2118.

WAR DIARY
or
INTELLIGENCE SUMMARY.

(Erase heading not required.)

Instructions regarding War Diaries and Intelligence Summaries are contained in F. S. Regs., Part II. and the Staff Manual respectively. Title pages will be prepared in manuscript.

Place	Date	Hour	Summary of Events and Information	Remarks and references to Appendices
LEALVILLERS	29/5		2nd Lt. F. FAZACKERLEY returned for duty & was posted to 330 C.F. Lieut. Owen returned to Brigade from G.H.Q. Reserve to v. Capt. Tyfferey Dixon the same. D.A.D.V.S. visited lines of 332 C.F.	B.
	30/5		2nd Lt. S. N. DEAN transferred to 331 C.F. 2nd Lt. L. JEFFERIES went on 14 days leave. No. 163 Pack Horse moved from Puchvillers to RAINCHEVAL & ARQUEVES HERISSART to ACHEUX 333 C.F. moved from HERISSART to ARQUEVES D.A.D.V.S. visited lines of 331 C.F. Every horse free to tie.	
	31/5		Visited D.H.Q. the same. Visited 320 C.M.T.C.	B.

1 8
/ 18.

R Duncan Lt Col
O. C. 38 (Welsh) Div. Vet Serv.

Army Form C. 2118.

W 33

WAR DIARY
INTELLIGENCE SUMMARY.
(Erase heading not required.)

Summary of Events and Information

of

Lt. Col. T. E. Bennett D.S.O.
Commanding
Army Service Corps
38th (Welsh) Divisional Train

Place	Date	Hour		Remarks and references to Appendices
From 8/15				To 31/15

Instructions regarding War Diaries and Intelligence Summaries are contained in F. S. Regs., Part II. and the Staff Manual respectively. Title pages will be prepared in manuscript.

Army Form C. 2118.

WAR DIARY
~~INTELLIGENCE SUMMARY.~~

(Erase heading not required.)

Instructions regarding War Diaries and Intelligence Summaries are contained in F. S. Regs., Part II. and the Staff Manual respectively. Title pages will be prepared in manuscript.

Place	Date	Hour	Summary of Events and Information	Remarks and references to Appendices
LEALVILLERS	1/8/18		Office routine	W.
	2/8/18		Office routine. Visited D.H.Q. Orderly Room	W.
	3/8/18		CAPTN E. E. CRANCH departed for ENGLAND for home service thro' shortage. Visited D.H.Q.	W.
	4/8/18		Office routine. Visited D.H.Q. 113 Bde moved to HERISSART 336 Coy. to TOUTENCOURT	W.
	5/8/18		Office routine. 115 Bde moved into the Line 333 Coy. to TOUTENCOURT Visited D.H.Q.	W.
	6/8/18		Office routine. Office routine. 173 Bde moved into the Line 331 Coy. to TOUTENCOURT	W.

A5834 Wt. W4973/M687 750,000 8/16 D. D. & L. Ltd. Forms/C.2118/13

Army Form C. 2118.

WAR DIARY
INTELLIGENCE SUMMARY.
(Erase heading not required.)

Instructions regarding War Diaries and Intelligence Summaries are contained in F. S. Regs., Part II. and the Staff Manual respectively. Title pages will be prepared in manuscript.

Place	Date	Hour	Summary of Events and Information	Remarks and references to Appendices
LEALVILLERS	7/5/18		Visited D.H.Q. Office routine. The Bde. moved into the line	W.
"	8/5/18		Visited D.H.Q. 331, 332 & 333 C's 2/Lt J.A. WALKER went on 14 days leave. Orderly Room. Office routine.	W.
"	9/5/18		Visited D.H.Q. 3/8 Cameron Regt at RUBEMPRE. Replying Busts of 113, 114 & 115 Bdes inspecting Transport. Office routine.	W.
"	10/5/18		Visited D.H.Q. Replying Busts of 113, 114 & 115 Bdes of J. Div. Troops inspecting Trans Transport. 330 C's Lines. Office routine. 2 horses killed & 1 driver wounded whilst carrying out R.E. work in forward area.	W.

A5834 Wt. W4973/M687 750,000 8/16 D. D. & L. Ltd. Forms/C.2118/13

Army Form C. 2118.

WAR DIARY
— or —
INTELLIGENCE SUMMARY.

(Erase heading not required.)

Instructions regarding War Diaries and Intelligence Summaries are contained in F. S. Regs., Part II. and the Staff Manual respectively. Title pages will be prepared in manuscript.

Place	Date	Hour	Summary of Events and Information	Remarks and references to Appendices
LEALVILLERS	11/8/18		Visited D.H.Q	H.
"	12/8/18		Office routine	
"	13/8/18		Visited D.H.Q.	H.
"			Office routine	
"			Visited D.H.Q.	
"	14/8/18		2°Lt C.F.K. MOORE went on 14 days leave	H.
"			Office routine	
"			Visited D.H.Q.	
"			Office routine	
"			Lt W.J.S. TAYLOR went on 14 days special leave	H.
"	15/8/18		2°Lt JEFFERIES returned from leave	
"			Visited D.H.Q.	
"			Office routine	
"	16/8/18		113 Bde relieved 113 Bde in the line	H.
"			113 Bde moved to TOUTENCOURT	
"			Visited D.H.Q.	H.
"			Office routine	

A 5834 Wt. W4973/M687 750,000 8/16 D. D. & L. Ltd. Forms/C.2118/13

Army Form C. 2118.

WAR DIARY
INTELLIGENCE SUMMARY.
(Erase heading not required.)

Instructions regarding War Diaries and Intelligence Summaries are contained in F. S. Regs., Part II. and the Staff Manual respectively. Title pages will be prepared in manuscript.

Place	Date	Hour	Summary of Events and Information	Remarks and references to Appendices
LEALVILLERS	17/8		Visited D.H.Q	
			Office routine	A.
	18/8		Visited D.H.Q	
			Reffing Points of 113, 114 & 115 Bdes & of Div. Troops	A.
	19/8		Visited D.H.Q	
			D.D. of S & T at 3rd Army H.Q	
			Office routine	A.
	20/8		114 Bde relieved the Left Bn of 113 Bde in the line	
			113 " moved into the line	
			Engaged on road reconnaissance in the forward area	
			Office routine	A.
	21/8		Visited D.H.Q	
			Engaged on road reconnaissance in the forward area	
			Lt. W.J.S. TAYLOR promoted ⁄ Captain whilst employed as Capt⁄ from 2/8/18	
			Railhead changed to FARM ROSEL near BELLE EGLISE.	
			Supplied by M.T. supplies drawn by Horse Transport	
			Visited D.D. of T. 3rd Army & fence change of Railhead.	A.

Army Form C. 2118.

WAR DIARY
or
INTELLIGENCE SUMMARY.
(Erase heading not required.)

Instructions regarding War Diaries and Intelligence Summaries are contained in F. S. Regs., Part II. and the Staff Manual respectively. Title pages will be prepared in manuscript.

Place	Date	Hour	Summary of Events and Information	Remarks and references to Appendices
LEALVILLERS	22/5/18		Visited D.H.Q	
			Engaged on road reconnaissance in the forward area	
			Office routine	
	23/5/18		Visited D.H.Q	U.
			CAPT E.C. NASH returned from leave	
			Office routine	
			Sundry Orders relating to Divisional move	
	24/5/18		The Division moved forward & crossed the ANCRE	U.
			All Train Co's moved to VARENNES area	
			Visited D.H.Q	
			Office routine	
			Engaged on road reconnaissance in the forward area	
			Sundry Orders relating to Divisional move	U
HEDAUVILLE	25/5/18		Lt WALKER returned from leave	
			Division moved forward	
			All Train Co's moved to HEDAUVILLE	
			T.H.Q	
			Visited D.H.Q	U
			Office routine	

Army Form C. 2118.

WAR DIARY
INTELLIGENCE SUMMARY.

(Erase heading not required.)

Instructions regarding War Diaries and Intelligence Summaries are contained in F. S. Regs., Part II. and the Staff Manual respectively. Title pages will be prepared in manuscript.

Place	Date	Hour	Summary of Events and Information	Remarks and references to Appendices
USNA HILL	26/8/18		CAPT. H.F. LAMBERT struck off strength 13/8/18	
			All Train Co's moved to near AVELUY WOOD	
			T.H.Q moved to USNA HILL	
			Visited D.H.Q.	
			Office routine	H.
	27/8		Visited D.H.Q	
			" 331-332 & 333 Co's	
			Surveying various selecting Refilling Points	
			Office routine	W.
	28/8/15		Visited D.H.Q	
			" all four Train Co's Camps	
			Orderly Room	
			Office routine	H.
	29/8/18		Visited D.H.Q	
			" all four Train Co's Camps	
			Office routine	W.

Army Form C. 2118.

WAR DIARY
INTELLIGENCE SUMMARY
(Erase heading not required.)

Instructions regarding War Diaries and Intelligence Summaries are contained in F. S. Regs., Part II. and the Staff Manual respectively. Title Pages will be prepared in manuscript.

Place	Date	Hour	Summary of Events and Information	Remarks and references to Appendices
USNA HILL	30/5/18		Visited D.H.Q.	
			330 C° moved to CONTAL MAISON	
			Visited camp of 330 C° d"	
			MAJOR C. WATT returned from leave	
			Office routine	
	31/5/18		Visited D.H.Q.	
			2nd L.T G.W. TEMPLER reported for duty & was posted to 330 C°	
			2d LT F. FAZACKERLEY was transferred from 330 to 332 C°	
			CAPTN A. ST JOHN MAC CALL was transferred from 332 to 333 C° & took over command of the latter C°	
			Office routine	

R. Bancroft / Lt Col
2/6/18.
O.C. 38/Welch / Div: Traut-

Army Form C. 2118.

WAR DIARY
or
INTELLIGENCE SUMMARY
(Erase heading not required.)

WO 34

Place	Date	Hour	Summary of Events and Information	Remarks and references to Appendices

Lt. Col. F. E. Bennett D.S.O.
Army Service Corps
Commanding
38th (Welsh) Divisional Train

Army Form C. 2118.

WAR DIARY
INTELLIGENCE SUMMARY
(Erase heading not required.)

Place	Date	Hour	Summary of Events and Information	Remarks and references to Appendices
CONTALMAISON	1/9/15		CAPT^N E.P. ROBATHAN went on 14 days leave	
			T.H.Q moved to CONTALMAISON	
			Issuing Orders relative to move of all Train Co's	
			Office routine	
			Visited D.H.Q	
	2/9/15		Selecting new Refilling Point's for Div: Troops & 3 Bde Groups	
			331. 332 /333 Co's moved to CONTALMAISON	
			Supplies drawn from AVELUY by M.T.	
			330 Co moved to between CONTALMAISON & BAZENTIN	
			Visited D.H.Q area	
			" Refilling Point's of all Bde Groups & of Div: Troops	
			" 330 & 332 Co's	
			" 113 Bde H.Q	
			Office routine	

Army Form C. 2118.

WAR DIARY
INTELLIGENCE SUMMARY
(Erase heading not required.)

Instructions regarding War Diaries and Intelligence Summaries are contained in F. S. Regs., Part II. and the Staff Manual respectively. Title Pages will be prepared in manuscript.

Place	Date	Hour	Summary of Events and Information	Remarks and references to Appendices
HIGH WOOD	3/9/15		Visited D.H.Q here. Selecting new Camps for 331.332 & 333 Co's & also new repairing points for 113.114 & 115 Bde Groups. 331.332 & 333 Co's moved to near MAMETZ WOOD. T.H.Q moved to near HIGH WOOD. Captⁿ E.C. NASH admitted to HOSPITAL. Lt MACLEAN took over temporary command of 331 C^o. Office routine.	
	4/9/15		Visited D.H.Q here. Selecting new Camps for 330 C^o. 330 C^o moved to near DELVILLE WOOD. Issuing Orders relative to Dis^t move out of the Line. Office routine.	

Army Form C. 2118.

WAR DIARY
INTELLIGENCE SUMMARY
(Erase heading not required.)

Place	Date	Hour	Summary of Events and Information	Remarks and references to Appendices
LES BŒUFS	5/7/15		Visited D.H.Q. Ruthven charged to BEAULENCOURT supplies drawn by M.T. Division moved out of line into rest T.H.Q. moved to LES BŒUFS Visited Ruthven at BEAULENCOURT Selecting new Rifling Butts in rear of a possible move of Bde Cos	W.
	6/7/15		CAPT^N TAYLOR returned from leave Visited 331 & 333 Cos Orderly Room Visited D.H.Q. Office routine	W.

Army Form C. 2118.

WAR DIARY
INTELLIGENCE SUMMARY

(Erase heading not required.)

Instructions regarding War Diaries and Intelligence Summaries are contained in F.S. Regs., Part II and the Staff Manual respectively. Title Pages will be prepared in manuscript.

Place	Date	Hour	Summary of Events and Information	Remarks and references to Appendices
LES BOEUFS	7/9/18		Visited D.N.Q. Issuing Orders for move of all Tran Co's Selecting new Camps for all Tran Co's & Refilling Points for Div. Troops & 3 Brigade Groups all Tran Co's moved to vicinity of BEAULENCOURT Office routine Visited Railhead at BEAULENCOURT	W.
	8/9/18		Supplies drawn by H.T from BEAULENCOURT Visited Railhead all Tran Co's inspecting New Camps & horses D.H.Q. twice Refilling Points of Div. Troops & 3 Bde Groups Office routine	W.

2449 Wt. W14957/Mg0 750,000 1/16 J.B.C. & A. Forms/C.2118/12.

Army Form C. 2118.

WAR DIARY
INTELLIGENCE SUMMARY
(Erase heading not required.)

Instructions regarding War Diaries and Intelligence Summaries are contained in F.S. Regs., Part II. and the Staff Manual respectively. Title Pages will be prepared in manuscript.

Place	Date	Hour	Summary of Events and Information	Remarks and references to Appendices
LES BŒUFS	9/9/18		Engaged on road & water reconnaissance in the CANAL DU NORD area.	
			Visited D.H.Q. here	
			Jammy. Orders relative to move of 115 Bde & 330 & 333 Co's	11
			Office routine	
"	10/9/18		Visited D.H.Q	
			115 Bde moved to LECHELLE	
			333 Co " " ROCQUIGNY	
			113 Bde " " MESNIL EN ARROUAISE	
			330 Co " " ROCQUIGNY	
			Supplies for Div. Troops & 115 Bde Group drawn by M.T. from BOULENCOURT	
			Visited 330 & 333 Co's & Repairing Parts of Div. Troops & 115 Bde	
			Visited Rearhead	
			" 49th M.V.S as to replacement of H.O. lorries	
			Office routine	Ch.

Army Form C. 2118.

WAR DIARY
or
INTELLIGENCE SUMMARY
(Erase heading not required.)

Instructions regarding War Diaries and Intelligence Summaries are contained in F.S. Regs., Part II. and the Staff Manual respectively. Title Pages will be prepared in manuscript.

Place	Date	Hour	Summary of Events and Information	Remarks and references to Appendices
ETRICOURT	11/9/15		Division relieved 17th Division in the line	
			Visited D.H.Q three times	
			" Ruchene	
			" 331 & 332 Co's	
	12/9/15		Army Orders received to move 331 & 332 Co's	K
			331 & 332 Co's moved to ROCQUIGNY	
			T.H.Q moved to ETRICOURT	
			2nd Lt F. FAZACKERLEY attached to No 5 CORPS TROOPS M.T.C° for	
			Supply duties for one month	
			CAPTn A. St J. MAC CALL went on 14 days leave	
			CAPTn W.J.S. TAYLOR took over temporary command of 333 Co.	K
			Visited D.H.Q three	
			" all four Train Co's	
			Office routine	
	13/9/15		Visited D.H.Q.	R.
			Office routine	

Army Form C. 2118.

WAR DIARY
INTELLIGENCE SUMMARY
(Erase heading not required.)

Instructions regarding War Diaries and Intelligence Summaries are contained in F. S. Regs., Part II. and the Staff Manual respectively. Title Pages will be prepared in manuscript.

Place	Date	Hour	Summary of Events and Information	Remarks and references to Appendices
ETRICOURT	14/9/18		Visited D.H.Q here	
			MAJOR C. WATT went on 14 day's Special Leave	
			CAPT. N. HODGSON took over temporary command of 330 C?	H.
			Office routine	
"	15/9/18		Visited D.H.Q	
			" all four Train Co's	
			" Relay Post of 113 Bde Group	
			Office routine	H.
		16/9/18	Visited D.H.Q	
			Office routine	H.
ROCQUIGNY	17/9/18		Visited D.H.Q here	
			" all four Train Co's	
			Orderly Room	
			Office routine	
			T.H.Q moved to between ETRICOURT and ROCQUIGNY	H.

2449 Wt. W14957/M90 750,000 1/16 J.B.C. & A. Forms/C.2118/12.

Army Form C. 2118.

WAR DIARY
or
INTELLIGENCE SUMMARY.
(Erase heading not required.)

Instructions regarding War Diaries and Intelligence Summaries are contained in F. S. Regs., Part II. and the Staff Manual respectively. Title pages will be prepared in manuscript.

Place	Date	Hour	Summary of Events and Information	Remarks and references to Appendices
ROCQUIGNY	18/9		Visited D.H.Q. Office routine	A
"	19/9		Visited D.H.Q. Engaged as President of a F.G.C.M. CAPT. ROBATHAN returned from leave & took over temporary command of 330 C. Sanitary Orders relative to Divisional move. Office routine	A
	20/9		114 Bde moved out of the line to EQUANCOURT. 115 Bde relieved 113 Bde in the line. 113 Bde moved to ROCQUIGNY. Rations changed to ROCQUIGNY & supplies drawn by H.T. Visited D.H.Q. Office routine	A

Army Form C. 2118.

WAR DIARY
— of —
INTELLIGENCE SUMMARY.

(Erase heading not required.)

Instructions regarding War Diaries and Intelligence Summaries are contained in F. S. Regs., Part II. and the Staff Manual respectively. Title pages will be prepared in manuscript.

Place	Date	Hour	Summary of Events and Information	Remarks and references to Appendices
ROCQUIGNY	21/9/18		105 Bde moved out of the line to the BEAULENCOURT area	
	22/9/18		Visited D.H.Q. three times	
			Office routine	
	23/9/18		Visited D.H.Q.	W.
			Office routine	
			114 Bde moved to LECHELLE	
	24/9/18		Visited D.H.Q. twice	W.
			" Railhead	
			" all Form C's	
			Office routine	
			Visited D.H.Q.	W.
	25/9/18		Office routine	
			Visited D.H.Q.	W.
			" 330 C⁰	
			" Railhead & Refilling Points	
			A. & Q.M.G. inspected Camps of 331 & 332 C⁰'s	
			Office routine	W.

Army Form C. 2118.

WAR DIARY
-or-
INTELLIGENCE SUMMARY.
(Erase heading not required.)

Instructions regarding War Diaries and Intelligence Summaries are contained in F. S. Regs., Part II. and the Staff Manual respectively. Title pages will be prepared in manuscript.

Place	Date	Hour	Summary of Events and Information	Remarks and references to Appendices
ROCQUIGNY	26/9/18		Visited D.H.Q. " 331 & 332 Co's " Rocheau Office routine	
"	27/9/18		Visited D.H.Q. twice " 330, 332 & 333 Co's " all four Refilling Points " 38 M.T.C. Office routine Issuing Orders relative to Divl move.	W.
"	28/9/18		Visited D.H.Q. twice Division moved to HEUDICOURT All Train C's moved to EQUANCOURT area Supplies drawn by M.T. Visited all Train C's at their new Camps " all four Refilling Points Office routine	W.

Army Form C. 2118.

WAR DIARY
INTELLIGENCE SUMMARY.
(Erase heading not required.)

Instructions regarding War Diaries and Intelligence Summaries are contained in F. S. Regs., Part II. and the Staff Manual respectively. Title pages will be prepared in manuscript.

Place	Date	Hour	Summary of Events and Information	Remarks and references to Appendices
ROCQUIGNY	29/8		Visited D.H.Q lines " all Town C.s " all four Refilling Points Office routine	
"	30/8		Railhead changed to FINS & Supplies drawn by H.T Visited D.H.Q lines " 330 Co Office routine	

R Deneuter Lt Col
O.C. 38 (Welsh) Div: Train.

2/18 10/18

Army Form C. 2118.

WAR DIARY
or
INTELLIGENCE SUMMARY.
(Erase heading not required.)

Vol /

Place	Date	Hour	Summary of Events and Information	Remarks and references to Appendices
From 1/10/18			of	To 31/10/18

Lt. Col. T. E. Bennell D.S.O.
Army Service Corps
Commanding
38th (Welsh) Divisional Train

Army Form C. 2118.

WAR DIARY
INTELLIGENCE SUMMARY.
(Erase heading not required.)

Instructions regarding War Diaries and Intelligence Summaries are contained in F. S. Regs., Part II. and the Staff Manual respectively. Title pages will be prepared in manuscript.

Place	Date	Hour	Summary of Events and Information	Remarks and references to Appendices
SOREL LE GRAND	1/8		Visited D.H.Q three times	
			" all Tram Co's	
			" Railhead	R.3
			T.H.Q moved to SOREL LE GRAND	
			Office routine	
"	2/8		All Tram Co's moved to HEUDECOURT area	
			Visited all Tram Co's at their new camps	
			" all Refilling Points	
			" D.H.Q.	
			Office routine	
			MAJOR W. THOMAS went on 14 days leave	
			CAPTN N. HODGSON took over duties of S.S.O. temporarily during absence of MAJOR THOMAS	
			LT. TEMPLER took over temporary command of 331 Co.	
"	3/8		Visited D.H.Q	W.
			Selecting sites for new Camps for all Tram Co's	

Army Form C. 2118.

WAR DIARY
INTELLIGENCE SUMMARY.
(Erase heading not required.)

Instructions regarding War Diaries and Intelligence Summaries are contained in F. S. Regs., Part II. and the Staff Manual respectively. Title pages will be prepared in manuscript.

Place	Date	Hour	Summary of Events and Information	Remarks and references to Appendices
SOREL LE GRAND	10/4/18		Marching new Brigade Transport lines. Water Bow's. Lorry Drivers unable to move of Train Co's. Office routine	
			All Train Co's moved to between HEUDECOURT & PEIZIERE. Supplies drawn from FINS by M.T. Visited D.H.Q. " all Train Co's " all Repairing Bow's. Orderly Room Office routine	A.
	5/15		Visited D.H.Q. three times 113 & 115 Boles moved to forward area CAPT. MAC CALL granted 10 days extension of leave from 28" ult on Medical Certificate MAJOR C. WATT granted 3 days extension of leave from 30" ult Visited all Train Co's Office routine	D.

Army Form C. 2118.

WAR DIARY
INTELLIGENCE SUMMARY.
(Erase heading not required.)

Instructions regarding War Diaries and Intelligence Summaries are contained in F. S. Regs., Part II. and the Staff Manual respectively. Title pages will be prepared in manuscript.

Place	Date	Hour	Summary of Events and Information	Remarks and references to Appendices
SOREL LE GRAND	6/10/18		Visited D.H.Q	W.
			MAJOR C. WATT returned from leave	
			CAPT^N ROBATHAN took over temporary Command of 331 C^o	
			L^T TEMPLER returned to 330 C^o	
			Office routine	
EPEHY	7/10/18		Visited D.H.Q	W.
			T.H.Q moved to EPEHY	
			113 & 115 B^{des} moved into the line	
			Office routine	
DE LA L'EAU	8/10/18		Visited D.H.Q.	W.
			114 B^{de} moved into the line	
			T.H.Q moved to DE LA L'EAU	
			Office routine.	
	9/10/18		Visited D.H.Q. three times	W.
			Issuing Orders relative to move of various C^o's	
			330 C^o moved to HONNECOURT	
			331. 332 & 333 C^o's moved to near BOIS-MAILLARD	

Army Form C. 2118.

WAR DIARY
INTELLIGENCE SUMMARY.
(Erase heading not required.)

Instructions regarding War Diaries and Intelligence Summaries are contained in F. S. Regs., Part II. and the Staff Manual respectively. Title pages will be prepared in manuscript.

Place	Date	Hour	Summary of Events and Information	Remarks and references to Appendices
DE LA L'EAU	9/10		The routine	
VILLERS-OUTREAUX	10/10		CAPT^N MAC CALL returned from leave	D.
			Visited D.H.Q hire	
			" all Train C^o's	
			all Train C^o's moved to new CLARY	
			T.H.Q moved to VILLERS OUTREAUX	
CLARY.	11/10		The routine	
			331 C^o moved to MALINCOURT	H.
			T.H.Q moved to CLARY	
			Visited D.H.Q hire	
			" 330. 331 & 332 C^o's	
			The routine	
BERTRY	12/10		330 C^o moved to between CLARY & BERTRY	H.
			333 C^o " " . BERTRY	
			331 C^o " " . "	
			T.H.Q " " . "	
			115 Base " " . TROISVILLES	
			113 " " . BERTRY	

Army Form C. 2118.

WAR DIARY
INTELLIGENCE SUMMARY.
(Erase heading not required.)

Instructions regarding War Diaries and Intelligence Summaries are contained in F. S. Regs., Part II. and the Staff Manual respectively. Title pages will be prepared in manuscript.

Place	Date	Hour	Summary of Events and Information	Remarks and references to Appendices
BERTRY	12/10/18		Visited D.H.Q. Div 330, 331 & 332 C's Office routine	
"	13/10/18		114 Bde moved to TROISVILLES. Visited all Two C's & Replying Points Orderly Room Visited D.H.Q 115 Bde moved into the line Office routine	A.
"	14/10/18		Visited D.H.Q Office routine	A.
"	15/10/18		Visited D.H.Q. Div 114 Bde moved to BERTRY 332 C. " near BERTRY Rockeau changes to MASNIERES Visited all Replying Points Office routine	A. A.

Army Form C. 2118.

WAR DIARY
INTELLIGENCE SUMMARY.
(Erase heading not required.)

Place	Date	Hour	Summary of Events and Information	Remarks and references to Appendices
BERTRY	16/10/8		Visited D.H.Q here	
			Office routine	
"	17/10/8		Visited D.H.Q here	
			relieved changes to FINS	
			Office routine	
"	18/10/8		Visited D.H.Q	
			Lt DEAN went on 14 days leave	
			Lt MOORE took over the duties of S.O. of 113 Bde whilst Lt DEAN was on leave	
			114 Bde relieved 115 Bde in the line	
			113 " went into the line	
			Office routine	
"	19/10/8		MAJOR W. THOMAS returned from leave	
			Visited D.H.Q here	
			Office routine	
"	20/10/8		Visited D.H.Q here	
			" all Train O's	
			Orderly Room	
			Office routine	

Army Form C. 2118.

WAR DIARY
or
INTELLIGENCE SUMMARY.
(Erase heading not required.)

Instructions regarding War Diaries and Intelligence Summaries are contained in F. S. Regs., Part II. and the Staff Manual respectively. Title pages will be prepared in manuscript.

Place	Date	Hour	Summary of Events and Information	Remarks and references to Appendices
BERTRY	21/10/18		115 Bde relieved 113 & 114 Bdes in the line	
			Visited D.H.Q	
			Office routine	
"	22/10/18		Visited D.H.Q twice	t
			115 Bde moved out of the line to TROISVILLES	
			Office routine	
"	23/10/18		Visited D.H.Q twice	
			113 & 114 Bdes moved forward in support	
			330 & 333 C's moved to TROISVILLES	
			Office routine	
			Railhead changes to CAUDRY supplies drawn by M.T	t
TROISVILLES	24/10/18		Visited D.H.Q	w
			331 C's moved to TROISVILLES	
			T.H.Q " " "	
			Office routine	

Army Form C. 2118.

WAR DIARY
of
INTELLIGENCE SUMMARY.
(Erase heading not required.)

Instructions regarding War Diaries and Intelligence Summaries are contained in F. S. Regs., Part II. and the Staff Manual respectively. Title pages will be prepared in manuscript.

Place	Date	Hour	Summary of Events and Information	Remarks and references to Appendices
FOREST	25/10/18		LT FAZACKERLEY returned from duty with V Corps Troops M.T.Co.	
			& resumed duty with 332 Co.	
			330 Co moved to CROISETTE	
			332 Co " " TROISVILLES	
			T.H.Q " " FOREST	
			Supplies drawn by M.T.	
			Visited D.H.Q here	
			" all Train Co's & Refilling Points	
			Office routine	
	26/10/18		Visited D.H.Q here	
			" Rucheval & all Refilling Points	
			113 Bde moved into the line	
			115 " " forward in support	
			111 " " into reserve	
			330 Co " to BERTRY	
			Issuing Orders relative to move of 3 Bde Co.	
			Office routine	

Army Form C. 2118.

WAR DIARY
INTELLIGENCE SUMMARY.
(Erase heading not required.)

Place	Date	Hour	Summary of Events and Information	Remarks and references to Appendices
FOREST	27/8/10		331, 332 & 333 Co's moved to between NEUVILLY & MONTAY	
			Visited all Train Co's & Refilling Points	
			" D.H.Q. here	
			Office routine	
"	28/8/10		Visited D.H.Q. here	Id.
			" all Train Co's & Refilling Points	
			Office routine	
"	29/8/10		Visited D.H.Q. here	Id.
			114 Bde relieved 115 Bde in the line	
			330 Co. moved to FOREST	
			Visited 38 M.T.Co.	
			" 333 Co.	
			Office routine	Id.

Army Form C. 2118.

WAR DIARY
INTELLIGENCE SUMMARY.
(Erase heading not required.)

Place	Date	Hour	Summary of Events and Information	Remarks and references to Appendices
RICHEMONT	30/8		Visited D.H.Q. three times T.H.Q. moved to RICHEMONT Visited 330. 331 & 332 Co's offices routine	D.
"	31/8		Visited D.H.Q. twice all Trans Co's & Repairing Points Office routine	D.

J. Bruce
Lt Col
31/8/18
O.C. 38 / Wood / Div Train

Army Form C. 2118.

WAR DIARY
or
INTELLIGENCE SUMMARY.
(Erase heading not required.)

Vol 36

30/11/18

Summary of Events and Information

of

Lt. Col. J. E. Bennett D.S.O

Army Service Corps

Commanding

38th (Welsh) Divisional Train

Instructions regarding War Diaries and Intelligence Summaries are contained in F. S. Regs., Part II. and the Staff Manual respectively. Title pages will be prepared in manuscript.

Place	Date	Hour		
From 1/11/18				

Army Form C. 2118.

WAR DIARY
INTELLIGENCE SUMMARY.
(Erase heading not required.)

Instructions regarding War Diaries and Intelligence Summaries are contained in F. S. Regs., Part II. and the Staff Manual respectively. Title pages will be prepared in manuscript.

Place	Date	Hour	Summary of Events and Information	Remarks and references to Appendices
RICHEMONT	1/11/18		Visited D.H.Q. twice. Office routine	A.
"	2/11/18		Visited D.H.Q. twice. Office routine. 113 Bde relieved 114 Bde in the line	A.
"	3/11/18		Visited D.H.Q. twice. Attending conference of all C.O. Commanders as to the use of roads & tracks in the forward area. Issuing Orders relative to move of all Tren. C's. Office routine	A.
"	4/11/18		All Tren. C's moved to neighbourhood of CROIX. Visited D.H.Q. twice. Lt HULLEY went on 14 days leave.	A.

Army Form C. 2118.

WAR DIARY
INTELLIGENCE SUMMARY.
(Erase heading not required.)

Instructions regarding War Diaries and Intelligence Summaries are contained in F. S. Regs., Part II. and the Staff Manual respectively. Title pages will be prepared in manuscript.

Place	Date	Hour	Summary of Events and Information	Remarks and references to Appendices
RICHEMONT	4/11/18		Visited all Tun Co's & Replacing Points of 331 Co. CAPTN E.C. NASH returned from Hospital & resumed command of 331 Co.	N.
ENGLEFONTEIN	5/11/18		Gue route. CAPTN ROBATHAN returned to 330 Co (from 331 Co) & resumed the duties of S.O. 330 Co moved to WAGNONVILLE T.H.Q ENGLEFONTEIN Visited D.H.Q Moving Orders received to move all Tunn Co's selecting sites for new Camps for all Tunn Co's & new Replacing Points.	N.
LOCQUIGNOL	6/11/18		All Tunn Co's moved to ENGLEFONTEIN Visited D.H.Q here T.H.Q moved to LOCQUIGNOL	N.

Army Form C. 2118.

WAR DIARY
INTELLIGENCE SUMMARY.
(Erase heading not required.)

Place	Date	Hour	Summary of Events and Information	Remarks and references to Appendices
LOCQUIGNOL	6/11/18		Issuing Orders relative to move of all Train Co's. Office routine	U.
	7/11/18		Visited D.H.Q three times. All Train Co's moved to LOCQUIGNOL. Lt DEAN returned from leave. Office routine	U.
	8/11/18		Visited D.H.Q twice. Issuing Orders relative to move of all Train Co's. Orderly Room. Office routine	U.
AULNOYE	9/11/18		Visited D.H.Q three times. All Train Co's moved to AULNOYE. T.H.Q moved to neighbourhood of BERLAIMONT. Office routine	U.

Army Form C. 2118.

WAR DIARY
INTELLIGENCE SUMMARY.
(Erase heading not required.)

Instructions regarding War Diaries and Intelligence Summaries are contained in F. S. Regs., Part II. and the Staff Manual respectively. Title pages will be prepared in manuscript.

Place	Date	Hour	Summary of Events and Information	Remarks and references to Appendices
AULNOYE	10/8		Visited D.H.Q. here	
"			" all from Co's Repelling Points	
"			Orderly Room	
"			Office routine	T.
"	11/8		Visited D.H.Q. here	
"			Office routine	T.
"	12/8		Visited D.H.Q.	
"			CAPTN N. HODGSON went on 14 days leave	
"			Office routine	T.
"	13/8		Visited D.H.Q.	
"			Office routine	
"			CAPTN & A.D.J.T W.H. HOOPER went on 14 days leave	T.

Army Form C. 2118.

WAR DIARY
~~INTELLIGENCE SUMMARY.~~
(Erase heading not required.)

Instructions regarding War Diaries and Intelligence Summaries are contained in F. S. Regs., Part II. and the Staff Manual respectively. Title pages will be prepared in manuscript.

Place	Date	Hour	Summary of Events and Information	Remarks and references to Appendices
AULNOYE	14/11		Visited D.H.Q	
			330. 332 & 333 Co's moved to PETIT MAUBEUGE	
			331 Co moved to East of ECLAIBES	
			Baggage turnouts of Divnly Bdes called in to Bde Co's	
			Horses of Divnl R.A called in to D. I. C.	
			Visited all Divnl Co's & Refilling Points	H.
"	15/11		Visited D.H.Q	
			Office routine	H.
"	16/11		Visited D.H.Q	
			Office routine	H.
"	17/11		Visited D.H.Q	
			Office routine	H.
"	18/11		Visited D.H.Q	
			Office routine	
			9th Pioneers moved to BERLAIMONT	H.

Army Form C. 2118.

WAR DIARY
INTELLIGENCE SUMMARY.
(Erase heading not required.)

Instructions regarding War Diaries and Intelligence Summaries are contained in F.S. Regs., Part II. and the Staff Manual respectively. Title pages will be prepared in manuscript.

Place	Date	Hour	Summary of Events and Information	Remarks and references to Appendices
AULNOYE	19/11/18		Visited D.H.Q.	
"			Office routine	
"	20/11/18		V Corps Cyclists N.I.H moved to BERLAIMONT	W.
"			Visited D.H.Q	
"			121 Bde R.F.A. moved to AULNOYE	
"			Office routine	
"	21/11/18		Visited D.H.Q.	W.
"			Office routine	
"			126 & 151 FIELD Co's R.E moved to BERLAIMONT	
"	22/11/18		Visited D.H.Q.	W.
"			Office routine	
"	23/11/18		113 Infantry Bde moved to SART-BARA area	W.
"			C.S.M. THOMAS & C.S.M. JAMES were presented with the M.S.M	
"			ribbon by the G.O.C 38th Div'n	
"			Visited D.H.Q.	
"			Office routine	
"			2º Lt WHOLLEY returned from leave	W.

Army Form C. 2118.

WAR DIARY
INTELLIGENCE SUMMARY.
(Erase heading not required.)

Instructions regarding War Diaries and Intelligence Summaries are contained in F. S. Regs., Part II. and the Staff Manual respectively. Title pages will be prepared in manuscript.

Place	Date	Hour	Summary of Events and Information	Remarks and references to Appendices
AULNOYE	24/18		Visited D.H.Q.	
"			Office routine	
"			2° Lt S. BIGGS admitted to Hospital	W.
"	25/18		Visited D.H.Q.	
"			Office routine	W.
"	26/18		Visited D.H.Q.	
"			Office routine	
"			2° Lt S. BIGGS died	W.
"	27/18		Visited D.H.Q.	
"			Lt J.J. COWAN went on leave	
"			Office routine	W.
"	28/18		Visited D.H.Q. in connection with Lt D.J. MACLEAN's promotion	
"			Lt G.W. TEMPLER proceeded on 14 days' leave	
"			Office routine	W.S.

Army Form C. 2118.

WAR DIARY
INTELLIGENCE SUMMARY.
(Erase heading not required.)

Place	Date	Hour	Summary of Events and Information	Remarks and references to Appendices
AULNOYE	29/12/18		Visited D.H.Q. Gue routine.	
"	30/12/18		Visited D.H.Q. Gue routine.	

5/12/18.

R Bennett
Lt Col
O.C. 23/Welsh Div: Train.

Army Form C. 2118.

WAR DIARY
or
INTELLIGENCE SUMMARY.
(Erase heading not required.)

Instructions regarding War Diaries and Intelligence Summaries are contained in F. S. Regs., Part II. and the Staff Manual respectively. Title pages will be prepared in manuscript.

Vol 3

From 1/12/18 to 31/1/19

L. Col. J. E. Bennett D.S.O
Royal Army Service Corps
Commanding
38th (Welsh) Divisional Train

Place	Date	Hour	Summary of Events and Information	Remarks and references to Appendices
From 12/18 1/18				

Army Form C. 2118.

WAR DIARY
or
INTELLIGENCE SUMMARY.
(Erase heading not required.)

Instructions regarding War Diaries and Intelligence Summaries are contained in F. S. Regs., Part II. and the Staff Manual respectively. Title pages will be prepared in manuscript.

Place	Date	Hour	Summary of Events and Information	Remarks and references to Appendices
AULNOYE	1/12/18		Visited D.H.Q.	
			Office routine	
"	2/12/18		C.R.E. 123. 124 & 151 Field Co's R.E. marched to Back area. Transport by road. Personnel by rail.	W.
			Visited D.H.Q.	W.
			Office routine	
"	3/12/18		Lt. F. FAZACKERLEY proceeded on leave.	
			Captn & Adjt. W. H. HOOPER returned from leave	
			Visit of H.M. the KING	
			Visited D.H.Q.	W.
			Office routine	
"	4/12/18		Visited D.H.Q.	W.
			" 330. 331 & 332 Co's 1 Repairing Points	
			Office routine	
"	5/12/18		Visited D.H.Q.	W.
			Office routine	

Army Form C. 2118.

WAR DIARY
INTELLIGENCE SUMMARY.
(Erase heading not required.)

Place	Date	Hour	Summary of Events and Information	Remarks and references to Appendices
AULNOYE	6/12/18		CAPTⁿ FOSTER went on 14 days leave. Lᵗ MACLEAN assumes temporary command of 332 Cᵒ. Presented his Distinguished Service Certificate to CPL HUGHES at a General Parade of 330 Cᵒ. Visited D.H.Q here. Office routine.	W.
"	7/12/18		Visited D.H.Q. CAPTⁿ N. HODGSON returned from leave. Issuing orders relative to runs of 19ᵗʰ WELSH to Back area. Office routine.	W.
"	8/12/18		Visited D.H.Q. 331, 332 & 333 Cᵒˢ. Office routine.	W.
"	9/12/18		Visited D.H.Q. Office routine.	W.

Army Form C. 2118.

WAR DIARY
or
INTELLIGENCE SUMMARY.
(Erase heading not required.)

Instructions regarding War Diaries and Intelligence Summaries are contained in F. S. Regs., Part II. and the Staff Manual respectively. Title pages will be prepared in manuscript.

Place	Date	Hour	Summary of Events and Information	Remarks and references to Appendices
AULNOYE	10/12/18		Visited D.H.Q	
"			Office routine	A.
"	11/12/18		Visited D.H.Q	A.
"			Office routine	
"	12/12/18		Visited D.H.Q	A.
"			Office routine	
"	13/12/18		Col T. E. Bennell left on 30 days Special leave. MAJOR C. WATT took over temporary command of the Train. CAPTN ROBATHAN took over temporary command of 330 Coy. Visited 330 / 332 Coys	W
"			. D.H.Q	
"			Office routine	
"	14/12/18		Visited D.H.Q	W
"			Office routine	
"	15/12/18		Visited D.H.Q	W
"			Office routine	

Army Form C. 2118.

WAR DIARY
INTELLIGENCE SUMMARY.
(Erase heading not required.)

Instructions regarding War Diaries and Intelligence Summaries are contained in F. S. Regs., Part II. and the Staff Manual respectively. Title pages will be prepared in manuscript.

Place	Date	Hour	Summary of Events and Information	Remarks and references to Appendices
AULNOYE	16/12/18		Visited D.H.Q. Office routine	W.
	17/12/18		Visited D.H.Q. Office routine. Lt. COWAN returned from leave	Co.
	18/12/18		Visited D.H.Q. Office routine. Residence changed to LE QUESNOY	W.
	19/12/18		Visited D.H.Q. Office routine	W.
	20/12/18		Visited D.H.Q. Office routine	W.
	21/12/18		Visited D.H.Q. Lt. TEMPLER returned from leave Lt. FAZACKERLEY " " Visited 330 Co. Office routine	W.

Army Form C. 2118.

WAR DIARY
or
INTELLIGENCE SUMMARY.
(Erase heading not required.)

Instructions regarding War Diaries and Intelligence Summaries are contained in F. S. Regs., Part II. and the Staff Manual respectively. Title pages will be prepared in manuscript.

Place	Date	Hour	Summary of Events and Information	Remarks and references to Appendices
AULNOYE	22/12/18		Visited D.H.Q.	(1)
			" 330. 331 & 333 Co's	
			The routine	
"	23/12/18		Visited D.H.Q.	(2)
			CAPTN ROBATHAN proceeded on 14 day's Steam leave	
			LT JEFFERIES was transferred to R.A.S.C. DEPOT BOULOGNE	
			The routine	
"	24/12/18		Visited D.H.Q.	(3)
			Posting Orders relative to Divisional move	
			The routine	
"	25/12/18		Visited D.H.Q.	(4)
			" all Train Co's	
			The routine	
"	26/12/18		Visited D.H.Q.	(5)
			" all Train Co's	
			The routine	

WAR DIARY
INTELLIGENCE SUMMARY.

(Erase heading not required.)

Place	Date	Hour	Summary of Events and Information	Remarks and references to Appendices
AULNOYE	27/12/18		Visited D.H.Q	
			113 Bde Group moved to Back area	
			MAJOR CAMERON reported for duty & took over command of 330 Co.	W.
			Office routine	
"	28/12/18		Visited D.H.Q	
			Artillery Group moved to Back area	W.
			Office routine	
"	29/12/18		Visited D.H.Q	
			115 Bde Group moved to Back area	W.
			Office routine	
INCHY	30/12/18		Visited D.H.Q	
			114 Bde Group moved to Back area	
			T.H.Q moved to INCHY	
			Lt MACLEAN evacuated to Hospital	
			Visited Railhead at CAMBRAI	W.

Army Form C. 2118.

WAR DIARY
~~INTELLIGENCE SUMMARY.~~
(Erase heading not required.)

Instructions regarding War Diaries and Intelligence Summaries are contained in F. S. Regs., Part II. and the Staff Manual respectively. Title pages will be prepared in manuscript.

Place	Date	Hour	Summary of Events and Information	Remarks and references to Appendices
GLISY	3/12/18		Voika D.H.Q T.H.Q moved to GLISY Office routine	

WAR DIARY
INTELLIGENCE SUMMARY.
(Erase heading not required.)

Army Form C. 2118.

From 1/1/19 To 31/1/19

Lt. Col. J. E. Bennett. D.S.O.

Royal Army Service Corps

Commanding

38th (Welsh) Divisional Train

Army Form C. 2118.

WAR DIARY
INTELLIGENCE SUMMARY.

(Erase heading not required.)

Place	Date	Hour	Summary of Events and Information	Remarks and references to Appendices
GLISY	1/9		Visited D.H.Q. 330/331 Co's	
			Office routine	
"	2/9		Visited D.H.Q. 330/331 Co's	
			Held Orderly Room at 331 Co.	
			Starting new Repairing Points for all Groups	(a)
			Office routine	
"	3/9		Visited D.H.Q. 333 Co.	
			Office routine	
"	4/9		Visited 332 Co.	
			CAPTN. FOSTER returned from leave	(a)
			Office routine	

Instructions regarding War Diaries and Intelligence Summaries are contained in F. S. Regs., Part II. and the Staff Manual respectively. Title pages will be prepared in manuscript.

WAR DIARY
INTELLIGENCE SUMMARY.

Place	Date	Hour	Summary of Events and Information	Remarks and references to Appendices
GLISY	5/9		331 C° moved to CONTAY	
			Visited D.H.Q	
			" all Train C°'s	
			Office routine	
"	6/9		MAJOR C. WATT proceeded to ENGLAND) I was struck	
			" W. S. CAMERON both new temporary Command of Train	
			Visited D.H.Q	
			" 330 C°	
			CAPTⁿ MAC CALL proceeded on 30 days Special leave	
			L^T WALKER proceeded on 14 days leave	
			Office routine	
"	7/9		MAJOR W. THOMAS proceeded on 14 days Special leave	
			Visited 330. 332 & 333 C°'s	
			Orderly Room at 333 C°	
			Visited D.H.Q	
			Office routine	

Army Form C. 2118.

WAR DIARY
INTELLIGENCE SUMMARY.
(Erase heading not required.)

Place	Date	Hour	Summary of Events and Information	Remarks and references to Appendices
GLISY	8/9		330 Coy moved to BUSSY	
		8¼	Visited 330 Coy	
			D.H.Q	
			Office routine	MQ
		9¼	Lt MACLEAN discharged from hospital & reported to 331 Coy for duty	MQ
			Visited D.H.Q	
			Office routine	
		10¼	Visited D.H.Q	MQ
			330 Coy & selected new Repairing Point for Div. Troops	
			Office routine	
		11¼	Visited D.H.Q	MQ
			330 Coy	
			Captn ROBATHAN returned from leave	
			Office routine	

Army Form C. 2118.

WAR DIARY
— or —
INTELLIGENCE SUMMARY.
(Erase heading not required.)

Instructions regarding War Diaries and Intelligence Summaries are contained in F. S. Regs., Part II. and the Staff Manual respectively. Title pages will be prepared in manuscript.

Place	Date	Hour	Summary of Events and Information	Remarks and references to Appendices
GLISY	12/9		CAPT^N TAYLOR proceeded on 14 days special leave L^T FAZACKERLEY (332 C^o) took over duties of S.O. 15/Bre temporarily	M<u>c</u>
			Visited D.H.Q " 330. 331 / 332 C^{os}	
"	13/9		Office routine Visited D.H.Q " 330 C^o Office routine	M<u>c</u>
"	14/9		Visited D.H.Q T.H.Q moved to PONT NOYELLE Office routine	M<u>c</u>
PONT NOYELLE	15/9		Visited D.H.Q Office routine	M<u>c</u>
	16/9		L^T COL: T.E. BENNETT returned from leave Office routine	F.B.

Army Form C. 2118.

WAR DIARY
INTELLIGENCE SUMMARY.
(Erase heading not required.)

Place	Date	Hour	Summary of Events and Information	Remarks and references to Appendices
PONT NOYELLE	17/9		Visited D.H.Q.	B.
			Office routine	
	18/9		CAPT. E.C. NASH took over duties of S.S.O vice MAJOR W. THOMAS (demobilyed)	W.
			Visited D.H.Q.	
			Office routine	
	19/9		Visited D.H.Q	B.
			Office routine	
	20/9		Visited D.H.Q	B.
			Office routine	
	21/9		Office routine	B.
	22/9		Visited D.H.Q "332 Cº"	
			Orderly Room here	
			G.O.C Division visited Camps of 330 Cº	B.
			Office routine	

Army Form C. 2118.

WAR DIARY
or
INTELLIGENCE SUMMARY.
(Erase heading not required.)

Instructions regarding War Diaries and Intelligence
Summaries are contained in F. S. Regs., Part II.
and the Staff Manual respectively. Title pages
will be prepared in manuscript.

Place	Date	Hour	Summary of Events and Information	Remarks and references to Appendices
PONT NOYELLE	23/9		Lt WALKER returned from leave	
			Office routine	B.
"	24/9		Visited D.H.Q	K.
			Office routine	K.
"	25/9		Visited D.H.Q	
			Office routine	
"	26/9		Supplies for 114 & 115 Bde Groups drawn by H.T	
			Supplies for 113 Bde Group & Div. Troops drawn by M.T	
			Visited D.D.S. 17 Third Army to discuss demobilization	
			Office routine	K.
"	27/9		Visited D.H.Q	K.
			Office routine	
"	28/9		Visited D.H.Q	K.
			Office routine	

Army Form C. 2118.

WAR DIARY
INTELLIGENCE SUMMARY.
(Erase heading not required.)

Place	Date	Hour	Summary of Events and Information	Remarks and references to Appendices
PONT NOYELLE	29/9		Office routine	A3.
"	30/9		Visited D.H.Q. Office routine. Attending Conference at D.H.Q as to use of Light Railways	A3.
"	31/9		Visited D.H.Q. Visited proposed Light Railway Railheads in company with D.A.Q.M.G. Division. Office routine	A3

R Bennet Lt Col
2/
1/19.

O.C. 38/Welsh/Divi: Train.

Army Form C. 2118.

WAR DIARY
or
INTELLIGENCE SUMMARY.
(Erase heading not required.)

WO 39/

War Diary of

Lt. Col. J. E. Bennell D.S.O. O.B.E.

R.A.S.C.

Commanding

38th (Welsh) Divisional Train.

Place	Date	Hour	Summary of Events and Information	Remarks and references to Appendices
From	1/2/19			to 28/2/19

Army Form C. 2118.

WAR DIARY
INTELLIGENCE SUMMARY.
(Erase heading not required.)

Instructions regarding War Diaries and Intelligence Summaries are contained in F. S. Regs., Part II. and the Staff Manual respectively. Title pages will be prepared in manuscript.

Place	Date	Hour	Summary of Events and Information	Remarks and references to Appendices
PONT NOYELLE	1/2/19		Visited D.H.Q.	
			Office routine.	
"	2/2/19		Visited D.H.Q.	
			"V CORPS" attending Conference regarding the forming of extraneous Unit's entrust the Divisional Area & as to the proper use of light Railways	
			Office routine.	
"	3/2/19		Visited D.H.Q.	
			Office routine.	
"	4/2/19		Visited D.H.Q.	
			Office routine.	
"	5/2/19		Visited D.H.Q.	
			Office routine.	

Army Form C. 2118.

WAR DIARY
INTELLIGENCE SUMMARY.
(Erase heading not required.)

Instructions regarding War Diaries and Intelligence Summaries are contained in F. S. Regs., Part II. and the Staff Manual respectively. Title pages will be prepared in manuscript.

Place	Date	Hour	Summary of Events and Information	Remarks and references to Appendices
PONT NOYELLE	6/2/19		H.R.H the PRINCE OF WALES & G.O.C DIVISION visited the Rifling Road of 113 Bde Group & also the Camps of 332 C⁰. Office routine.	1/
"	7/2/19		H.R.H the PRINCE OF WALES & G.O.C DIVISION visited Camp of 333 C⁰. Visited D.H.Q. Office routine.	1/
"	8/2/19		H.R.H the PRINCE OF WALES & G.O.C DIVISION visited 330 C⁰. CAPT^N MAC CALL returned from leave. Visited D.H.Q. Office routine.	1/
"	9/2/19		Visited D.H.Q. " 330 C⁰. Office routine.	2/

WAR DIARY
INTELLIGENCE SUMMARY.

(Erase heading not required.)

Army Form C. 2118.

Place	Date	Hour	Summary of Events and Information	Remarks and references to Appendices
PONT NOYELLE	10/2/19		Visited D.H.Q.	
			Orderly Room	
			In company with A.A.& Q.M.G. Div. visiting GLISSY and neighbourhood selecting Transport Park when Division returned to Corps	Ns.
			Office routine	
	11/2/19		Visited D.H.Q.	
			Office routine	
			350 Co moved to QUERRIEU	
			353 Co " " BUSSY	
	12/2/19		Radical changes to POULAINVILLE & supplies delivery from Here to repairing Points by Light Railway	Ns.
			Visited D.H.Q.	
			Office routine	
			Orderly Room	Ns.

Army Form C. 2118.

WAR DIARY
or
INTELLIGENCE SUMMARY.
(Erase heading not required.)

Instructions regarding War Diaries and Intelligence Summaries are contained in F. S. Regs., Part II. and the Staff Manual respectively. Title pages will be prepared in manuscript.

Place	Date	Hour	Summary of Events and Information	Remarks and references to Appendices
PONT NOYELLE	13/9		Visited D.H.Q	
			Office routine	U
"	14/9		CAPTN. ROBATHAN admitted to Hospital	
			Visited D.H.Q	
			Rejoining Point of Divi: Troops Group	
			Office routine	
			Orderly Room	U.
"	15/9		Visited D.H.Q	
			Orderly Room	
			Office routine	
"	16/9		Office routine	U.
"	17/9		Visited Rochêne	U
			D.H.Q	
			Office routine	U.

Army Form C. 2118.

WAR DIARY
INTELLIGENCE SUMMARY.
(Erase heading not required.)

Place	Date	Hour	Summary of Events and Information	Remarks and references to Appendices
PONT NOYELLE	18/2/9		Visited D.H.Q	20
			" 331 C⁰ 1 Repelling Point of 113 Bde Group at CONTAY	
			Office routine	
"	19/2/9		Visited D.H.Q	20
			" 332 C⁰ 1 Repelling Point of 114 Bde Group at ALLONVILLE	
			Office routine	
"	20/2/9		Visited D.H.Q	20
			Office routine	
			Lt J.A.WALKER proceeded to 9th Div: Train & Struck off Strength	
"	21/2/9		Visited D.H.Q	20
			Office routine	
"	22/2/9		Visited D.H.Q	20
			Office routine	

Army Form C. 2118.

WAR DIARY
INTELLIGENCE SUMMARY.
(Erase heading not required.)

Place	Date	Hour	Summary of Events and Information	Remarks and references to Appendices
PONT NOYELLE	23/2/19		CAPT^N N. HODGSON proceeded on 7 days special leave	
			Office routine	
"	24/2/19		Visited D.H.Q	
			Office routine	
"	25/2/19		Visited D.H.Q	
			Office routine	
"	26/2/19		Visited D.H.Q	
			Office routine	
			Orderly Room	
"	27/2/19		Visited D.H.Q	
			Orderly Room	
			Office routine	
"	28/2/19		Visited D.H.Q	
			Office routine	

Bennett J.C.
1/3/19 O.C. 32/W est Con

Army Form C. 2118.

WAR DIARY
INTELLIGENCE SUMMARY.
(Erase heading not required.)

Vol 40

Place	Date	Hour	Summary of Events and Information	Remarks and references to Appendices
From 3/1/19				To 3/31/19

Lt. Col. T. C. Bennett D.S.O. O.B.E.
R.A.S.C.
Commanding
38th (Welsh) Divisional Train

Army Form C. 2118.

WAR DIARY
— of —
INTELLIGENCE SUMMARY.
(Erase heading not required.)

Instructions regarding War Diaries and Intelligence
Summaries are contained in F. S. Regs., Part II.
and the Staff Manual respectively. Title pages
will be prepared in manuscript.

Place	Date	Hour	Summary of Events and Information	Remarks and references to Appendices
PONT NOYELLE	1/3/19		Visited D.H.Q.	W.
			" 332 C°.	
			Orderly Room here	
			Office routine	
"	2/3/19		Visited D.H.Q.	W.
			Orderly Room	
			Office routine	
"	3/3/19		Lt HOWSON evacuated to 130 F.A	W.
			Lt MOORE handover temporarily to 332 C°. to take over	
			duties of Lt HOWSON	
			Visited D.H.Q	
			Office routine	
"	4/3/19		Visited D.H.Q.	W.
			Office routine	

Army Form C. 2118.

WAR DIARY
— of —
INTELLIGENCE SUMMARY.
(Erase heading not required.)

Instructions regarding War Diaries and Intelligence
Summaries are contained in F. S. Regs., Part II.
and the Staff Manual respectively. Title pages
will be prepared in manuscript.

Place	Date	Hour	Summary of Events and Information	Remarks and references to Appendices
PONT NOYELLE	5/3/19		Visited D.H.Q.	W.
			Office routine	
"	6/3/19		Lt COWAN proceeded to ENGLAND to report to W.O. for Slemie	W.
			duty at home	
"	7/3/19		Visited D.H.Q.	W.
			Office routine	
"	8/3/19		Visited D.H.Q.	W.
			Office routine	
"	9/3/19		Visited D.H.Q.	W.
			333 C°	
			Office routine	
"	10/3/19		Visited D.H.Q.	W.
			Office routine	

Army Form C. 2118.

WAR DIARY
INTELLIGENCE SUMMARY.
(Erase heading not required.)

Instructions regarding War Diaries and Intelligence Summaries are contained in F. S. Regs., Part II. and the Staff Manual respectively. Title pages will be prepared in manuscript.

Place	Date	Hour	Summary of Events and Information	Remarks and references to Appendices
PONT NOYELLE	11/3/19		Visited D.H.Q. Office routine.	Id.
"	12/3/19		Visited D.H.Q. Office routine. CAPTN HODGSON returned from leave having been granted 7 days extension	Id.
"	13/3/19		Issuing Orders relative to move of 331 C: to QUERRIEU Office routine	Id.
"	14/3/19		Visited D.H.Q. Office routine	Id.
"	15/3/19		CAPTN HODGSON proceeded on 3 days Special leave Office routine	Id.
"	16/3/19		Visited D.H.Q. Office routine	Id.

Army Form C. 2118.

WAR DIARY
INTELLIGENCE SUMMARY.
(Erase heading not required.)

Instructions regarding War Diaries and Intelligence Summaries are contained in F. S. Regs., Part II. and the Staff Manual respectively. Title pages will be prepared in manuscript.

Place	Date	Hour	Summary of Events and Information	Remarks and references to Appendices
PONT NOYELLE	17/3/19		331 C⁰ moved to QUERRIEU	
"	18/3/19		113 Bde moved to CLISY	
			Visited 333 C⁰	
			Office routine	⅟
"	19/3/19		Office routine	⅟
			CAPTⁿ MAC CALL proceeded on 7 days Special leave	
			Visited D.H.Q	
"	20/3/19		Office routine	⅟
			Army Orders relative to move of 332 C⁰ to BUSSY	
			Office routine	
"	21/3/19		Office routine	⅟
			CAPTⁿ HODGSON returned from Special leave	
"	22/3/19		Office routine	⅟
			Move of 332 C⁰ cancelled	

Army Form C. 2118.

WAR DIARY
or
INTELLIGENCE SUMMARY.
(Erase heading not required.)

Instructions regarding War Diaries and Intelligence Summaries are contained in F. S. Regs., Part II. and the Staff Manual respectively. Title pages will be prepared in manuscript.

Place	Date	Hour	Summary of Events and Information	Remarks and references to Appendices
PONT NOYELLE	23/3/19		Visited D.H.Q. Office routine	W.
"	24/3/19		Visited D.H.Q. Office routine. Issuing Orders relative to move of 332 Co. & of Cadres of 330 & 331 Co's	
"	25/3/19		CAPTN. HODGSON proceeded to ENGLAND for Demob. Service. Visited D.H.Q. Office routine	W.
"	26/3/19		LT TEMPLER proceeded to ENGLAND to report for Service there. Visited Third Army H.Q. Office routine	W.
"	27/3/19		332 Co. moved to BLANGY BUSSY Cadres of 330 & 331 Co. moved to BLANGY. Visited D.H.Q. 330 Co. & 333 Co. Office routine	W.

Army Form C. 2118.

WAR DIARY
INTELLIGENCE SUMMARY.
(Erase heading not required.)

Instructions regarding War Diaries and Intelligence Summaries are contained in F. S. Regs., Part II. and the Staff Manual respectively. Title pages will be prepared in manuscript.

Place	Date	Hour	Summary of Events and Information	Remarks and references to Appendices
PONT NOYELLE	28/3/19		MAJOR W.S. CAMERON took over temporary command of Train during absence of Lt Col T.E. BENNETT on Special duty	MC
"	29/3/19		Office routine	MC
"	30/3/19		Office routine	MC
"	31/3/19		Visited D.H.Q Office routine	MC

W.S. Cameron Major
T/Comdg 38th (Welsh) Div'l Train

Army Form C. 2118.

WAR DIARY
or
INTELLIGENCE SUMMARY.
(Erase heading not required.)

Instructions regarding War Diaries and Intelligence Summaries are contained in F. S. Regs., Part II. and the Staff Manual respectively. Title pages will be prepared in manuscript.

Place	Date	Hour	Summary of Events and Information	Remarks and references to Appendices
From	4/1/19		Major W. S. Cameron T/ Commanding 38th (Welsh) Divisional Train	To 30/9

Army Form C. 2118.

WAR DIARY
INTELLIGENCE SUMMARY.
(Erase heading not required.)

Instructions regarding War Diaries and Intelligence Summaries are contained in F. S. Regs., Part II. and the Staff Manual respectively. Title pages will be prepared in manuscript.

Place	Date	Hour	Summary of Events and Information	Remarks and references to Appendices
PONT NOYELLE	1/4/19		Office routine	
"	2/4/19		Visited 332 C⁰.	M.C.
			" Cadre of 331 C⁰.	
			Office routine.	
"	3/4/19		Issuing Orders relative to move of Cadres of 332 & 333 C⁰'s to	M.C.
			BLANGY & of the remainder of the C⁰'s to QUERRIEU	
			Office routine.	
"	4/4/19		Visited D.H.Q.	M.C.
			Office routine.	
"	5/4/19		Visited D.H.Q.	M.C.
			Office routine.	
"	6/4/19		Visited D.H.Q.	M.C.
			Office routine.	

Army Form C. 2118.

WAR DIARY
INTELLIGENCE SUMMARY.
(Erase heading not required.)

Place	Date	Hour	Summary of Events and Information	Remarks and references to Appendices
PONT NOYELLE	7/4/19		Office routine. T.H.Q. moved to QUERRIEU	WC
QUERRIEU	8/4/19		332 & 333 Co's (less Cadres) moved to QUERRIEU. Office routine.	WC
"	9/4/19		Office routine. Cadres of 332 & 333 Co's moved to BLANCY. Orderly Room	WC
"	10/4/19		Lt. S.H. DEAN proceeded to Base Supply Depot ANTWERP for duty. Office routine. Orderly Room	WC
"	11/4/19		Visited Railhead & Refilling Point of 113 Bde Group. Cadres of 331, 332 & 333 Co's at BLANGY. Office routine.	WC

Army Form C. 2118.

WAR DIARY
INTELLIGENCE SUMMARY.
(Erase heading not required.)

Instructions regarding War Diaries and Intelligence Summaries are contained in F. S. Regs., Part II. and the Staff Manual respectively. Title pages will be prepared in manuscript.

Place	Date	Hour	Summary of Events and Information	Remarks and references to Appendices
QUERRIEU	12/9		LT FAZACKERLEY admitted to Hospital	M/C
			One cordue	
	13/9		CAPT: MAC CALL rejoin Unit, wounded on leave	M/C
			One cordue	
	14/9		Visited D.D.V.T. III Army	M/C
			One cordue	
	15/9		Rail head changed to MERICOURT	
			Visited Cadre Park	
			Cadres of 351, 352 & 353 Cos	M/C
	16/9		One cordue	M/C
	17/9		One cordue	M/C

Army Form C. 2118.

WAR DIARY
or
INTELLIGENCE SUMMARY.
(Erase heading not required.)

Place	Date	Hour	Summary of Events and Information	Remarks and references to Appendices
QUERRIEU	18/9		Visited D.H.Q	
	19/9		"Convoy of 331, 332 & 333 C's	M/c
			Fine weather	
			Fine weather	M/c
BLANGY	20/9		T.H.Q moved to BLANGY	
			Convoy of 330 C. & had M.C. moved to BLANGY. Remainder	
			330 C. moving to GLISY	
			Fine weather	M/c
	21/9		Visited D.H.Q	M/c
			Fine weather	
			Fine weather	M/c
	22/9		Visited D.H.Q	M/c
	23/9		" Adv Corps H.Q	
			Fine weather	M/c

Army Form C. 2118.

WAR DIARY
INTELLIGENCE SUMMARY.
(Erase heading not required.)

Place	Date	Hour	Summary of Events and Information	Remarks and references to Appendices
BLANGY	24/9		Office routine	W.C.
"	25/9		Visited D.AD.O.S 35" Div.	W.C.
"			Office routine	
"	26/9		MAJOR W.S. CAMERON went on 4 days PARIS leave	W.C.
"			CAPTN E.C. NASH took over temporary command of Coy.	E.N.
"	27/9		Office routine	E.N.
"	28/9		Office routine	E.N.
"			Visited D.H.Q	
"			Lt FAZACKERLEY returned from 9 days leave	E.N.
"	29/9		Office routine	E.N.
"	30/9		Visited D.H.Q	E.N.
"			MAJOR W.S. CAMERON returned from Paris leave & resumed command of Coy.	E.N.
"			Office routine	

W.S. Cameron
Major R.A.S.C
O/C Coy 38 (Welsh) Div: Train

Army Form C. 2118.

WAR DIARY
or
INTELLIGENCE SUMMARY.
(Erase heading not required.)

May 1919.

Lt. Col. T. E. Bennett D.S.O. O.B.E.

R.A.S.C

Commanding

38th (Welsh) Divisional Train

Place	Date	Hour	Summary of Events and Information	Remarks and references to Appendices
From 1/5/19				To 31/5/19

No 10

Army Form C. 2118.

WAR DIARY
INTELLIGENCE SUMMARY.
(Erase heading not required.)

Place	Date	Hour	Summary of Events and Information	Remarks and references to Appendices
BLANGY	1/5/19		Visited D.H.Q. Office routine	MC
"	2/5/19		Visited D.H.Q. Office routine	MC
"	3/5/19		Visited D.H.Q. Office routine	MC
"	4/5/19		Visited D.D.J.S. Third Army. Office routine	MC
"	5/5/19		CAPTN. E.C.NASH proceeded on 14 days leave. Office routine	MC
"	6/5/19		Visited D.H.Q. Office routine	MC

Army Form C. 2118.

WAR DIARY
INTELLIGENCE SUMMARY.
(Erase heading not required.)

Instructions regarding War Diaries and Intelligence Summaries are contained in F. S. Regs., Part II. and the Staff Manual respectively. Title pages will be prepared in manuscript.

Place	Date	Hour	Summary of Events and Information	Remarks and references to Appendices
BLANGY	7/5/19		Office routine	MC
"	8/5/19		Office routine. Orderly Room. Visited D.H.Q	MC
"	9/5/19		Office routine	MC
"	10/5/19		Lt. FAZACKERLEY proceeded to report for duty to Base Supply Depot HAVRE. Visited Railhead. " D.H.Q	MC
"	11/5/19		Office routine. Office routine	MC

Army Form C. 2118.

WAR DIARY
or
INTELLIGENCE SUMMARY.
(Erase heading not required.)

Place	Date	Hour	Summary of Events and Information	Remarks and references to Appendices
BLANGY	12/5/19		MAJOR W.S. CAMERON proceeded to join 40th DIV: TRAIN. CAPTN. W.H. HOOPER assumed temporary command of the Train. LT J.W. HULLEY took over command of 330 C°. Visited Railhead. " D.H.Q. Office routine	WZH.
"	13/5/19		Visited D.H.Q. Office routine.	WZH.
"	14/5/19		Visited D.H.Q. " Railhead Office routine Cadre Vehicles of 331 C° moved to CANGAS	WZH.

Army Form C. 2118.

WAR DIARY
or
INTELLIGENCE SUMMARY.
(Erase heading not required.)

Place	Date	Hour	Summary of Events and Information	Remarks and references to Appendices
BLANGY	15/5/19		CAPT^N E.C. NASH returned from leave (having two months) over Command of the Train. In conformity with V CORPS wire S.M 653 to D.H.Q the following releasable personnel were posted as follows :- 16 O.R's to 16 R.W.F 14 " " 13 R.W.F 4 " " 10 S.W.B D.A.A.G. Div: informed me by phone that G.H.Q. authority has been obtained for this.	E.C.N.
	16/5/19		20 O.R's (releasable personnel) were to-day posted to 13 WELSH. Visited D.H.Q. to obtain leave to buy back vehicles of 331 Cane from CANGAS but D.A.A.G informed me that no horses could be supplied made Sunday on account of shortage. Office routine	E.C.N.

Army Form C. 2118.

WAR DIARY
or
INTELLIGENCE SUMMARY.
(Erase heading not required.)

Instructions regarding War Diaries and Intelligence Summaries are contained in F. S. Regs., Part II. and the Staff Manual respectively. Title pages will be prepared in manuscript.

Place	Date	Hour	Summary of Events and Information	Remarks and references to Appendices
BLANGY	17/9		Office routine	S.W.
"	18/9		Visited Railhead	S.W.
"	19/9		Office routine	S.W.
"	20/9		Visited Railhead	S.W.
"			Office routine	
"	21/9		Visited D.D.S. & T. Third Army Area. D.H.⊙ Orderly Room. Office routine	S.W.
"	22/9		Visited Railhead. Lt MACLEAN proceeded on 14 days leave. Office routine	S.W.

Army Form C. 2118.

WAR DIARY
INTELLIGENCE SUMMARY.
(Erase heading not required.)

Instructions regarding War Diaries and Intelligence
Summaries are contained in F. S. Regs., Part II.
and the Staff Manual respectively. Title pages
will be prepared in manuscript.

Place	Date	Hour	Summary of Events and Information	Remarks and references to Appendices
BLANGY	23/5/19		Lt COL: BENNETT returned from detached duty & resumed command of the Train.	R.B.
"	24/5/19		Office routine. Visited D.H.Q.	R.B.
"	25/5/19		Office routine. Visited D.H.Q.	R.B.
"	26/5/19		Office routine.	R.B.
"	27/5/19		Office routine. CAPTN NASH proceeded on 14 days leave. Lt HULLEY " "	R.B.
"	28/5/19		Office routine. Orderly room Office routine.	R.B.

Army Form C. 2118.

WAR DIARY
INTELLIGENCE SUMMARY.

(Erase heading not required.)

Instructions regarding War Diaries and Intelligence Summaries are contained in F. S. Regs., Part II. and the Staff Manual respectively. Title pages will be prepared in manuscript.

Place	Date	Hour	Summary of Events and Information	Remarks and references to Appendices
BLANGY	29/5/17		The routine	R.
"	30/5/17		The routine	R.
"	31/5/17		The routine	R.
			JFBennett Lt Col Comdg Welsh Div: Train
9.6.38
6/A.	

S.A.212.

[stamp: AMIENS SUB-AREA. No...... Date......]

D.A.G.
British Troops in France & Flanders,
(RECORDS SECTION).

     Herewith WAR DIARY of 38th. WELSH DIVISIONAL TRAIN from 1/6/19 to 16/6/19.

                                     Captain S.C.
                                for Cdt. Amiens Sub-Area.

18/6/19.

38

Army Form C. 2118.

T.F.135/132 43

WAR DIARY
or
INTELLIGENCE SUMMARY.
(Erase heading not required.)

Place	Date	Hour	Summary of Events and Information	Remarks and references to Appendices

From 1/6/19 — to 16/6/19

Ceased

Lt. Col. T. E. Bennett D.S.O. O.B.E.
R.A.S.C
Commanding
38th (Welsh) Divisional Train

Instructions regarding War Diaries and Intelligence Summaries are contained in F. S. Regs., Part II. and the Staff Manual respectively. Title pages will be prepared in manuscript.

(A8c.04) D. D. & L., London, E.C. Sch. 52 Form./C2118/14
Wt W1771/M2031 750,000 5/17

Army Form C. 2118.

WAR DIARY
INTELLIGENCE SUMMARY.
(Erase heading not required.)

Place	Date	Hour	Summary of Events and Information	Remarks and references to Appendices
BLANGY	1/6/19		Office routine	
"	2/6/19		Office routine	
"	3/6/19		Equipment of 331, 332 & 333 Co's handed in to I.C.S at POULAINVILLE	
"	4/6/19		Office routine	
"	5/6/19		Office routine	
"	6/6/19		Office routine	
"	7/6/19		Office routine	
"	8/6/19		Office routine	
"	9/6/19		Office routine	
"	10/6/19		Office routine	

Army Form C. 2118.

WAR DIARY
INTELLIGENCE SUMMARY.
(Erase heading not required.)

*Instructions regarding War Diaries and Intelligence Summaries are contained in F. S. Regs., Part II. and the Staff Manual respectively. Title pages will be prepared in manuscript.

Place	Date	Hour	Summary of Events and Information	Remarks and references to Appendices
BLANGY	11/6/19		Office routine	
"	12/6/19		Visited D.D.S.& T. 3rd Army Area	
			Office routine	
			CAPTN NASH returned from leave	
"	13/6/19		Office routine	
			LT HULLEY returned from leave	
"	14/6/19		Visited D.D.S.& T. 3rd Army Area	
			Office routine	
"	15/6/19		Office routine	
			LT HULLEY proceeded to 61st DIV: TRAIN	
"	16/6/19		Personnel proceeded to Embarkation Camps for dispersal	
			CAPTN NASH " " " "	
			" HOOPER " " " "	
			COL BENNETT proceeded to ENGLAND for duty.	

H Bennett Lt Col
O.C. 88/Welsh Div. Train
16/6/19

www.ingramcontent.com/pod-product-compliance
Lightning Source LLC
Chambersburg PA
CBHW080836010526
44114CB00017B/2317